Solo Literature
for
Low Brass and Organ

A Guide to Unexplored Music
for Recitals and Liturgical Settings

Patrick Lawrence, DMA

Solo Literature for Low Brass and Organ

WM

A **Write Mind** Book

ISBN: 978-0-9989076-2-8

A Personal Note...

Whether you are a low brass musician or an organist, you have an opportunity to explore a new and rewarding musical collaboration.

My interest in low brass and organ began with an opportunity to play with a gifted and willing organist during my master's study. It grew into research for a doctoral paper. It's morphed into a mission to have this literature played more widely. Try it! It will inject welcome variety into routine academic recitals. And it's a feast for the ears for the many who have never heard this rich combination of instruments.

In here, you'll find solos spanning every dimension, from starched-collar serious to utterly laughable. From serene and reflective to bold and bombastic. From baroque to avant-garde. From easy to extremely challenging. Some are perfectly straightforward. Others require an array of mutes and every tricky technique that composers can imagine (and some you may wish they hadn't). There's something for everyone and every situation.

Patrick Lawrence

To Megan, Norah, and Claire.

Preface

The timbre of low brass and organ is complementary. Few instruments match the organ's volume, color, and depth of sound as well as trombone, euphonium, and tuba.

Despite the existence of numerous original compositions for low brass and organ, there lacks an annotated guide for these works. This book is intended to correct that deficiency, to create interest in this body of literature and to broaden the repertory and performance opportunities for low brass players outside the typical performance venues.

This project originated as my doctoral dissertation at Arizona State University in 2009. The original dissertation included 168 original solos with organ, written specifically for alto, tenor and bass trombone. In the subsequent years I have continued my research in this area. This expanded publication contains 221 compositions and includes newly discovered pieces for trombone and works for euphonium and tuba.

Annotations for each work include information about the composer, general stylistic comments, performance notes and available recordings. Sections in the back include a list of works by difficulty, a discography and a list of publishers with their contact information. Works with multiple editions or different publishers will be listed separately with annotations highlighting the differences between publications. A few works listed are unpublished. In these cases, information about where the works can be found is included.

Many of the works are available for purchase using the publisher contact information.

Table of Contents

Introduction

The bulk of music written for low brass and organ has been composed for the trombone. This is due to the fact that the trombone's history is deeply rooted in sacred music. Additionally, the tuba and euphonium are much younger, developed in the nineteenth century. From the sixteenth to eighteenth centuries, the trombone was used in liturgical settings as a solo instrument, but it also doubled choir parts, since the expressive versatility and timbral qualities of the instruments blended with the voices. Church employment records dating back to the late sixteenth-century show the practice of hiring city and court trombonists to play for special church occasions. Permanent performers were common during the seventeenth-century.[1]

In Germany, the trombone played such a significant role in sacred music that Martin Luther used the word *posaune* (trombone) in his versions of the German Bible instead of the traditional *trumpet.*

Early on, literature for the trombone was non-existent. Players were able to memorize parts, later recalling them for use as a solo or in a polyphonic setting. The first parts labeled for trombone began appearing in the sixteenth-century.[2] The use of the trombone in church music grew in Europe during the seventeenth century, but waned in the following century, when it was more often used, as in present times, for important occasions during the church year.

We often see the word *limited* in articles and reviews about the repertoire for trombone and organ. This may hold true in comparison to the literature pool for low brass and piano; however, considerable

---

[1] Trevor Herbert, *The Trombone* (New Haven, CT: Yale University Press, 2006), 100- 108.

[2] Ibid., 92.

literature exists which may be undocumented. I believe that solos for low brass with organ constitute an untapped source of performance and educational opportunities.

The Organ

It is important for a low brass performer to have at least a rudimentary understanding of the pipe organ for performance practices and to communicate effectively with the organist. When playing with an organist, a brass player must put more effort into sustaining since notes can be held indefinitely on the organ. This is unlike playing with a piano which has a natural decay to the sound as soon as a note is played. An organist refers to *the organ*, meaning the pipes, whether visible or hidden behind a screen; the *console* is where the keyboards or *manuals* (two or more) are played. The console also includes a *pedal board*, which allows two or more notes to be played with the feet, usually in the bass register.

Ultimately, the organ console functions to turn on or off the air supply to the organ pipes. The various types of organ pipes produce a wide range of timbres. *Flue* pipes produce sound in the same manner as a whistle or recorder. The *principals* are flue pipes that imbue the foundational character of the organ with considerable bite. The *flutes* are flue pipes with a much lighter and purer tone.

Reed pipes, or *the reeds*, function much like an oboe reed made of metal, rather than cane. Shape and design of the various pipes produce a wide range of timbres. Some are light in character and used as a solo voice in quiet passages. Others are loud and brash, used in an ensemble of other stops for power and grandeur.

Each chromatic *rank* of pipes is activated with a *stop tab* or *stop knob*. On organs using purely mechanical action, pushing in the stop knob stops the air supply to that rank of pipes. Pulling it out activates the air supply. This is the origin of the phrase "pulling out all the stops." *Tracker organs* feature mechanical linkages directly from the keys and pedals to the pipes. This arrangement has the organ console close to the pipes. Modern consoles send electronic signals to the pipe mechanisms by wire or fiber optic cable, which allows the console to be set further away from the pipes.

The names of the various stops vary by style of the organ and preferences of the organ builder. Many names are unique to organ vernacular. Other stops are named after instruments of the orchestra with timbre reminiscent of their namesake. Stop names also include an indication of length in feet. The so-called *8-foot* stops (group of pipes) sound at unison pitch. The longest, lowest-pitched pipe in this *rank*, or group of pipes, is approximately eight feet in length and sounds two octaves below middle C. The pipe that produces a middle C pitch in the same group of pipes is approximately two feet long.

Sixteen-foot stops are the lowest-pitched stops on many organs and sound one octave below the pitch played. A 4-foot stop plays an octave above the pitch played. A 32-foot stop, found only on large organs, sounds two octaves below the pitch played. When several stops are selected, a single key can sound pipes over multiple octaves. Other *mutation* and *mixture* stops sound one or more pipes at harmonically related pitches, adding brightness and sparkle. With hands and feet, the organist can produce a wide range of pitch—from growling bass to sparkling high treble notes.

Air flow is supplied by the *blower*. Air pressure to each pipe is regulated and constant. The volume created from each pipe cannot be changed. Enough air is supplied to sustain continuous sound, even if all stops are selected (*full organ*) and a large chord is played. A vibrato effect can be created by activating *tremulant* which vibrates the air supply.

Overall sound volume is determined by the type and number of stops selected. Stops can be added selectively, creating a terraced increase in volume with an attendant change in timbre. Organs of the Baroque period often have most or all their pipes exposed and visible. Organs of this type can only modulate volume by controlling the type and number of stops selected. Modern organs have most or all pipes *under expression*, enclosed in one or more chambers with movable vanes or shutters that allow varying sound to pass into the listening area. The *expression pedal* controls the shutters, allowing continuous control of the volume without terracing. This expressive capability is essential in romantic and more expressive music.

On most modern organ consoles, selection of the stops can be programmed by setting *pistons*. This allows the organist to quickly select commonly used combinations of stops. Modern organs also provide a *crescendo pedal*, adding stops gradually in a predetermined manner.

By selecting the various stops, an organist can produce an extraordinary range of pitch and timbre. The selection of various stops to create the desired effect is called *registration*. Registration may be suggested by the composer in the organ score using shorthand notation or may be left to the judgment and taste of the organist. Different registration can be set on the manuals (keyboards) allowing, for example, a solo reed stop to be played with one hand, accompanied by an ensemble sound with the other hand on another manual.

Organs vary dramatically in style, *voicing*, size and character. Each has a personality and quirks. An organist must learn and adjust to an unfamiliar organ far more than a pianist to a piano.

Modern electronics has allowed satisfactory or, at least, useful imitation of pipe organs. Though the means of sound production is completely different, console function and terminology remain the same. These electronic "pipe organs" should not be confused with organs used in jazz and popular music which are not intended to replicate the sound and operation of a pipe organ.

The trombone, euphonium, and tuba are among a select few instruments that can balance and blend with the full range and power of a large pipe organ. Woodwind instruments such as oboe, flute or clarinet, for example, would be easily overpowered by full organ sonorities. Though some literature is written for a variety of solo instruments with organ accompaniment, the trombone allows the composer to creatively explore the full range and power of both instruments.

Organs are built in a variety of styles roughly corresponding to musical periods. Baroque and classically voiced organs are often bright in sound with the majority of pipes free-standing, not under expression. Later, more romantic instruments provide greater expressive capabilities by enclosing most pipes in chambers with shutters that can be gradually opened and closed. Modern instruments are mostly built in the latter style, to suit a wide range of musical styles.

About This Repertoire

Solos for trombone and organ constitute a significant part of the trombone repertoire, but are rarely performed since they are unknown. An examination of David Guion's article, *Twenty-five Years of Trombone Recitals: An Examination of Programs Published by the International Trombone Association*, indicated that Krol's *Sinfonia Sacra*, was listed as the only original composition for trombone and organ performed on recital from 1982-1997, and not a single work listed for this duo among the fifty most frequently performed works.[3] These data may be misleading since despite the organization's title of International Trombone Association, it rarely includes information about recitals outside the United States and Canada.[4]

Unaware of this literature, many performers and educators focus instead on the repertoire for trombone, euphonium, and tuba with piano. Several prominent performers including Alain Trudel, Christian Lindberg, Armin Rosin and Branimir Slokar have commissioned new

---

[3] David M. Guion, "Twenty-five Years of Trombone Recitals: An Examination of Programs Published by the International Trombone Association," *International Trombone Association Journal* (Winter 1999), 22.

[4] Ibid.

works and released recordings of works for trombone and organ, but these isolated instances do not reflect the richness of this repertory.

By collecting and annotating the works, this document serves as a catalyst for creating awareness and interest in the solo literature for low brass with organ, by broadening the repertory and performance opportunities for performers outside the typical venues.

Much of the music described in this volume is challenging and covers a broad musical spectrum from sacred to avant-garde. The majority of solo literature for low brass with organ was written in the twentieth-century, gaining momentum since the 1970s.[5] Many of these works are published by small European printing houses, or are available directly from the composer. To facilitate access to this repertory, this thesis provides information on how to access these scores.

---

[5] Klaus Winkler, "Posaune und Orgel- Dialog zweier Instrumente," *Brass Bulletin*, no. 56 (1986): 75-89.

Review of Related Literature

There is little documentation pertaining to music for low brass with organ. The most comprehensive annotated bibliographies of solo low brass music today have few, if any, entries for this combination. The *Annotated Guide to Bass Trombone Literature,* by Thomas Everett,[6] lists six entries for bass trombone and organ, three of which meet the criteria of this document. *French Music for Low Brass Instruments: An Annotated Bibliography,* by J. Mark Thompson and Jeffrey Jon Lemke[7], has only one entry for trombone with organ. Vern Kagarice's *Solos for the Student Trombonist: An Annotated Bibliography,*[8] does not have any annotations for solo trombone and organ.

The *Guide to the Euphonium Repertoire: The Euphonium Source Book,*[9] Compiled and edited by Lloyd E. Bone Jr. and Eric Paull, has a short section devoted to euphonium and organ music, however most of the works are adapted from other instruments.

---

[6] Thomas Everett, *Annotated Guide to Bass Trombone Literature* (Nashville, TN: The Brass Press, 1978).

[7] J. Mark Thompson and Jeffrey Jon Lemke, *French Music for Low Brass Instruments: An Annotated Bibliography* (Bloomington, IN: Indiana University Press, 1994).

[8] Vern Kagarice, Solos for the Student Trombonist: An Annotated Bibliography (Nashville, TN: The Brass Press, 1979).

[9] *Bone Jr., Lloyd E et al.* The Guide to the Euphonium Repertoire: The Euphonium Source Book. (IN: Indiana University Press, 2007).

The Guide to Tuba Repertoire: The New Tuba Source Book,[10] also has a section titled Tuba and Keyboard Other than Piano, which lists pieces that meet the criteria.

Lastly, James H. Laster's Catalogue *of Music for Organ and Instruments* is an excellent reference guide of the music for organ in combination with a variety of other instruments. Since this volume covers all instruments, and subsequent combinations of small ensemble involving the organ, it contains little information about specific works and is not exhaustive.[11]

Articles on Low Brass & Organ Literature

There have been several publications pertaining to this topic in the professional journals. Klaus Winkler wrote a two-part article, entitled *Bibliographie der Kompositionen für Posaune und Orgel,* published in the *Brass Bulletin* in 1985 and 1986.[12] This article is a bibliography that lists works both alphabetically and chronologically. The chronological section is divided in two categories: before 1960 and since 1970, leaving the decade between undocumented. Winkler cites a total of forty-one works. Twenty-nine citations are in the material since 1970 and include the following attributes: year, composer, title, movements, range, notation, and technical notes. The thirteen citations before 1960 lack information beyond the composer and title, except in a few entries which

---

[10] Morris, R. Winston and Perantoni, Daniel. The *Guide to Tuba Repertoire: The New Tuba Souce Book.* (IN: Indiana University Press, 1996).

[11] James H. Laster, *Catalogue of Music for Organ and Instruments* (Lanham, MD:Scarecrow Press, 2005).

[12] Klaus Winkler, "Bibliographie der Kompositionen für Posaune und Orgel," *Brass Bulletin* no. 51(1985): 63-66.

include publisher and date. This article serves as an adequate reference; however, it is almost thirty-five years old and therefore out-of-date.

The second article is *20ᵗʰ- Century Music for Trombone and Organ* by Charles Isaacson.[13] This publication in the *International Trombone Journal* includes an annotated bibliography of 114 works. The information listed includes: composer, title, year of composition or copyright, instrument required (alto trombone, B-flat/F: tenor trombone with f-attachment, bass trombone, euphonium, and tuba), number of movements, duration, performance requirements, range, level of difficulty, source/availability and a discography. The information presented seems to be useful and well-documented; unfortunately, a quarter of the annotations state "no further information available," often listing no more than the composer and title of the piece.

These two articles establish an important precedent in this area of literature; however, they are not inclusive and are out-of-date.

---

[13] Charles Isaacson, "20ᵗʰ- Century Music for Trombone and Organ, *International Trombone Association Journal* (Winter 1996): 24-29.

Methods and Procedures

The following section—Solos by Composer—is in the form of an annotated bibliography. All entries are listed alphabetically by the composer's last name. Each citation includes the following information when available:

- Composer's name and dates
- Title
- Publication information including: company name, address, publication date
- Instrument required
- Range, notated with the clefs used in the piece
- Level of difficulty
- Technique requirements
- Mutes indicated
- Movement names

Range is notated for each entry showing the encompassing range of that work, notated in the clefs used in the score.

For example:

In instances where specific notes are mentioned within the annotation, the following system of notation is used:

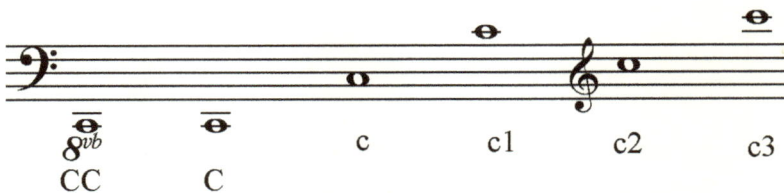

The difficulty of each work is assessed and graded as *Easy, Moderate,* or *Advanced.* A section in the back contains a list of solos by difficulty level.

When available, the annotations for each piece include biographical and historical information about the composer and background information about the piece, including its premiere, duration, style and character.

When possible, the composer was contacted and pertinent comments are included in the annotations.

These citations should serve as a reference guide for performers to select works according to their needs. Although discussion of the worth of the works is not addressed in this volume, the author makes suggestions about the appropriateness of a work for use in traditional liturgical settings.

Intended as a reference, this document limits discussion of organ technique. Each listing contains information about the organ score, including the number of staves, manuals required, registration and dynamics. All other details pertaining to organ parts have been obtained from a professional organist while rehearsing this literature. All available recordings are listed in the discography.

Solos by Composer

Akerwall, Martin (b. 1965)

Meditation for tuba and organ: Just Sheet Music. http://www.justsheetmusic.com, 2001.

- Tuba
- Difficulty: Easy
- Technique: Nothing unusual
- Mutes: None

Martin Akerwall, a Dutch conductor, percussionist, and composer studied at the Sibelius Academy in Helsinki, and at the Music Academy of Copenhagen. Several of his compositions have won distinguished prizes.

Meditation, is a two-minute work written in the unusual meter 16/4. The piece begins with tuba alone, playing long lyrical lines that are reminiscent of Gregorian chant. The organ enters with a simple accompaniment, which adds tension through dissonance. This work is appropriate for a recital and for use in a liturgical setting.

The organ part is on three staves with registration suggested and dynamics clearly marked.

Aho, Kalevi (b. 1949)

Epilog für Posaune und Orgel. Helsinki, Finland: Fennica Gehrman, 2002.

- Tenor trombone
- Difficulty: Moderate
- Technique: Nothing unusual
- Mutes: None

I.   ♩ = 60

Aho, one of Finland's leading composers, studied at the Sibelius Academy in Helsinki, later to return as a professor of composition before devoting himself entirely to freelance composition. A prolific writer, he composed fourteen symphonies, four operas and numerous chamber works. His Symphony No. 9 for Trombone and Orchestra (1993-94) was recorded by Christian Lindberg and the Lahti Symphony Orchestra on the disc BIS-CD-706.

Composed in 1998, this three-and-a-half minute single-movement work maintains a soft lyrical style throughout, only briefly reaching a dynamic of forte. The beginning of the work, marked "dolcissimo," shows off the singing quality of the trombone with expressive shaping and dynamics creating musical interest.

There are frequent meter changes. It requires a strong sense of pulse, due to complex rhythmic lines functioning independently of the organ. This work is appropriate for a recital and for use in a liturgical setting.

The organ part is on three staves with registration suggested and dynamics clearly marked.

Allers, Hans Gunther (b. 1935)

Pavane Opus 62 für Posaune und Orgel. Kassel, Germany: Verlag Merseburger, 1995.

This work from 1960 was unavailable at the time of this publication.

Angerer, Paul (1927-2017)

Luctus et Gaudium für Altposaune und Orgel. Vienna, Austria: Musikverlag Ludwig Doblinger, 1983.

- Alto trombone
- Difficulty: Moderate
- Technique: Glissandi
- Mutes: None

    I.   Luctus
    II.   Gaudium

Angerer, an Austrian composer conductor and violist, received his formal musical training at the Vienna Music Academy. After graduating, he played in several European orchestras before obtaining the position of principal violist in the Vienna Symphony Orchestra. On the podium, Angerer held several music director positions for well-known orchestras located in major European centers including Vienna, Bonn and Salzburg. His compositional style has been described as having a strong influence by Hindemith. He won first prize in 1954 for one of his organ compositions.

Composed in 1977-78, this twelve-minute work is originally for trombone and strings with the reduction for organ done by the composer. The two movements are a typical slow-fast pairing. *Luctus* (Sorrow) is expressive and sweet. This movement, marked "Lento" uses the voice-like timbre of the alto trombone. This section is slow, however, momentum is created in a 3/8 section before returning to simple meter. The second movement, *Gaudium* (Joy) is marked "Allegro" and is nimble. It begins in 4/4 meter, but most of the movement is in 7/8. This compound meter could present rhythmic challenges. This work is appropriate for a recital and for use in a liturgical setting.

The organ part is on three staves with no registration indicated. Dynamics are clearly marked.

This work has been recorded by Branimir Slokar on the CD *Trombonist* (Claves D707).

Argast, Felix (b. 1936)

Partita für Posaune in C/B & Orgel. Köln, Germany: Wolfgang G. Haas – Musikverlag Köln E.K., 2008.

- Tenor trombone
- Difficulty: Moderate
- Technique: Nothing unusual
- Mutes: Cup

    I.   Intrada

    II.   Air

    III.   Gaillarde

Argast, a keyboardist, trumpeter and composer was born in Basel, Switzerland. He received his formal musical training at the Academy of Basel. After graduation, he was employed by several European orchestras as a trumpet player. He is currently a freelance composer and a member of the Swiss Arts Work Alliance.

Partita was composed in 2008, a twelve-minute, three-movement work. The first movement marked "Maestoso" begins with a dramatic recitative section, easing into a contrasting lyrical section with a quarter and half-note triplet melody. After a grand pause, the conclusion repeats the opening material.

The second movement, marked "Largo espressivo," is lyrical with long, contoured phrases, which take place over meter changes between 3/4 and 4/4. The use of a mute is optional, however in the prefatory notes, the composer indicates his preference for a cup mute. The first section of the final movement, marked "Festivo," is in 3/4 meter, and has a stately dance character, which should be felt in one. The contrasting B section of this movement is lyrical, marked "Tranquillo," and should be played slightly slower then the adjoining A sections. Again, the conclusion repeats the opening material.

In the performance notes, the composer suggests that the movements could be played independently; however, when played together, the end of the second movement should be *attacca* into the final movement. This transition could be problematic with the removal of the trombone mute. This work is suited for a recital and for a liturgical setting.

The organ part is on three staves. Some registrations are indicated and dynamics are clearly marked.

Ayerst, Jonathan (b. 1971)

Victimae Paschali. Coventry, England: Warwick Music, 2002.

- Tenor trombone
- Difficulty: Advanced
- Technique: F attachment tuned to E, Lip trill, Glissandi across the harmonic series
- Mutes: None

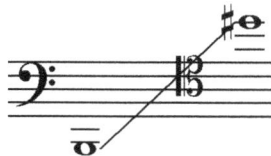

I.   Grave

Ayerst, an English composer and keyboardist, received his formal musical training at the Royal Academy of Music. He has written several chamber works, a ballet for two pianos and percussion, and *Exodus,* a fifty-minute oratorio for orchestra and choir. Ayerst currently performs with Remix Ensemble, a contemporary music ensemble in Portugal.

This modern single-movement, five-minute work bears the inscription "to my friend Jonathan Pippen." The piece is one of a series of paraphrases on Gregorian chant for brass and organ. The work begins with a slow lyrical trombone cadenza including several glissandi from (BB) to (f#1). The score indicates that in measure six the trombonist should pull the F attachment slide to be tuned in E to facilitate the low B. The publisher, however, neglected to include this notation in the trombone part. A brief powerful section, marked "Majestic," contrasts the preceding section before a lengthy organ cadenza. The trombone returns with slower lyrical playing including the same repeated glissandi figures. The trombonist retunes the F attachment slide for the ending, which also has a cadenza-like quality. This work is not inherently difficult; however, there are several large leaps marked with slurs that could be challenging in addition to the glissandi across the harmonic series. This work is best suited for a recital.

The organ part is on three staves some registration indicated and dynamics are clearly marked.

Baratto, Paolo (1926-2008)

Andante Cantabile. Vuarmarens, Switzerland: Édition Bim, 1931.

- Tenor trombone
- Difficulty: Easy
- Technique: Grace notes
- Mutes: None

I.   Andante cantabile

Baratto was born in Switzerland in 1926. He received his early musical training on trumpet from his father with later formal musical studies at the Zurich Conservatory. A well-known trumpeter, he made a career performing with several European orchestras. His compositional output of over eighty pieces consists primarily of works for trumpet.

Composed in 1965, *Andante Cantabile* is a simple four-minute piece. The work remains in common meter and stays within E-flat major and its relative minor without any tempo or style changes. This piece would be suitable for a young trombonist with only a few sixteenth note patterns and grace notes added for embellishment. Although not mentioned in the score, some catalogues suggest that this work was originally composed for horn and organ. This work is well-suited for a recital and for a liturgical setting.

The organ part is indicated for organ-piano and is on two staves with the pedal doubling. No registration is indicated and dynamics are clearly marked.

Bartmuss, Richard (1859-1919)

Recitativ und Arioso Op 24. Ditzingen, Germany: Edition Musica Rinata E. Hofmann, 1994.

- Tenor trombone
- Difficulty: Easy
- Technique: Grace notes
- Mutes: None

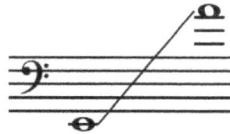

    I.   Moderato assai

Bartmuss, a German composer was born into a musical family. His father was a well-known organist and music scholar. Richard became the organist at the Schlosskirche St. Marien in Dessau, and the court organist of Duke Friedrichs I.

Recitativ und Arioso is primarily lyrical without any technical challenges for the trombonist. There is a large ossia section in the trombone part which avoids the extended high tessitura and tenor clef (up to C^2). This work is well-suited for a recital and for a liturgical setting.

The organ part is on two staffs with pedal part notated.

This work has been recorded by trombonist Sebastian Krause and organist Gabrielle Wadewitz on the CD *Sonntagsposaunenstück: Romantic music for trombone and organ* (Raum Klang RK 9805).

Bausznern, Dietrich von (1928-1980)

Konzert für Posaune und Orgel. Kassel, Germany: Verlag Merseburger, 1981.

- Tenor trombone
- Difficulty: Advanced
- Technique: Glissandi, Lip trills, Flutter tonguing, Grace notes
- Mute: Straight

I.	♩ = ca.76	
II.	♩ = ca.48	
III.	Schnell ♩ = 100-108	

Bausznern, born in East Prussia (modern day Poland) was a composer, organist, cantor and music teacher. He was a prolific writer with a compositional repertoire of over 300 works composed in a wide range of styles. He is best-known for his church music and chamber works, but his repertoire includes opera—even a funk opera.

Konzert für Posaune und Orgel is a twenty-minute work in three movements. Both the trombone and organ parts are demanding. The first movement is angular and disjointed with chromatic interplay between the trombone and organ. The second movement includes triple tonguing, horn calls and a cadenza. The opening of the third movement marked "Schnell," features the organist. The rapid staccato sixteenth-note figures are demanding for the trombonist.

The organ part is on three staves has difficult passages in the pedal including pedal trills. No registration indicated and dynamics are clearly marked.

Bendix, Hermann (1859-1935)

Elegie für Posaune und Orgel op. 92 Nr. 2. Köln, Germany: Verlag Christoph Dohr, 2008.

- Tenor trombone
- Difficulty: Moderate
- Technique: Nothing unusual
- Mutes: None

    I.   Andante

Bendix, a German composer, cantor and church musician, received his formal musical training at the Royal Institute of Music. Although his musical output was primarily for organ and harmonium, he also wrote sacred music for choir and small chamber ensembles.

The estate of Hermann Bendix rediscovered this work along with two other original, previously unpublished manuscripts, for instrument and organ. The publisher believes the work was composed in the 1920s, likely written for his son Rudolf Bendix, who played trombone. Publication of this work was made possible through the efforts of Guido Johannes Joerg.

Elegie, a nine-minute, single movement work, is based on the tune "Was mein Gott will, gescheh' allzeit," a sixteenth-century melody. The somber work is in ABA form, beginning with solo organ. The trombone presents the delicate legato main theme. The middle section changes key, the trombone playing simple chant-like half note figures, then passing the lead role to the organ. The final section of the work returns to opening material. Because of the high tessitura, slow tempo, and few rests, endurance may be a concern. This work is suited for a recital and for use in a liturgical setting.

The organ part is on three staves with no registration indicated and dynamics clearly marked.

Beraldo, Primo (1924-2006)

Dialogo per Trombone e Organo. Horgen, Switzerland: Pizzicato Verlag Helvetia, 1980.

- Tenor trombone
- Difficulty: Moderate
- Technique: Grace notes
- Mutes: Straight

    I.   Quarter note = 60

Dialogo is a four-minute, single-movement work. After a soft, slow introduction, the piece changes abruptly. The style becomes aggressive with the loud dynamics and a shift to 5/4 meter. The organ holds two notes a half step apart in the pedal. Twelve-tone sonorities and angular figures are pervasive throughout. The piece is in ABA form slowing to a lento section The B section is slightly more legato than the A material. This work is suited for a recital. However, it might be considered too modern for a traditional liturgical setting.

The organ part is on three staves with registration and dynamics clearly marked.

Berg, Fred Jonny (b. 1973)

Paralysing Atmosphere Op.11. Bodø, Norway: Symbiophonic, 2008.

- Tenor trombone
- Difficulty: Moderate
- Technique: Nothing unusual
- Mutes: None

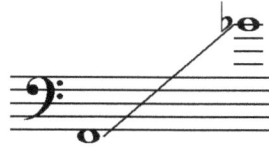

I.   Spiritoso

Berg, a Norwegian composer, movie director and producer, has written a wide range of compositions from small chamber works to film scores and large-scale orchestral works. His composition, *Flute Mystery*, was performed by Sir James Galway and the National Symphony Orchestra conducted by Leonard Slatkin in 2008.

Paralysing Atmosphere is a three-minute work composed in 1992 and premiered in Tromsø, Norway in 1997 by trombonist Gunnar Høgseth and organist Patricia Manwaring. The dramatic work explores the full range of color and dynamics of both instruments. The work remains in 9/4 meter which creates unusually long phrases. The piece is well-balanced, blending old choral traditions with new energetic concepts. A reflective mood is established beginning with a brief organ interlude prior to the trombone's entrance above a pedal point played by the organ. The thin texture is soon replaced with the organ and trombone parts building in intensity with dark harmonies, and ends with both instruments playing in full voice. This work is best suited for a recital. It might be considered too modern for a traditional liturgical setting.

The organ part is on three staves with no registration indicated, and dynamics clearly marked.

Beuerle, Herbert (1911-1994)

Kleine Studie für Posaune (Violoncello, Fagott) und Orgel. Munich, Germany: Strube Verlag, 1986.

- Tenor trombone
- Difficulty: Moderate
- Technique: Nothing unusual
- Mutes: None

    I.   Half note = 60-76

This three-minute single-movement work is fifty measures long, based on a theme by Heinrich Schütz set to Psalm 3: 5-9. The work alternates between 4/2 and 6/2 meter with several "ritardando—a tempo" sections. The chorale theme is played by the trombone. The organ part is from the German organ tradition, featuring broad harmonies and a variety of inner moving parts. This piece is well-suited for a recital or for a liturgical setting.

The organ part is on three staves with some registration suggested and dynamics clearly marked.

Böhler, Friedel W. (b. 1946)

Fünf Miniaturen für Posaune und Orgel. Munich, Germany: Strube Verlag, 1986.

- Tenor trombone
- Difficulty: Moderate
- Technique: Flutter tonguing, Grace notes, Glissandi
- Mutes: None

I.   Präludium

II.   Tanz

III.   Wie ein Ländler

IV.   Lied

V.   Scherzo

Böhler, a German composer and church musician, received his formal musical training in Berlin. From 1954 until his retirement, he served as a cantor and music director in the cathedral in Gelnhausen, Germany. Although his compositional output is primarily church music, many of his compositions are adaptations of North American spirituals.

These five movements are eight minutes in length. The work is "dedicated in friendship to Friedhelm Flammein." The first movement, *Präludium*, marked "langsam," serves as a short introduction in the form of a subdued fanfare. This opening is attacca into the next movement, S*chnell und tänzerisch,* a nimble dance in 2/4 meter. The third movement, *Wie ein Ländler,* is a waltz with a modal flavor, starting and ending softly. There is a puzzling optional ending which has one fewer measure than the actual part, but does not omit anything difficult. The fourth movement is the shortest of the set—just fourteen measures in length. Marked, "Sehr ruhig und cantabel," this movement is mostly in common meter and features a simple melody. The final movement is the most technically demanding. Marked, "sehr lebhaft," is in cut time with the half note equivalent 76-84 a tempo faster than the previous sections. Independent lines and interesting dialogue between the two instruments along with an optional short trombone cadenza add drama to the conclusion of this work. Several of these movements could function independently. This piece is well-suited to a young trombonist with a strong high range.

The organ part is on three staves with some registration and manual indications marked.

Böhler, Friedel W. (b. 1936)

In the Upper Room, 15 Spirituals für Posaune und Orgel. Munich, Germany: Strube Verlag, 1999.

- Tenor trombone
- Difficulty: Easy
- Technique: Flutter tonguing, Grace notes, Glissandi
- Mutes: Straight

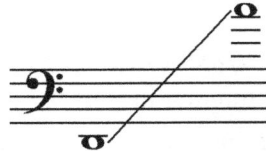

I.	In the upper room
II.	Standin' in the need of prayer
III.	I couldn't hear nobody pray
IV.	Steal away
V.	By and by
VI.	Sometimes I feel like a motherless child
VII.	Ev'ry time I feel the spirit
VIII.	Gospel-Sound
IX.	I'm gonna sing
X.	Go down, Moses
XI.	Wade in the water
XII.	Deep river
XIII.	Didn't my Lord deliver Daniel
XIV.	O happy day
XV.	O freedom

This collection features a wide range of gospel styles from slow tunes full of emotion to upbeat numbers that instill hope and pride. Characteristics of African-American music are evident throughout the work, including call and response figures between the two instruments, the use of blue-notes and syncopation. The final movement, *O freedom,* begins with trombone alone and suggests a field holler. The average movement is three to four minutes and would be well-suited to a young trombonist. It is not intended to be performed in its entirety due to its length. Several selections would work well for a recital or in a liturgical setting. In one section, the organist is required to snap fingers while playing in the pedal.

The organ part is on three staves with a few registrations indicated and dynamics clearly marked.

Borg, Kim (1919-2000)

Church Music for Trombone and Organ, op.26. Helsinki, Finland: Finnish Music Information Centre, 1991.

- Tenor trombone
- Difficulty: Advanced
- Technique: Grace notes, Glissandi
- Mutes: Velvet tone

    I.   Psalm
    II.   Meditation
    III.   Prayer

Borg, a Finnish composer and vocalist, received his formal musical training at the Sibelius Academy in Helsinki. After graduation, he continued with advanced studies in Vienna, Rome and New York. As a bass-baritone singer, Borg performed on the international opera scene in many of the world's renowned opera houses. Upon retiring from performance, he became a professor of voice at the Copenhagen Conservatory. His compositional repertoire includes two symphonies and many chamber works including a concerto for trombone, double bass and orchestra.

Composed in 1977 and dedicated to trombonist Carsten Svanberg, *Church Music* is a three-movement, twelve-minute piece which covers a broad range of styles from reflective to grand. The opening of the first movement, marked "Poco pesante," begins with a cantabile chant-like melody played by the trombone over a long pedal point played by the organ. This switches to a soft dolce melody, providing contrast with the opening. A fermata divides this movement into two sections. After the hold, the style becomes more marcato. An unusual effect is created with the two instruments scored in opposition, creating a sense of instability. The movement ends with a grandioso conclusion with both instruments playing in full voice. As the title suggests, the second movement is meditative. This section features slow-moving figures which develop chromatically. Due to the slow tempo, high tessitura and delicate playing, this movement requires a controlled command of the trombone. The end of the movement concludes with the trombonist holding out b1 for twelve measures. An optional attacca segues to the third and final movement marked, "Appassionato Allegro Moderato," which is primarily in 5/4 meter with transitions from rubato to a tempo. This work covers a wide array of dynamics and emotions, but is not difficult. There are few rests for the trombonist, so the piece needs to be carefully programmed.

The organ part is on three staves with no registration indicated and dynamics clearly marked; it is difficult and requires an accomplished organist.

Bornefeld, Helmut (1906-1990)

LITUUS für Posaune und Orgel. Echterdingen, Germany: Carus Verlag.1977

- Tenor trombone
- Difficulty: Advanced
- Technique: Multiphonics, Alternate notation, Quarter tone adjustments, Grace notes,

- Mutes: Straight

  I.   Bedächtig (Carefully)

Bornefeld, a German keyboardist, composer, organ builder and educator, originally wanted to become a garden architect. After a change of heart, he studied keyboard and church music at the Stuttgart Conservatory of Music. In conflict with the Nazis, Bornefeld left Germany during World War II and relocated to Prague where he served in the Russian military. After the war, he returned to Germany and taught church Music as a Lecturer in choral practice.

Composed in 1977, *LITUUS für Posaune und Orgel,* a seventeen-minute modern work, bears the inscription, "As a monument for Hans-Arnold Metzer." The program notes describe a "LITUUS" as an ancient crooked signal horn. The trombone part is played from the score, resulting in difficult page turns. The work has a free or open quality, created by long pauses with rests over fermatti and open notation lacking measures. There are instances where the trombonist hums through the instrument creating effects. The work becomes more structured at the "Conductus I" section with the arrival of the 6/4 time signature. This shifts to the unusual meter, 5/8/9. Here the measures have either five, eight or nine eighth notes per measure, but are arranged in no particular order. The moving eighth-note lines build in intensity ending with an upward trombone glissando to an indefinite pitch, played as high as possible. "Conductus II and III" are similar, both returning to 6/4 meter. "Elegie" features an extended trombone cadenza with organ interjections. The Chorale Section is based on Bach's BWV 495. The chorale text is included in the trombone part for reference. The work concludes with the trombone and organ building in intensity for a powerful ending, but at the last moment the style changes abruptly and the work ends softly and peacefully. This piece is difficult and requires a highly-skilled trombonist and organist. This piece is suited to a recital.

The organ part is on three staves with registrations indicated and dynamics clearly marked.

This work has been recorded by Armin Rosin on the CD *Posaune & Orgel* (Teldec 6.42164AW).

Bottje, Will Gay (b. 1925)

LITTLE SONATA NR.VI for Trombone and Organ. New York, NY: American Composers Alliance, 1983.

- Tenor trombone
- Difficulty: Advanced
- Technique: Grace notes, Glissandi, Alternate notation
- Mutes: Straight

     I.   Very Deliberate

An American composer, Bottje earned a Bachelor's degree in Flute Performance and a Master's Degree in Composition at the Juilliard School of Music before completing a Doctor of Musical Arts at the Eastman School of Music. Dr. Bottje served as a professor of Music at Southern Illinois University in Carbondale from 1957 to 1981 teaching composition and electronic music. He has since retired to Grand Rapids, Michigan.

LITTLE SONATA NR.VI is part of a series of sonatas composed for various wind and string instruments combined with organ. This nine-minute, single-movement work has several shifts in tempo, style and meter. Most of the piece could be characterized as declamatory and deliberate, at times even aggressive. There are several notes which are indicated to be played flat, with lengthened slide positions. A short legato section provides contrast concluding with a jazz feel. This work is best suited for a recital. It should be noted that measure 25 has an impossible mute change.

The organ part is quite virtuosic in places with difficult runs in the pedal. The composer writes: "No specific registration is indicated. Dynamics, balance, taste and the particular instrument should all be important considerations. The composer welcomes unusual timbral effects."

Braun, Peter Michael (b. 1936)

Jericho – die fallenden Mauern, Geistliche Musik für Posaune und Orgel. Berlin, Germany: Bote & Bock, 1982.

- Tenor trombone
- Difficulty: Advanced
- Technique: Flutter tonguing, Alternate notation, Trills and glissandi over the harmonic series, Tremolo
- Mutes: Straight, Straight with plunger, Velvet tone

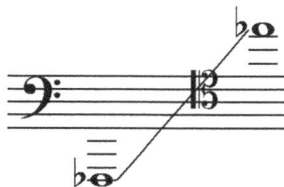

I.	Konfrontation
II.	Zerstörung
III.	Trauer

Braun, a German composer and pianist, received his formal musical training at the National Academy in Cologne and Detmold, where he studied composition with Frank Martin. From 1978 to 2001, Braun was a Professor of Composition and Theory at the National University of Music and Performing Arts in Mannheim. His earlier works are considered aleatory and atonal, this piece, one of his later works, combines stylistic elements from the past and present.

This modern work, dedicated to Armin Rosin, was premiered in November 1982 by trombonist Eberhard Merz and organist Wolfgang Dallmann in Heidelberg Germany. *Jericho – the falling walls, Music for*

Trombone and Organ is a ten-minute work inspired by Joshua 5: 13-15. Although a single movement work, the piece is divided into three main sections. *Konfrontation* (Confrontation) begins with tremendous energy as the composer attempts to depict God's wrath through angry marcato lines, permeated with large leaps and angular figures. The style becomes only slightly more legato near the end of the section, and has several glissandos over the harmonic series. The second movement, *Zerstörung* (Destruction), is similarly styled. Harmonic ideas are developed with the bitonal chords of the organ and recitative figures of the trombone. A passage of long notes and organ chords marked, "as loud as possible" builds to frantic section with both instruments playing tremolos, glissandi and sixteenth note chromatic figures.

Tension breaks in the final movement, *Trauer* (Grief), a softer more pensive section. Here, the phrases are stretched and more legato. The conclusion of the work incorporates several Bach chorale fragments. It should be noted that the piece requires the trombonist to play down to pedal E-flat with straight mute. This work is highly virtuosic and has an extreme range; an outstanding trombonist and organist are required. This work is suited for a recital.

The organ part is on three staves with registration indicated and dynamics clearly marked.

Breimo, Bjørn (b. 1958)

Postludium for alt-trombone og orgel. Oslo, Norway: Norwegian Music Information Centre, 1983.

- Alto trombone
- Difficulty: Moderate
- Technique: Nothing unusual
- Mutes: None

I.   Adagio

A Norwegian composer and pianist, Breimo's formal musical training took place at the Norwegian State Academy of Music with Robert Riefling and Einar Steen-Nøkleberg. After graduation, he returned to the same institution and completed a degree in composition. Mr. Breimo currently teaches music theory at the Foss School of Music in Oslo and is an active freelance composer.

Postludium, a one-and-a-half minute work is light and expressive in character. Marked "Adagio," the piece remains in common meter except for the penultimate measure, which is in 3/2 meter and functions as a written-out ritardando. The alto trombone melody consists primarily of triplet figures. The upper manual of the organ has an interesting rhythmic augmentation—a trill pattern begins with thirty-second-notes then shifts through sextuplets, sixteenth-notes, eighth-notes and finally quarter-notes. This deceleration occurs while the trombone plays an expressive lyrical line above, creating an unusual effect. This work is not difficult, but the chromatic passages on alto trombone could present a challenge for some players. This work is well-suited for a recital and for a liturgical setting.

The organ part is on three staves with no registrations indicated, and dynamics clearly marked.

Breman, Niklas (b. 1966)

Intrata for Organ and Trombone. Stockholm, Sweden: Swedish Music Information Center, 1995.

- Tenor trombone
- Difficulty: Moderate
- Technique: Nothing unusual
- Mutes: None

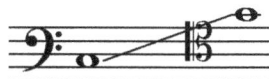

I.   Andante tranquillo ♩ = 64

Composed in 1995, *Intrata* is a four-minute, single-movement work. The form of this piece is ABA, beginning with a trombone fanfare set over slow moving organ harmonies. This trombone melody moves around dissonant organ pedal points built on two sets of perfect fourths played a major second apart. The B section has lyrical trombone lines over repeating sixteenth-note patterns played by the organ, again using the same dissonant pedal points from the previous section. The piece reaches a climax in this middle section, creating an arch form from beginning to end. The work concludes with material which is similar to the opening and ends softly. The piece is not technically demanding for the trombonist with the exception of a few quintuplets and sixteenth-note triplets. This work is best suited for a recital.

The organ part is on three staves with no registrations indicated and dynamics clearly marked.

Bresgen, Ceaser (1913-1988)

Meditation for Trombone and Organ. Berlin, Germany: Edition Gravis, 1993.

- Tenor trombone
- Difficulty: Moderate
- Technique: Nothing unusual
- Mutes: None

    I.   Sostenuto

Bresgen, an Italian composer, studied composition in Munich and became a Professor of Music at the Mozarteum in Salzburg. His music is strongly influenced by folk song and dance. These simple melodies were adapted in numerous stage works for young performers.

Written in 1982, and revised in 1985, *Meditation* is a twelve-minute work premiered by trombonist Werner Hacl and organist Rudolf Scholz on September 11, 1993. The opening is pensive with rich harmonies. This slow introduction reflects the work's title. The composer's use of meter changes and organ harmonies carry over the bar-lines, creating a floating effect. A chant-like melody emerges with the trombone playing the primary theme. The pulse is blurred in two meno mosso sections with offset triplet figures that play against each other between the two instruments. This ensemble playing is challenging and requires extra attention in rehearsal. The piece ends softly, as in the beginning. This piece uses close harmony and dissonance. It would be suitable for a recital and for a liturgical setting.

The organ part is written on three staves and has sections of double pedaling. No registration indicated and dynamics are clearly marked.

Brown, Rayner (1912-1999)

Meditation for Trombone and Organ. Greeley, CO: Western International Music.

Brown, an American composer, organist and music teacher, was born in Des Moines, Iowa. He received his formal music training at the University of Southern California where he graduated with Bachelors and Masters degrees in Music. Brown served as the principal organist for the Wilshire Presbyterian Church in Los Angeles from 1941 to 1977.

At the time of this writing, this work was temporarily out-of-print.

Brown, Rayner (1912-1999)

Prelude and Fugue for Trombone and Organ. Greeley, CO: Western International Music.

At the time of this writing, this work was temporarily out-of-print.

Brown, Rayner (1912-1999)

Sonata for Trombone and Organ. Composer's Library, 1985

- Tenor trombone
- Difficulty: Moderate
- Technique: Nothing unusual
- Mutes: Cup

    I.   Prelude and Fugue

    II.   Scherzo

    III.   Canzonetta

    IV.   Postlude and Fugue

Composed in 1985, *Sonata for Trombone and Organ* is a seven-minute work in four movements. The first movement, *Prelude and Fugue,* is in 3/2 meter is marked "Allegro." It begins with trombone alone, later joined by a contrasting theme played in the organ pedal. A fugue-like section begins in measure 63, where the theme is passed between the organ and trombone three times. The movement concludes with the trombone playing long phrases over the organ's toccata like figures. The second movement, *Scherzo,* is in 6/8 meter. The playful trombone melody is accompanied by humorous staccato interjections of the organ using the principal and flute stops. The third movement, *Canzonetta,* is slow and reverent. Here, the trombone uses a cup mute and the organ plays with the string stops. This section also features an extended trombone cadenza. The finale, *Postlude and Fugue,* returns to 3/2 meter and builds to an energetic finish. This work is suited for a recital and in a liturgical setting.

The organ part is on three staves with both registration and dynamics clearly indicated.

Burgmann, J. Hartmut (b. 1936)

4 Choralvorspiele in traditionellem Stil mit Chorälen für Posaune und Orgel, Band I. Ingersheim, Germany: Musikverlag Castellano, 1998.

- Tenor trombone
- Difficulty: Easy
- Technique: Nothing unusual
- Mutes: None

I.	Ach bleib mit deiner Gnade, EG 347
II.	Der Herr ist mein getreuer Hirt, EG 274
III.	Preis, Lob und Dank sei Gott, dem Herren, EG 245
IV.	Christe, du bist der helle Tag, EG 469

Composed in 1998, this collection is the first in a series of seven books for trombone and organ. These settings are written for a church service. All selections begin with a prelude, followed by one or two short chorales. The first setting, *Ach bleib mit deiner Gnade* (Oh remain with your mercy) is based on the tune,"Christus, der ist mein Leben" (Christ, who is my life). The second setting, *Der Herr ist mein getreuer Hirt* (The Lord is my faithful shepherd) is based on the tune, "Du Lebensbrot, Herr Jesu Christ" (You are the life bread, Lord Jesus Christ). This setting alternates between 2/2 and 4/4 meter, and is followed by two chorales with repeated sections. Movement three, *Preis, Lob und Dank sei Gott, dem Herren* (Praise, laud thanks is God, the Lord) is based on the tune, "*Nun segnet dankt und lobt den Herren*" (Now bless, offer thanks and praise to the Lord). This setting remains in 4/2 meter, and has one longer chorale. The final setting, *Christe, du bist der helle Tag* (Christ, you are the bright day) is in 4/4 meter, followed by one chorale. The majority of these simple settings would be appropriate for a young trombonist. Along with the score, the publisher provides two trombone parts—one in bass clef, the other in tenor clef.

The organ part is on three staves with no registration indicated and dynamics clearly marked.

Burgmann, J. Hartmut (b. 1936)

4 Choralvorspiele in traditionellem Stil mit Chorälen für Posaune und Orgel, Band II. Ingersheim, Germany: Musikverlag Castellano, 1998.

- Tenor trombone
- Difficulty: Moderate
- Technique: Nothing unusual
- Mutes: None

I.   Nun bitten wir den Heiligen Geist, EG 124

II.   Jesu, meine Freude, EG 396

III.   Der Tag bricht an und zeiget sich, EG 438

IV.   Nun jauchzt dem Herren alle Welt, EG 288

Book II in this series for trombone and organ features simple settings structured as preludes with one or two short chorales. The first setting, *Nun bitten wir den Heiligen Geist* (Now we ask the Holy Spirit) is legato in style, written in 4/2 meter followed by a single chorale. This setting is intended to be used at Pentecost. The second setting, *Jesu, meine Freude* (Jesus, my joy) one of the more difficult preludes in the collection, is composed in several compound meters with challenging rhythmic figures for the trombone. The two chorales which follow are in 2/2 meter. The third setting *Der Tag bricht an und zeiget sich* (The day breaks) is intended to be used in an early morning service and is based on the familiar "Wach auf" theme. The final setting, *Nun jauchzt dem Herren alle Welt* (Now, rejoice in the Lord everyone) is in 6/4 meter with an obbligato trombone line. Along with the score, the publisher provides two trombone parts—one in bass clef, the other in tenor clef.

The organ part is on three staves with no registration indicated and dynamics clearly marked.

Burgmann, J. Hartmut (b. 1936)

5 Choralvorspiele in taditionellem Stil mit Chorälen für Posaune und Orgel, Band III. Ingersheim, Germany: Musikverlag Castellano, 1998.

- Tenor trombone
- Difficulty: Moderate
- Technique: Nothing unusual
- Mutes: None

I.	O Heiland reiss die Himmel auf, EG 7
II.	Es kommt ein Schiff geladen, EG 8
III.	Nun singet und seid froh, EG 35
IV.	Ich steh an deiner Krippen hier, EG 37
V.	Fröhlich soll mein Herze springen, EG 36

Book III in this series for trombone and organ features settings of preludes with one or two shorter chorales intended for Advent and Christmas services. The first setting, *O Heiland reiss die Himmel auf* (O Lord open the heavens) has a simple lyrical prelude followed by two chorales with flowing variations. The second setting, *Es kommit ein Schiff geladen* (There comes a ship loaded) is intended as a prelude during Advent, followed by five short Christmas settings. The third setting, *Nun singet und seid froh* (Now sing and be glad) begins with trombone alone, joined by the organ accompaniment. This setting is longer than most in this collection. The fourth setting, *Ich steh an deiner Krippen hier* (I stand here at your crib) is emotional, yet subdued. The final setting, *Fröhlich soll mein Herze springen* (My heart shall leap with happiness), joyful in nature and is intended for a Christmas service. Along with the score, the publisher provides two trombone parts—one in bass clef, the other in tenor clef.

The organ part is on three staves no registration indicated, and dynamics clearly marked.

Burgmann, J. Hartmut (b. 1936)

6 Choralvorspiele in traditionellem Stil für Posaune und Orgel, Band IV. Ingersheim, Germany: Musikverlag Castellano, 1998.

- Tenor trombone
- Difficulty: Moderate
- Technique: Grace notes
- Mutes: None

I.	Korn, das in die Erde, EG 98
II.	Herr Jesu, deine Angst und Pein, EG 89
III.	Auf, auf, mein Herz, mit Freuden, EG 112
IV.	Der schöne Ostertag, EG 117
V.	Herzlich tut mich erfreuen, EG 148
VI.	Jerusalem, du hochgebaute Stadt, EG 150

Book IV in this series for trombone and organ features settings of preludes with one or two short chorales. This collection is intended for Easter and the end of the church year services. The first setting, *Korn, das in die Erde* (The seed that is in the earth) is written in 4/4 meter followed by two short chorales. The second setting, *Herr Jesu, deine Angst und Pein* (Lord Jesus, Thy fear and pain) is similar to the first setting in style and tempo, with two short chorales which remain in common meter. The third setting, *Auf, auf, mein Herz, mit Freuden* (Rise up, my heart, with joy) is inteneded for Easter service, and is written in

6/4 meter. The fourth setting, *Der schöne Ostertag* (The beautiful Easter day) is in 4/4 meter and has a high tessitura. The last two settings are intended for the end of the church year. *Herzlich tut mich erfreuen* (I rejoice heartily) is in 4/4 meter and is followed by two mixed meter chorales. The final setting, *Jerusalem, du hochgebaute Stadt* (Jerusalem, you high-built city) begins in 2/2 meter followed by two short chorales in 4/4 meter. Along with the score, the publisher provides two trombone parts, one in bass clef; the other in tenor clef.

The organ part is on three staves with no registration indicated, and dynamics clearly marked.

Burgmann, J. Hartmut (b. 1936)

7 Choralvorspiele in traditionellem Stil mit Chorälen für Posaune und Orgel, Band V. Ingersheim, Germany: Musikverlag Castellano, 1999.

- Tenor trombone
- Difficulty: Moderate
- Technique: Nothing unusual
- Mutes: None

I.	Verleih uns Frieden gnädiglich (1), EG 421
II.	Verleih uns Frieden gnädiglich (2), EG 421
III.	Sonne der Gerechtigkeit, EG 262
IV.	Das ist köstlich, dir zu sagen Lob und Preis, EG 284
V.	Komm in unsre stolze Welt, EG 428
VI.	Sollt ich meinem Gott nicht singen, EG 325
VII.	Lobe den Herren, den mächtigen König, EG 316

Book V in this series for trombone and organ features settings of preludes with one or two short chorales. This collection is intended for peace prayer services. The first two settings are based on the same tune,

Verleih uns Frieden gnädiglich (Grant us peace). The first setting is simple, written in 3/4 meter with a chorale. The second setting is in a flowing 7/8 meter, with two short chorales. The third setting, *Sonne der Gerechtigkeit* (Sun of Justice) is short and simple with two chorales. The fourth setting, *Das ist köstlich, dir zu sagen Lob und Preis* (It is delicious, to give you praise) is intended for Psalm and Canticles. This prelude is longer than the others, with two interesting chorales in mixed meter. The fifth setting, *Komm in unsre stolze Welt* (Come into our proud world) is a song of creation and peace. Both somber and hopeful, it is written in 6/4 meter. The sixth setting, *Sollt ich meinem Gott nicht singen* (Should I not sing to my God) is a tune of praise and thanks. The final setting, *Lobe den Herren, den mächtigen König* (Praise the Lord, the mighty King) is in 3/4 meter. The two chorales that follow are in 9/4 meter. Along with the score, the publisher provides two trombone parts—one in bass clef, the other in tenor clef.

The organ part is on three staves with no registration indicated, and dynamics clearly marked.

Burgmann, J. Hartmut (b. 1936)

Choralvorspiele in taditionellem Stil mit Chorälen für Posaune und Orgel, Band VI. Musikverlag Castellano, 2000.

- Tenor trombone
- Difficulty: Moderate
- Technique: Nothing unusual
- Mutes: None

I.	Macht hoch die Tür, EG 1
II.	O du fröhliche, EG 44
III.	Nun lasst uns gehn und treten, EG 58
IV.	Wie schön leuchtet der Morgenstern, EG 70
V.	Ein Lämmlein geht und trägt, EG 83

VI.   Erschienen ist der herrlich Tag, EG 106
VII.   Gen Himmel aufgefahren ist, EG 119
VIII. Komm, Gott Schöpfer, EG 126
IX.   Brunn alles Heils, dich ehren wir, EG 140
X.   Aus tiefer Nor schrei ich zu dir, EG 299
XI.   Es ist gewisslich an der Zei, EG 149

Book VI in this series for trombone and organ features settings of preludes with one or two short chorales. This collection includes eleven-movements to be used throughout the church year. The first setting, *Macht hoch die Tür* (Make high the door) is intended to be used in advent. Written in 6/4 meter, the prelude and two chorales have a high tessitura with few rests. The second setting, *O du fröhliche* (Oh thou joyful) is written in 5/8 and 6/8 meter. The following three chorales are in 4/4 meter and use dotted eighth-sixteenth figures. The third setting, *Nun lasst uns gehn und treten* (Now let us go and walk) is based on the tunes, *Wach auf, mein Herz, und singe* (Wake up, my heart, and sing) and *Die ihr bei Jesus bleibet* (The ones that remain with Jesus). This section is legato and remains in 3/2 meter. The fourth setting, *Wie schön leuchtet der Morgenstern* (How beautiful shines the morning star) is intended for Epiphany and is based on the tune, *O Heilger Geist, kehr bei uns ein* (Oh, Holy Ghost enter our home). The fifth setting, *Ein Lämmlein geht und trägt* (A little lamb walks and bears) is written in 2/2 and 3/2 meter, based on the tune, *Du Werk des Vaters, rede du* (Work of the Father, speak!). The sixth setting, *Erschienen ist der herrlich Tag* (A wonderful day has dawned) remains in 6/4 meter and is intended for Easter service. The seventh setting, *Gen Himmel aufgefahren ist* (Ascended to heaven is) is simple with two short chorales. The eighth setting, *Komm, Gott Schöpfer* (Come, God creator) remains in 4/4 meter throughout. The ninth setting, *Brunn alles Heils, dich ehren wir* (Source of all salvation, we honor thee) is light and joyous. The final two settings, *Aus tiefer Not schrei ich zu dir* (Out of deep despair I cry out to you thee) and *Es ist gewisslich an der Zeit* (It is certainly time) are intended for the end of the church year. Along with the score, the publisher provides two trombone parts, one in bass clef; the other in tenor clef.

The organ part is on three staves with no registration indicated, and dynamics clearly marked.

Burgmann, J. Hartmut (b. 1936)

10 Choralvorspiele in taditionellem Stil mit Chorälen für Posaune und Orgel, Band VII. Ingersheim, Germany: Musikverlag Castellano, 2001.

- Tenor trombone
- Difficulty: Moderate
- Technique: Nothing unusual
- Mutes: None

I.	Ihr lieben Christen freut euch nun, EG 6
II.	Es ist ein Ros entsprungen, EG 30
III.	Hilf, Herr Jesu, lass gelingen, EG 61
IV.	Der Morgenstern ist aufgedrungen, EG 69
V.	O Traurigkeit o Herzeleid, EG 80
VI.	Heut trimphieret Gottes Sohn, EG 109
VII.	Jesus Christus herrscht al König, EG 123
VIII.	Komm, Heiliger Geist, Herre Gott, EG 125
IX.	Befiehl du deine Wege, EG 361
X.	Die Sonn hat sich mit ihrem Glanz gewendet, EG 476

Book VII in this series for trombone and organ features settings of preludes with one or two short chorales. This collection includes ten movements to be used throughout the church year. The first setting, *Ihr lieben Christen freut euch nun* (My Dear Christians Rejoice now) is intended for advent, based on the tunes, "Du Morgenstern, du Licht vom

Licht" (You morning star, Light of Light) and "Steht auf, ihr lieben Kinderlein" (Get up my dear children). The first setting is a simple prelude, written in common meter with two chorals, written in 4/2 meter. The second setting, *Es ist ein Ros entsprungen* (He has arisen) is short with two chorales, also in common meter intended for Christmas service. The third setting, *Hilf, Herr Jesu, lass gelingen* (Help, Lord Jesus, Let Succeed). This prelude is in 6/4 meter, with two short chorales also in the same meter. The fourth setting, *Der Morgenstern ist aufgedrungen* (The Morning star has risen) is in common meter and has a high tessitura. Both choral sections are in 2/2 meter. The fifth setting, *O Traurigkeit o Herzeleid* (O sadness O heartache) is a song of passion. The three chorales are in 3/3 meter. The sixth setting, *Heut trimphieret Gottes Sohn* (Today the Son of God triumphs) is based on the theme "Wir danken dir, Herr Jesu Christ" (Thank you, Lord Jesus Christ) is intended for an Easter service. Written in 6/4 meter the trombone part has long eighth-note runs. The seventh setting, *Jesus Christus herrscht al König* (Jesus Christ is King) is intended for an assention service. Because of the high tessitura of this work, it should be programmed with endurance considerations. The eighth setting, *Komm, Heiliger Geist, Herre Gott* (Come Holy Spirit, Lord God) is intended for a Pentecostal service. The ninth setting, *Befiehl du deine Wege* (Come thou, thy ways) is simple, written in common meter. The final setting, *Die Sonn hat sich mit ihrem Glanz gewendet* (The sun has turned its luster) is in 4/2 meter. The two chorales that follow are in 2/2 meter. Along with the score, the publisher provides two trombone parts, one in bass clef; the other in tenor clef.

The organ part is on three staves with no registration indicated, and dynamics clearly marked.

Burgmann, J Hartmut (b. 1936)

Die Nacht ist vorgedrungen für Posaune und Orgel. Ingersheim, Germany: Musikverlag Castellano, 1996.

- Tenor trombone
- Difficulty: Moderate
- Technique: Nothing unusual
- Mutes: None

    I.   Vorspiel
    II.   Choral I
    III.   Choral II

Die Nacht ist vorgedrungen, (The Night is Progressing) is a two-and-a-half minute theme and variation consisting of a prelude and two short chorales. The prelude marked, "ruhig half note = 88," is in 3/2 meter and is composed with simple rhythmic figures. Both chorales are shorter than the prelude section, and shift between 3/2 and 2/2 meter. The highest note in this work is (c2), however, there is an optional lower line which only has the trombone playing up to g1. Along with the score, the publisher provides two trombone parts—one in bass clef, the other in tenor clef. This work is suited for a recital and for a liturgical setting.

The organ part is on three staves with no registration indicated, and dynamics clearly marked.

Burgmann, J. Hartmut (b. 1936)

Südtiroler Brugen-Suite für Posaune und Orgel. Ingersheim, Germany: Musikverlag Castellano, 2003.

- Tenor trombone
- Difficulty: Moderate
- Technique: Glissandi, Flutter tonguing
- Mutes: None

    I.   Sentiero per il castello Andraz
    II.   Trostburg

III.   Wolkenstein
IV.   Untermontani
V.   Haderburg

This nine-minute piece incorporates several themes by Oswald von Wolkenstein (1377-1445). Each of the five movements is a musical depiction of a specific European castle. The first movement, *Path to the Castle Andraz,* portrays the journey to an imposing castle located in the province of Belluno in the Italian Alps. The movement is marked, "quasi intrada" and features a stately main theme in 6/4 meter. The end of this section should segue directly into the next movement which depicts *Trostburg*, a castle located in Waidbruck, Germany. The primary theme for this section is based on *"Wach aug mein hort"* (Wake up my heart) The third movement depicts the ruins of the castle Wolkenstein. This thirteenth-century German castle, destroyed in the fifteenth-century, was never rebuilt. This section is dissonant and has the organ playing a repeated rhythmic figure consisting of two simultaneous major triads set a whole step apart. The movement has a canonic march-like quality. The fourth movement, *Untermontani,* depicts a 14th century German castle and features the tune *"Ach senliches leiden."* (Oh heartfelt suffering) The high tessitura of this movement, which has few rests, may present endurance challenges for the trombonist. The final movement, *Haderburg,* depicts a medieval castle in the German Rhineland. The movement is based on the tune "Wer die Augen will verschüren" (Who will close his eyes). This section begins with a chant-like theme played by trombone alone before the organ enters, building to a dramatic ending. The composer and publisher have included a 4 x 6 color photograph of each of the castles (or ruins) in a separate envelope. The publisher includes trombone parts in bass and tenor clef. This work is suited for a recital and for a liturgical setting.

The organ part is on three staves with no registration indicated and dynamics are clearly marked.

Büsing, Otfried (b. 1955)

Nox für Bass-Posaune und Orgel. Berlin, Germany: Edition Gravis, 2002.

- Bass trombone
- Difficulty: Advanced
- Technique: Flutter tonguing, Glissandi
- Mutes: Straight

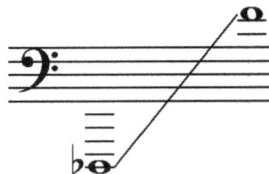

I.	Cantus 1
II.	Interludium 1
III.	Cantus 2
IV.	Interludium 2
V.	Cantus 3
VI.	Interludium 3
VII.	Cantus 4

Büsing, a German composer, received his formal musical training at the Musikhoschule in Hanover. After graduation he became a Professor of Music at the Hochschule für Musik in Freiburg.

Composed in 2003, *Nox* (Night) is an eleven-minute fantasie in seven-movements. The piece was premiered by bass trombonist Christoph Auerbach and organist Rainer Fritzsch, in Radeberg, Germany, July 2003. The work consists of four Cantus sections, each followed by an Intermezzo. This modern work begins with, *Cantus 1,* which is marked "Andante." An organ introduction sets the character of the piece and is joined by the organ playing muted phrases. Interludium 1, marked "Con moto, energico," contrasts the somber opening with a dialogue between the two instruments featuring accented figures. Cantus 2, marked "Andante, con calma" returns to the chorale-like melodies. Interludium 2, marked "Agitato," again features angry figures played by the trombone. Cantus 3, marked "Andantino" has several short trombone cadenzas written in a medative style. Interludium 3, is far less aggressive and is a waltz written in 11/8 meter. The final section, Cantus 4 returns to a dialogue similar to the opening of the work and ends softly. This work is suited for a recital.

The organ part is on three staves with some registration indicated and dynamics clearly marked.

Callahan, Charles (b. 1951)

In the Beginning, Biblical Poem for Tuba (Cello) and Organ. St Louis, MO: MorningStar Music Publishers a division of E.C.S Schirmer Music Company, 1994.

- Tuba
- Difficulty: Moderate
- Technique: Nothing unusual
- Mutes: None

I.   Expressively and freely

Callahan, an American composer and organist studied at the Curtis Institute of Music, and at the Catholic University of America. His compositions include works for orchestra, choir, chamber ensembles, and several solo works with organ.

In the Beginning is based on Genesis 1:1-5, and is a beautiful, meditative four-minute work. There is nothing overly challenging about the piece other than several meter changes and the high tessitura for the tuba, which is scored above the staff for most of the piece. This work is suited for a recital and for a liturgical setting.

The organ part is on three staves with no registration indicated and dynamics are clearly marked.

Callahan, Charles (b. 1951)

Out of the Depths I Cry to You, O Lord, for trombone, euphonium, or tuba and organ. Fenton, MO: Briamwood Publications, a division of MorningStar Music Publishers a division of E.C.S Schirmer Music Company, 2008.

- Trombone, Bass Trombone Euphonium or Tuba
- Difficulty: Moderate
- Technique: Nothing unusual
- Mutes: Straight

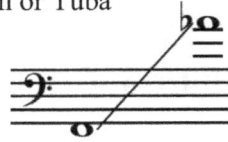

      I.   Lento

Out of the Depths I Cry to You, O Lord is a beautiful three-minute, single-movement work based on Martin Luther's hymn tune: *Aus Tiefer Not.* The piece begins with muted solo instrument. The organ joins with rich harmonies. The piece is in a slow cut-time meter and moves through several different keys. The high tessitura could be a challenge, especially for tuba. This work is suited for a recital and for a liturgical setting.

The organ part is on three staves with no registration indicated and dynamics are clearly marked.

Callhoff, Herbert (1933-2016)

5 Versetti sopra "VENI SANCTE SPIRITUS" for Trombone and Organ. Berlin, Germany: Edition Gravis, 2004.

- Tenor trombone
- Difficulty: Advanced

- Technique: Multiple tonguing, Flutter tonguing, Grace notes, Multiphonics. Lip Trills (half and whole step) Alternate notation
- Mutes: Harmon, Straight, Cup

I.	Moderato
II.	Tanquillo
III.	Allegro con moto
IV.	Andante sostenuto
V.	Allegro vivace

Composed in 2004, this seventeen-minute work provides an avant-garde approach to ancient music. Each of the five movements is based on a specific ancient chant, with reproductions included in the score. They require twentieth-century trombone techniques. The first movement is primarily a cadenza with organ interjections, both parts lacking meter and bar-lines. The second movement begins in common meter played by the organ alone, shifting to an atypical 3/4 + 1/8 meter. The third movement is dramatic, featuring an assortment of extended trombone techniques. Similar to the first movement, the bar-lines are dissolved, which creates an improvised character. The fourth movement is an interlude for solo organ. The final movement is the most technically demanding for both instruments. This work is suited for a recital.

The organ part is on three staves with registrations and dynamics clearly marked. The organ part requires a three-manual instrument, improvised sections, and double pedaling.

Callhoff, Herbert (1933-2016)

Vier Meditationen für Posaune und Orgel. Bergisch Gladbach, Germany: Musikverlag Hans Gerig, 1976.

- Tenor trombone
- Difficulty: Advanced
- Technique: Flutter tonguing, Alternate notation, Grace notes, Half and whole step trills, Slide vibrato
- Mutes: Harmon, Straight

I.	Antiphon
II.	Organum
III.	Motettus
IV.	Tropus

Composed in 1974, this thirteen-minute modern work begins in common meter, but the time signature is quickly abandoned, resulting in a free or alternate form of notation. The first movement, *Antiphone,* begins softly, emerging from the organ pedal and develops into abstract exchanges between the trombone and organ. With the use of a stem-in Harmon mute, the trombone creates a speech-like dialogue, a "wah-wah" effect. This continues in the second movement, *Organum,* marked "Adagio," where the trombonist sings through the instrument, creating eerie sounds. *Motettus,* marked, "Moderato," features a trombone cadenza set over tone clusters from the organ. The final movement, *Tropus,* begins with a cadenza using non-traditional sounds including a passage in which the trombonist is instructed to "proceed from singing into blowing the note." This work is suited for a recital.

The organ part is on three staves with registration indicated and dynamics clearly marked.

Campbell, Bruce (b. 1948)

Meditation for Euphonium and Organ, San Antonio, TX: Southern Music Company a division of Lauren Keiser Music Publishing, 1990.

- Euphonium
- Difficulty: Easy
- Technique: Nothing unusual
- Mutes: None

Campbell is an American composer. This four-minute work is dedicated to Barbara W. Ward. The piece is pleasant and lyrical, there are no challenges and the piece would be suitable for a young performer and would work well in a liturgical setting.

The organ part is on two staves with registration suggested and dynamics clearly marked.

Cejka, Petr D. (b. 1939)

Through for Trombone and Organ. 1998.

- Bass trombone

Through, is an eight-and-a-minute, single-movement work. A copy of this work was unobtainable at the time of this writing. *Through* has been recorded by trombonist Gaute Vikdal on the CD *Skybrudd* (EUCD 007).

Cesare, Giovanni Martino (1590-1667)

La Hieronyma from Musicali Melodie, 1621. Pembroke, MA: Robert King, 1972.

- Tenor trombone
- Difficulty: Moderate
- Technique: Nothing unusual
- Mutes: None

I.   Andante

Cesare, an Italian born composer and court musician, worked in Günzberg, and was the cornetto player in the Bavarian Court Band in 1612.

La Hieronyma is an early baroque piece. The original score identifies the piece as a trombone or viola solo. In this publication, the editor has retained the original key, added tempo suggestions, dynamics, slurs, and phrasing. In addition to the bass clef trombone part there is an optional continuo realization. There are many publications of this work available, this Robert King publication edited by Glen Smith also includes a french horn part (solo part). This work is appropriate for a recital and for use in a liturgical setting.

The organ part is on two staves with registration suggested and dynamics clearly marked.

This work has been recorded by trombonist Abbie Conant and organist Schnorr Klemens on the CD *Posaune und Orgel* (Audite 97.410).

Christensen, Bernhard (1906-2004)

Concerto for trombone and organ. Copenhagen, Denmark: Society for Publication of Danish Music (Samfundet), 1977.

- Tenor trombone
- Difficulty: Moderate
- Technique: Trills, Grace notes
- Mutes: None

    I.   Chaconne
    II.   Aria Concerto

Christensen, a Danish church organist and composer, graduated from the Royal Academy of Music in Copenhagen in 1929. He led the jazz scene in Denmark during the early 1930s. His compositional output covers a range of styles from classical works to big band charts, and includes two jazz oratorios.

There is a discrepancy concerning the title of this ten-minute work, possibly from a mistranslation. The hand-written title page, penned by the composer, is *Koncert for basun (evt. Fagot aller violincello) og orgel,* but the publisher lists the work as *Concerto for trombone and organ.* The title *Koncert* better suits the work because of its two-movement structure, which is closer to a vocal cavatina than a concerto. The first movement, a stately chaconne, has two time signatures notated, which allows the performer to think in either 6/4 or 3/2 meter. The piece begins with trombone alone stating the theme marked, "solo ad lib. " This theme is soon passed to the organ, where the section becomes more structured with the marking, " ♩ = 104." This evolves into a true duo, both the trombone and organ alternate and share important solo lines. The movement concludes with a short cadenza. The second movement, *Aria Concerto,* has two meter options, 6/8 or 3/4. More playful then the previous movement, this section makes a strong musical statement. This work is suited for a recital and in a liturgical setting.

The organ part is on three staves with some registrations indicated and dynamics clearly marked.

This work has been recorded by trombonist Niels-Ole Bo Johansen and organist Ulrich Spang-Hanssen on the CD *Alpha and Omega* (Paula PACD 87).

Cohen, Jules (1835-1901)

Andante pour Trombone et Orgue (Piano). Paris, France: Editions Musicales Européenes, 1995.

- Tenor trombone
- Difficulty: Moderate
- Technique: Turns, Grace notes
- Mutes: None

I.   Andante

Cohen, a French composer, keyboardist, and vocalist was born in Marseilles and received his formal musical training at the Paris Conservatory. After graduation, he remained at the conservatory as a vocal instructor, as well as chorus master for the Grand Opera. He composed four unsuccessful operas and several symphonies, but is best known for his vocal and keyboard works, composing over 200 of each. Cohen wrote several works for the trombone, including *Andantino for trombone quartet in D-flat major*, which is reminiscent of Liszt.

This single movement, three-and-a-half minute work is an excellent example of nineteenth-century French bel canto style. The prefatory notes states, "suitable for church performance at the Offertory." Appropriately marked "Andante," this work in B-flat major features a singing style throughout, and would provide a complementary performance piece for any student working on etudes from the Bordogni-Rochut books. *Andante* remains in 3/4 meter with simple rhythms, but requires control, sensitivity, and shaping from the trombonist. The high tessitura may test a young player. This work is suited for a recital and for a liturgical setting.

The organ part is on two staves with a few registration indicated, and dynamics clearly marked.

This work has been recorded by trombonist Benny Sluchin on the CD *French Bel Canto Trombone* (ADDA 581247).

Cresswell, Lyell (b. 1944)

Canzone for trombone and organ. Wellington, New Zealand: Center for New Zealand Music, 1992.

- Tenor trombone
- Difficulty: Advanced
- Technique: Multiple tonguing, Grace notes, Glissandi
- Mutes: Straight

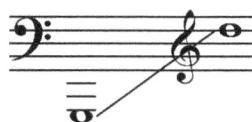

      I.   ♩ = 72

Cresswell, a New Zealand composer, received his first musical training as a member of a Salvation Army brass band. His formal studies took place in New Zealand, Canada and Europe. Currently, he is a Professor of Music in Scotland. He maintains a close association with the BBC Scottish Symphony Orchestra, which premiered several of his works.

Composed in 1992, this fifteen-minute, single-movement work was commissioned by trombonist John Kenny who also premiered the work with organist John Kitchen at the Paisley Organ Festival in 1992.

Cresswell writes:

The Italian word *canzone* (song), or sometimes *canzona*, has several musical applications. From the 13th to the 17th centuries in Italian poetry it referred to a type of lyrical poem in stanzas of eight lines; in the 12th and 13th centuries to a type of troubadour song; in the 16th century a type of madrigal; in the 16th and 17th centuries an instrumental composition of clear texture and sectional structure often involving repetition—an ancestor of the sonata; and in the 18th and 19th centuries a song or instrumental piece of lyrical character. My composition, *Canzone*, draws on all of these types. It is a work in stanzas following a pattern ABACDA (but with many cross-references) and it emphasizes the vocal qualities of the trombone. The trombone is, perhaps, the instrument closest to the human voice; it has the ability to slide between notes and the player must breathe.[14]

The piece begins with the muted trombone playing alone with rhythmic figures almost entirely connected with glissandi. This establishes an impressionistic quality evident throughout the work. A delicate slow section showcases the trombone and organ pedal playing the melody in unison. The work builds in complexity and intensity to the end. The trombone score is notated in bass and treble clef. This work is suited for a recital.

The organ part is on three staves and requires a large organ. Registration and dynamics are clearly marked.

Cresswell, Lyell (b. 1944)

Canzone for trombone and organ. Coventry, England: Warwick Music, 1992.

This is the same work as the one listed above from a different publisher.

Daetwyler, Jean (1907-1994)

Sérénade au Clair de Lune pour Trombone Alto et Orgue. Crans-Montana, Switzerland: Editions Marc Reift, 1991.

---

[14] Lyell Cresswell, personal E-mail, March 25, 2008.

- Alto trombone
- Difficulty: Moderate
- Technique: Nothing unusual
- Mute: None

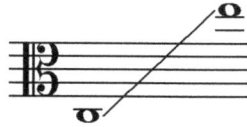

I.   Quasi recitativo

Daetwyler, a Swiss composer, studied composition at the Paris Conservatory. After graduation he became a professor of music, teaching theory and composition at the Sion Conservatoire in Switzerland. His compositions have a strong connection to his native Switzerland, with the use of alphorn and other traditional Swiss instruments.

Sérénade au Clair de Lune, a playful eight-and-a-half minute, single-movement work, journeys through many tempo and stylistic changes. The opening, marked "Quasi Recitativo ♩ = 72," is essentially for trombone alone, but has several organ exclamations. This opening leads to a cantabile section which is slightly slower but continues in a similar style. The work accelerates in the section after a fermata marked, "Grazioso ♩ = 144," and continues building to the Allegro section. A slight change in character occurs when the meter shifts to 2/4, and features sixteenth-note runs played by the trombone. The piece concludes with the return of the A section material with the addition of a trombone cadenza before ending softly. This work is suited for a recital and for a liturgical setting.

The organ part is on two staves no registration indicated, and dynamics clearly marked.

This work has been recorded by Branimir Slokar on his recording *Fantasia* (Marcophon CD 922).

de Haan, Jacob (b. 1959)

Missa Brevis for trombone and Organ. Heerenveen, Holland: De Haske Publications, 2004.

- Tenor trombone
- Difficulty: Easy
- Technique: Nothing unusual
- Mutes: None

I.	Kyrie
II.	Gloria
III.	Credo
IV.	Sanctus
V.	Benedicus
VI.	Agnus Dei

de Haan was born in Heerenveen, Netherlands. He received his formal musical training at the Conservatory in Leeuwarden where he studied composition, organ, and trumpet. After graduation, he returned to his alma mater as a professor of music. Aside from his teaching duties, de Haan is in demand as a music editor for several European publishers.[15]

Missa Brevis, an eighteen-minute work in six-movements, was commissioned by the Department of Music and Culture in Guebwiler, France, and premiered in June 2002. The movements are simple and suited to a young trombonist. The composers notes indicate the piece is intended to be used in a liturgical setting, but it would work equally as well for a recital. The piece includes a play-along CD and features Dutch

---

[15] Prefatory notes.

trombonist Jilt Jansma. *Missa Brevis* is also available for choir with organ or wind band accompaniment.

The organ part is on two staves with dynamics and registration clearly indicated.

Diemer, Emma Lou (b. 1927)

Psalm 1 for Bass or Tenor trombone & Organ or Piano. Ithaca, NY: Ensemble Publications, 2002.

- Bass or Tenor trombone
- Difficulty: Moderate
- Technique: Nothing unusual
- Mutes: None

    I.   Slowly, Expressively

Diemer, an American keyboardist and composer, was identified as a musical prodigy at an early age. She studied composition with Gardner Read while still in high school. She received her formal musical training at Yale, where she studied with Hindemith. This was followed by a Ph.D. in composition from the Eastman School of Music. She was employed as a professor of music at several American universities, and remained an active organist. In 1995, Diemer was named "Composer of the Year" by the American Guild of Organists. She is best known for her instrumental and choral works which are often in a neo-classical or neo-romantic style, featuring free tonality.

Psalm 1, a four-minute, single-movement work, dedicated to Brian Anton and Joan DeVee Dixon, who premiered the work in November 1998. This piece is slow and expressive, written in 2/2 meter without any style or meter changes. The piece develops three separate themes which consist mostly of quarter and eighth-notes, and would be suited to a young trombonist. Because of the high tessitura, this piece would be more comfortably played on tenor trombone rather than bass trombone. This work is suited for a recital and for a liturgical setting.

The organ part is on two staves no registration indicated, and dynamics clearly marked.

This work has been recorded by Byron Anton, bass trombone and Joan DeVee Dixon, organ on the CD *The Psalms of Emma Lou Diemer* (vol. 2. RBWCD015).

Diemer, Emma Lou (b. 1927)

Psalm 122 for Bass Trombone (Tuba) & Organ (Piano). Ithaca, NY: Ensemble Publications, 1999.

- Bass trombone
- Difficulty: Advanced
- Technique: Flutter Tonguing, Tremolos, Glissandi
- Mutes: None

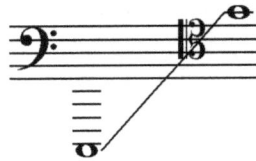

     I.   Allegro Moderato

Commissioned by Alvin C. Broyles, *Psalm 122,* a six-and-a-half minute work written for Brian Anton, Joan DeVee Dixon and Mark Lusk in 1998 to expand the limited repertoire for bass trombone and organ. This dramatic work has a wide range of style changes throughout. The opening features fanfare passages from the bass trombone, alternating between 2/4 and 3/4 meter. A sequence of sixteenth-notes creates a transition to the slower lyrical section where the composer suggests a jazz style with syncopation, flutter tonguing and glissandi played by the trombone. The final section returns to the style of the opening, concluding with the trombone playing a high F- G tremolo. The piece ends with a stinger on B-flat1. This work is suited for a recital.

The organ part is on three staves and requires a three manual instrument. No registration is indicated and dynamics are clearly marked.

This work has been recorded by Byron Anton, bass trombone and Joan DeVee Dixon, organ on the CD *The Psalms of Emma Lou Diemer* (RBWCD013), this recording is also released on, *The Psalms of Emma Lou Diemer*, Volume 2 (RBWCD015).

Donati, Guido (b. 1949)

...Buccina parva canente per Trombone barocco e Organo (oppure Trombone e Pianoforte). Sondrio, Italy: Animando Edizioni Musicali, 2002.

- Tenor trombone
- Difficulty: Moderate
- Technique: Nothing unusual
- Mutes: None

I.   Lento espressivo

Donati, an Italian composer, keyboardist, and choir director, received his musical training at the Conservatorio Giuseppe Verdi in Turin, Italy. After graduation, he became a professor of music, teaching organ at the same institution. An active performer, he is in demand in classical and jazz realms. Donati has published over one-hundred compositions, mostly chamber instrumental works.

Dedicated to Florino Rosini, this single-movement, four-and-a-half minute work is marked, "Lento espressivo," and begins with a four-measure legato organ introduction. The trombone enters with a similar cantabile melody, accelerating into a short animated recitative section. The piece ends softly. The high tessitura, combined with soft dynamics, requires control and endurance from the trombonist. This work is suited for a recital and for a liturgical setting.

The organ part is on two staves with no registration indicated and dynamics clearly marked.

Drude, Matthias (b. 1960)

Solo für Tuba. Aurich, Germany: ADU Verlag, 2000.

- Tuba
- Difficulty: Advanced
- Technique: Nothing unusual
- Mutes: None

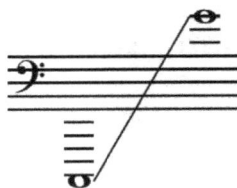

      I.   Andante

Drude, a German composer, also teaches at the College of Sacred Music in Dresden. He has an extensive compositional portfolio, including an impressive list of works for brass.

Composed in 1998 for Markus Hötzen, *Solo für Tuba* is a technically challenging sixteen-minute, single-movement work. Commanding, emotional, and powerful, the piece alternates between lyrical cadenza-like sections played by the tuba set over thinly orchestrated chords in the accompaniment. This is contrasted with strong rhythmic motives shared between the two instruments. The work remains dark and moody throughout, ending pensively. The tuba part is technically challenging with rapid runs and large leaps. Endurance might be a consideration since there are only two measures of rest for the tuba during the piece.

This work is suited for a recital. The organ part is on three staves with registration indicated and dynamics are clearly marked.

This work has been recorded by tubist Markus Hötzen on the CD *Matthias Drude Sonaten* (Audiolis).

Eben, Petr (1929-2007)

Two Invocations for Trombone and Organ, Essex, England: United Music Publishers, 1996.

- Tenor trombone
- Difficulty: Moderate
- Technique: Nothing unusual
- Mutes: Straight

     I.   Moderato
    II.   Resoluto

Eben, is regarded as the most renowned contemporary Czech composer. His early musical education began at the piano and organ in the medieval town of Cesky Krumlov. During the atrocities of World War II, he and his family were held captive at the Buchenwald concentration camp until its liberation in 1945. After the war, he studied at the Prague Academy of Music and Dramatic Arts. His compositional output includes over 200 works in many genres.

This eleven-minute, two-movement work was commissioned in 1988 by the Czech Music Alliance of the USA, and premiered by trombonist Joel Blahnik in New Prague, Minnesota. *Two Invocations,* is based on the theme from the "St. Wencelas Chorale" which dates back to the Middle-Ages. *Invocation I*, marked "Moderato," begins lyrically and presents the theme in its diatonic form. The piece changes character as the movement develops. The texture becomes thicker and the interaction between organ and trombone becomes more frenetic as the tempo accelerates. The movement concludes with a return of the main theme played by the trombone. *Invocation II*, marked "Risoluto," features the same theme, developed more chromatically than the first movement, the use of syncopation creates interesting effects. This work is suited for a recital and a liturgical setting.

The organ part is on three staves with registration indicated and dynamics clearly marked. This piece requires an accomplished organist because of its virtuosic nature.

This work has been recorded by: Trombonist Christian Lindberg and organist Gunnar Idenstam on the CD *The Sacred Trombone* (BIS CD-488), trombonist Kalfus Votava on the recording *Eben: Religious Works* (Supraphone 111438-1231), Invocation No. 1 by trombonist Lars-Göran Carlsson on the recording *A composer portrait 2 "Bittere Erde"—Petr Eben* (OPUS 3 OP9301CD), trombonist Niels-Ole Bo Johansen and organist Ulrich Spang-Hanssen on the CD *Holst: Duo Concertante for Trombone & Organ; Works by Elgar, Guilmant, Liszt, Ropartz, Vaughan Williams & Eben.* (Classico CLASSCD 122).

Ehmann, Heinrich (1938-1998)

Drei Stücke für Tuba und Orgel. Wolfenbüttel, Germany: Mösler Verlag, 1982.

- Tuba
- Difficulty: Moderate
- Technique: free meter sections
- Mutes: None

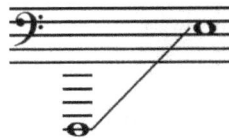

    I.   Ruhig

    II.   Bewegt

    III.   Etwas breite Viertel, frei im Tempo

This four-and-a-half-minute work is a collection of three movements. *Ruhig*, is slow and has a predominate triplet motive. The second movement *Bewegt* is in a playful 7/8 meter. The final movement *Etwas breite Viertel, frei im Tempo* is without an indicated meter. There are sections without barlines, so both instrumentalists play-off each other in a rubato-like feel.

This work is well-suited for a recital and for a liturgical setting.

The organ part is on three staves with no registrations indicated, and dynamics clearly marked.

Erdmann-Abele, Veit (b. 1944)

Epilog für Posaune und Orgel. Reutlingen, Germany: Veit Erdmann-Abele, 1985.

- Tenor trombone
- Difficulty: Moderate
- Technique: Alternate notation
- Mutes: None

    I.   Rezitativo
    II.   Cadenza
    III.   Aria

Erdmann, a German composer, received his formal musical training at the Musikhochschule in Stuttgart. After graduation, he became the music editor of the *Süddeutsche*, a publication of Stuttgart Radio. He is also the director of the Musica-Nova-Konzertreihe, a new music festival in his home town of Reutlingen.

Composed in 1985, this six-and-a-half minute modern work is dedicated to Hermann Egnet. The first movement, *Rezitativo,* without bar-lines, features a trombone recitation developed around triplet figures. The second movement, *Cadenza*, is for trombone alone, again notated without meter. The final movement, *Aria,* is more structured and shifts between 2/2 and 3/2 meter, "marked ♩ = 100." The musical line is angular and stark, in a march-like character. There are a few contrasting lyrical phrases which create a dialogue between the organ and trombone. This work is suited for a recital and a liturgical setting.

The organ part is on three staves with no registration indicated, and dynamics clearly marked.

Eversole, James (1929-2015)

ESQUISSES for Trombone and Organ. Seattle, WA: Ars Nova Press, 2006.

- Tenor trombone
- Difficulty: Moderate-Advanced
- Technique: Grace notes
- Mutes: None

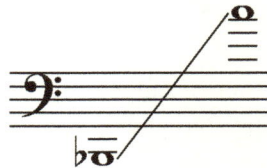

    I.   Lively

Eversole, an American trombonist and composer, received his formal musical training from the University of Kentucky, the old Cincinnati Conservatory of Music and earned an Ed.D. in Composition at Columbia University. He taught composition at the University of Connecticut until his retirement in 1989 and now resides in Missoula, Montana. He has a large compositional body of work, ranging from operas to chamber works.

Composed in 1993, this single-movement, ten-minute piece was written for Dr. Jim Robertson, who premiered the work with organist Sandra Rabas in Billings, Montana in 1994. *ESQUISSES* (sketches) is in four sections and is intended to be played without pause. The subtitle, "Athedra," refers to a series of works by the composer for trumpet, baritone, horn, trombone, and tuba and also includes two works for brass quintet. [16] The first section of this piece is energetic with continuous sixteenth-note runs played by the trombone, at times doubled by the

---

[16] Prefatory notes.

organ. Proficient slide technique is required to play at the indicated tempo "quarter-note = 112." The second section is lighter and playful. A canon is introduced by the trombone and echoed by the organ. An expressive lyrical section provides contrast before returning to material which is similar to the opening section. The conclusion of the work is exuberant. This piece is also arranged for solo trombone and six trombones. This work is suited for a recital and for a liturgical setting.

The organ part is on three staves with registration and dynamics clearly marked. .

Fischer, Carl August (1829-1892)

Fantasie für Solo-Posaune (oder violoncello) und Orgel (oder pianoforte) op.21. Leipzig, Germany: C.F. Kahnt, 1978.

- Tenor trombone
- Difficulty: Moderate
- Technique: Grace notes
- Mutes: None

    I.   Maestoso e energico

Fischer, a celebrated German composer and organist, played for many churches in Dresden. The majority of his compositions use the organ, including four symphonies for orchestra and organ, and numerous chamber works for organ and various instruments.

Fantasie, a nine-minute, single-movement romantic work bears the inscription, "dedicated to my good friend Mr. A. Bruns." Composed in a fast-slow-fast, ABA form, the work begins with a recitative section. The following A-tempo section incorporates typical baroque styling, using scale patterns and sequences. The B section is slower, marked "Andante Cantabile." This lyrical section requires expressive playing. The final section is similar to the opening.

The organ part is on three staves with no registration indicated and dynamics clearly marked.

This work has been recorded by trombonist Sebastian Krause and organist Gabrielle Wadewitz on the CD *Sonntagsposaunenstück: Romantic music for trombone and organ* (Raum Klang RK 9805).

Foreman, Roger (b. 1985)

Resolution for Trombone and Organ, Unpublished, 2009.

- Trombone
- Difficulty: Advanced
- Technique: Nothing unusual
- Mutes: Bucket Mute

Foreman, an American composer, has had works performed by the Tucson Symphony Orchestra, the Tucson Pops Orchestra, and the Arizona Balalaika Orchestra. He studied composition at the University of Arizona, and Florida State University.

Resolution was commissioned by Patrick Lawrence and the Southern Arizona Chapter of the American Guild of Organists; and premiered by Patrick Lawrence and Pamela Decker at the University of Arizona in February 2010. The seven-minute work begins with a chant-like melody in the trombone, which develops along with the organ accompaniment; the music then proceeds through an introspective section filled with piquant harmonies and a tumultuous period of dissonant conflict before culminating in a bold and triumphantconclusion. Influenced by Barber and Hindemith, the work has a strongmelodic sense and makes use of quartal and extended tertian harmonies.

The organ is scored on three staves with registration suggested and dynamics clearly marked.

Fork, Gunter (1930-1998)

Kanzone, Fuge, und Madrigal für Posaune und Orgel. Renningen, Germany: C.F. Schmidt, 1992.

- Bass or Tenor trombone
- Difficulty: Advanced
- Technique: Glissandi, Flutter tonguing
- Mutes: Straight

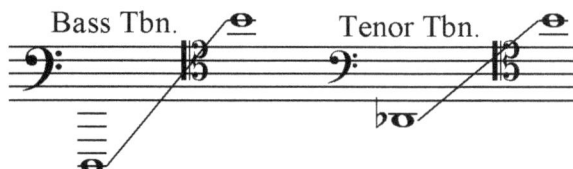

    I.   Kanzone
    II.   Fuge
    III.   Madrigal

This twelve-minute, three-movement work was written for bass trombone. The publisher includes an adaptation for tenor trombone written by Joachim Elser. All three movements begin with trombone alone. The first movement, *Kanzon,* marked "Andante ♩ = 72," after the opening recitation played by the trombone, the organ enters playing colorful harmonies set in a thin texture. This style continues, becoming a duet for trombone and organ pedal, which builds in intensity and later fades to nothing to conclude the section. The second movement, *Fuge,* marked "Allegro ♩ = 132," is technically demanding with rhythmic patterns shifting between simple and compound meter. Like the previous movement, the organ joins the trombone in the established principal theme. A march-like section provides contrast prior to returning to material similar to the beginning. The final movement, *Madrigal,* marked "Molto cantabile ♩ = 66," begins with a theme by Orlando di

Lasso.[17] The composer has organized the three movements in an unusual format, with the slow lyrical movement as the finale. This work is suited for a recital.

The organ part is on three staves and requires an accomplished organist. No registration indications provided, however, dynamics are clearly marked.

This work has been recorded by Joachim Elser on the CD *Posaune und Orgel* (Mitra CD 16228).

Forsyth, Malcolm (1936-2011)

Soliloquy, Epitaph and Allegro for trombone and organ. Markham, Canada: Counterpoint Musical Services, 1988.

- Tenor trombone
- Difficulty: Advanced
- Technique: Alternate notation, Grace notes, Glissandi
- Mutes: None

I.	Soliloquy
II.	Epitaph
III.	Allegro

Forsyth, a composer and trombonist, was born in South Africa. He received his formal musical training at the University of Cape Town. After graduation, he was a member of the Cape Town Symphony Orchestra for several years prior to immigrating to Canada, where he became a Professor of Music at the University of Alberta in Edmonton.

---

[17] Prefatory notes.

His South African roots are evident in his compositions. He has received awards for his work including three Juno awards (the Canadian equivalent of the American Grammy). He was recognized as Canadian Composer of the Year in 1989.

This twelve-minute, three-movement contemporary work was commissioned and premiered by trombonist James Montgomery with organist Willis Noble in Windsor, England in 1989. The first movement, *Soliloquy,* marked "freely," has no bar-lines. This section features chant-like figures played by the trombone over repeating organ patterns. This movement is powerful yet moving and is rich in chromatic harmonies. The second movement, *Epitaph*, is a peaceful lament which bears the inscription "To the memory of Alan Paton (1903-1988)." The final movement, *Allegro*, is the longest and most technically demanding for both instruments with rapid sequences of sixteenth-note figures weaving through different meters. A contrasting meno mosso section provides some calm and lyricism before the flashy double-time ending section. The piece concludes dramatically with a harmonic slur followed by an optional glissando up to f3. This work is suited for a recital and a liturgical setting.

The organ part is on three staves with registration indicated and dynamics clearly marked.

Forsyth, Michael (1936-2011)

Welzheim Flourish for Trombone and Organ. Granville, Australia: Trombonis Australis Editions, 1998.

- Tenor trombone
- Difficulty: Advanced
- Technique: Nothing unusual
- Mutes: None

I.   Andante Maestoso ♩ = 60

Welzheim Flourish, a four-and-a-half-minute, single movement work begins in 5/4 meter, marked "Andante Maestoso ♩ = 60." The first three trombone phrases are technically demanding with figures constructed from: triplets, sixteenth-notes, sextuplets and thirty-second-notes. Although these patterns look exceedingly difficult, they are actually quite manageable due to the slow tempo. After a fermata, the piece moves into the next section, marked "Allegro Moderato, dotted half = 60," and remains in a light 6/8 and 5/8 meter. The work returns to the opening flourishes, ending dramatically with the trombone holding the note d2. This work is suited to a recital or a liturgical setting.

The organ part is on three staves with registration and dynamics clearly indicated.

Frith, John (b. 1947)

Meditation for bass trombone and organ. Coventry, England: Warwick Music, 2010.

- Bass trombone
- Difficulty: Moderate
- Technique: Nothing unusual
- Mutes: None

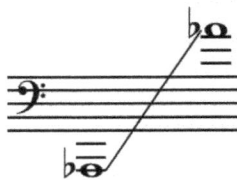

John Frith, an English composer and hornist, studied at Dartington College of Arts and The Guildhall School of Music. He has written extensively for brass and winds.

Meditation for bass trombone and organ was composed in 2010 for Jonathan Warburton. The piece begins slowly and pensively. The piece traverses several key and meter changes before building in intensity near the end with showering sixteenth-note figures on the organ manuals. An accessible piece, nothing is technically difficult for the bass trombonist.

The organ part is not demanding, written on three staves with no registration indicated. This piece is suited for a recital and for use in a liturgical setting. A sample score and midi excerpt can be found at: www.warwickmusic.com. A review by Patrick Lawrence can be found in the ITA Journal, January 2014, Vol.42 (1), p. 47.

Gadsch, Herbert (1913-2011)

Konzert für Posaune und Orgel. Ditzingen, Germany: Edition Musica Rinata E. Hofmann, 1997.

- Tenor trombone
- Difficulty: Moderate
- Technique: Grace notes, Lip trills, Glissando
- Mutes: None

    I.   Präludium "Gwinea lay down"
    II.   Improvisation "Lay this body down"
    III.   Tokkata "I'm arolling"

Gadsch, a German composer and organist, was raised in a musical family. He received his formal musical training at the Leipzig Conservatory of Music. He served as a German soldier in World War II and was held captive for several years in Russia. Upon his release in 1950, he found work as a church music director and organ teacher at the Academy of Music in Dresden.

Composed in 1997, this ten-minute, three-movement modern work has many rhythmic features. The composer does not provide any form of tempo indication with the exception of a ritardando at the end of each movement. *Präludium,* has an etude-like quality passing syncopated sequences and motivic ideas between the trombone and organ. Because of this strong rhythmic drive, many of the trombone lines sound similar to Morse code. The second movement, *Improvisation,* has a thinner texture, allowing the trombonist opportunity to play expressively. The final movement, *Tokkata,* is similar to the first, requiring flexibility and dexterity. This work is suited for a recital.

The organ part is on three staves with no registration indicated, and dynamics clearly marked.

Gadsch, Herbert (1913-2011)

Spiritual-Suite für Posaune und Orgel. Ditzingen, Germany: Edition Musica Rinata E. Hofmann, 1997.

- Tenor trombone
- Difficulty: Moderate
- Technique: Nothing unusual
- Mutes: None

I.	Tokkata "Listen to the Lambs"
II.	Ostinato "Nobody Knows"
III.	Kanon "This Train is Bound"
IV.	Pastorale "Every Time"
V.	Fuge "Go Down, Moses"

This eight-minute suite is a collection of five movements based on African-American spirituals. The first movement, *Tokkata "Listen to the Lambs,"* is in common meter and features light syncopation with off-the-beat figures. There are arpeggiated sixteenth-note patterns which are technically demanding. The second movement, *Ostinato "Nobody Knows,"* is based on the familiar theme, and is developed over an organ accompaniment with a prominent walking bass line in the pedal. The third movement, *Kanon "This Train is Bound,"* features triplet figures and a driving musical line. The penultimate movement, *Pastorale "Every Time,"* is soft and lyrical in 6/8 meter. The final movement, *Fuge*

"Go Down, Moses," is a fuguetta on the title theme, ending dramatically with organ and trombone. The trombone part is primarily in bass clef with a few measures notated in treble clef. This work is suited for a recital and for a liturgical setting.

The organ part is on three, no registrations indicated, and dynamics clearly marked.

Gárdonyi, Zsolt (b. 1946)

Rhapsodie für Posaune und Orgel, Frankfurt, Germany: Musikverlag Zimmermann, 1982.

- Tenor trombone
- Difficulty: Moderate
- Technique: Glissandi over the harmonic series
- Mutes: Straight

I.   Adagio, quasi recitative, molto rubato

Gárdonyi, a Hungarian composer and organist, is the son of the well-known composer and musicologist Zoltán Gárdonyi who studied with Kodály and Hindemith. He is currently employed as a Professor of Music Theory at the State Conservatory in Würzburg, Bavaria. He composes primarily choral and chamber works, with a strong emphasis on organ. In the year 2000, he was awarded an Honorary Doctorate by the Reformed Theological University of Debrecen, Hungary, for his contributions in the field of church music.

Rhapsodie, a single-movement ten-minute work was composed in 1980 for the International Organ Week of Wiesbaden. The first half, marked "Adagio, quasi reciativo, molto rubato," features soft expressive trombone phrases set over sustained organ chords in close harmony. The middle section has an abrupt shift in character, becoming loud and bombastic with the trombone playing fanfare-like figures. It builds in intensity in the ensuing allegro section, before returning to material based on the espressivo opening theme.

Dr. Gárdonyi comments on this work:

You can observe the alternation of acoustic chords and those based on the distance principle. There is ample precedent for this type of composition among the great composer-organists is the history of music. Through several pieces, J.S. Bach in his Orgelbüchlein and César Franck in L'Organiste gaveadequate guidelines for the possibilities of organ improvisation andcomposition.[18]

Gárdonyi's other works for brass and organ include, *Sonata da Chiesa for Trumpet, Trombone and Organ*, and *Fantasie for Four Trombones and Organ,* available through Edition Walhall Magdeburg and Musikverlag Zimmermann Frankfurt respectively. This work is suited for a recital and a liturgical setting.

The organ part is on three staves with no registration indicated and dynamics clearly marked.

Rhapsodie has been recorded by trombonist Sándor Hegedüs on the CD *Works by Zsolt Gárdonyi* (Psalmus Records OVA-002), and by trombonist Martin Goss and organist Jakob Hans-Otto on the CD *Musik für Orgel und Posaune* (Hänssler Classics 98.945).

Genzmer, Harald (b. 1909)

Sonate Für Posaune und Orgel. New York, NY: Litolff/C.F.Peters, 1989.

---

[18] Zsolt Gárdonyi, personal E-mail, March 24, 2008.

- Tenor trombone
- Difficulty: Advanced
- Technique: Multiple tonguing, Glissandi
- Mutes: Straight, Cup

I.	Moderato
II.	Adagio
III.	Finale-Vivo

Genzmer, a German composer, studied with Hindemith. He later served as Professor of Composition at the Musikhochschule in Freiburg and Chair of the Composition Department at the Hochschule für Musik, Munich. He has a compositional repertoire of over 300 works. Genzmer, known as "a humanist among musicians," strives to place the human being at the center of his compositional activities with a particular interest in young and amateur musicians.

Sonate Für Posaune und Orgel, a fourteen-and-a-half-minute work composed in 1977, is dedicated to Armin Rosin. In the first movement, *moderato,* Gezmer blends the timbre of the two instruments, adding tension with a reoccurring three-against-two rhythmic figure. The second movement, *adagio,* opens with the instruments conversing in a slow expressive call and response section that leads to a vivace segue into the third movement.

The final movement, *Finale-Vivo,* is technically demanding for both trombonist and organist. This work is suited for a recital. The organ part is on three staves.

This work has been recorded by Armin Rosin on his recording *Posaune In Unserer Zeit* (FCD 91 407), and by Alain Trudel on the CD *The Art of The Trombone* Naxos (8.553716).

Gerlach, Günter (1928-2003)

Introduktion und Choral für Posaune und Orgel. Köln,Germany: Verlag Christoph Dohr, 1996/2002.

- Tenor trombone
- Difficulty: Moderate
- Technique: Nothing unusual
- Mutes: None

     I.   Grave
    II.   Choral

Gerlach, a German born composer, studied keyboard and sang in choirs as a child. He secured his first position as a church organist by the age of fourteen. After completing his formal training, he continued to serve as an organist until his retirement in 1995.[19]

Composed in 1969, *Introduktion und Choral*, is a four-minute, two movement work. The introduction, marked "Grave," begins with a brief organ prologue followed by a trombone fanfare. The remainder of this movement is stately and regal, shifting between simple and compound meter. The second movement, *choral,* is simple, yet lyrical with opportunity to showcase the resonant quality of the trombone, aided by the acoustic properties of a good performance hall or church. The section builds in intensity and then settles into a trombone cadenza near the end of the work. This work is suited for a recital and a liturgical setting.

The organ part is on three staves with registrations and dynamics clearly indicated.

---

[19] Prefatory notes.

Gerlach, Günter (1928-2003)

Sonatine : "Wie schön leucht' uns der Morgenstern": für Posaune und Orgel. Glendale, NY: C.F. Peters, 1992.

- Tenor trombone
- Difficulty: Moderate
- Technique: Nothing unusual
- Mutes: None

    I.   Feierlich – rezitativisch
    II.   Adagio
    III.   Vivo

Sonatine, an eight-minute work in three movements bears the inscription "How beautifully luminous is the morning star." The first movement, *Feierlich – rezitativisch*, is solemn, beginning primarily in recitative style, before settling into a trombone and organ dialogue in a mournful lento section. The second movement, *Adagio*, shifts between alla breve meter 2/2, 3/2 and 4/2 meter. In this section, the two solo instruments exchange thematic material, playing together only for a few measures. Numerous rests marked with fermati and a trombone cadenza marked, "libero," create an expansive quality. The second movement segues directly into the final movement, *Vivo*. Together, the two instruments play fanfare-like figures while building in intensity to the end of the piece. This work is suited for a recital and a liturgical setting.

The organ part is on three staves with no registration indicated and dynamics clearly marked.

Glauser, Max (b. 1937)

Canzona Für Posaune und Orgel (Klavier). Crans-Montana, Switzerland: Editions Marc Reift, 1992.

- Tenor trombone
- Difficulty: Advanced
- Technique: 3/8+3/8+2/8 meter
- Mutes: None

       I.   Fliessend bewegt

Glasuer, a German composer and organist, received his formal musical training at the Bern Conservatory, and studied with Dr. M. Zulaf, Fritz Indermühle and Gerhard Aeschbacher. Many of his works are for solo wind instrument and organ. He is currently a music instructor at the Muristalden Teachers' Seminar in Bern.[20]

Canzona, an eight-minute, single-movement work, has many tempo and style changes. The piece begins with a simple ostinato pattern established in the lower manual of the organ. The trombone and upper manual join playing the main theme in canon. This melody is challenging for the trombone, with rapid sixteenth-note runs that venture to the upper reaches of the practical range of the instrument. The second section, marked "allegro," features the unusual meter 3/8+3/8+2/8; which could present ensemble challenges with the organ. This section also has a high tessitura which can be taxing on the performer. The work slows in a section marked, "moderato," built on triplet figures before a return to a 3/8 allegro section. The piece concludes with a "vivace" section, demanding strong technique from both performers. In addition to the score, the publisher provides trombone parts in C bass clef, C tenor clef,

---

[20] Prefatory notes.

and B-flat treble clef. This work is suited for a recital and a liturgical setting.

The organ part is on two staves with some registration indicated and dynamics clearly marked.

Glauser, Max (b. 1937)

Trilogie für Posaune & Orgel. Crans-Montana, Switzerland: Editions Marc Reift, 1992.

- Tenor trombone
- Difficulty: Moderate
- Technique: Lip trill
- Mutes: None

    I.   Toccata "Herr Gott dich loben wir"
    II.   Passacaglia "Christe du Lamm Gottes"
    III.   Fantasie "Nun bitten wir den heiligen Geist"

From the Collection Branimir Slokar, *Trilogie,* is a ten-minute work in three movements, designed to represent the Trinity: God the Father, Christ the Son, and the Holy Spirit. The first movement, *Toccata "Herr Gott dich loben wir,"* (Lord God we praise thee) is based on the "Te Deum" melody. The trombone and the upper manual of the organ play offset sixteenth-note passages set in canon, over long, descending pedal points. The second movement, *Passacaglia* is based on the theme "Christe du Lamm Gottes" (Christ thou lamb of God). This melody, shared between the organ pedal and the trombone, is somber and chromatic. The dissonance portrays the pain suffered by Jesus at his death. The final movement, *Fantasie*, is based on the cheerful hymn tune "Nun bitten wir den heiligen Geist" (Now we ask the Holy Spirit). The melody is presented in the form of a fugue, developing into a trombone cadenza near the end of the work. This work is suited for a recital and a liturgical setting.

The organ part is on three staves with registration indicated and dynamics clearly marked.

This work has been recorded by Branimir Slokar on the CD *Fantasia* (Marcophon CD 922-2).

Goddard, Philip (b. 1942)

The Unknown, Opus 24, Lagny-sur-Marne, France: Musik Fabrik Music Publishing, 1999.

- Tuba
- Difficulty: Moderate
- Technique: Nothing unusual
- Mutes: None

Goddard was born in Middlesex England during the Second World War. He describes himself as a "self-realized composer, writer, and nature photographer" Goddard has written ten symphonies and numerous choral and instrumental works.

This thirteen-minute work was commissioned by Carson Cooman, a composer and keyboardist. According to the program notes, the piece is often associated with Charles Ives' *The Unanswered Question*. Goddard writes:

"In my mind was this haunting musical question loaded with a burden of an intense longing for something beyond all understanding (i.e. what people, in their ignorance of what spirituality *really* is, would widely call a 'spiritual' longing)—a three-note motif—which it seemed would be most effectively rendered on the tuba, its questions echoing in the mysterious space evoked by exotic registrations on the organ."

The composer writes "A tuba in F is preferred, with or without an additional euphonium for the highest phrases only; A euphonium for the whole work would not have the intended weight of tone." Aside from the range written for the tuba, the organ part is more difficult than the solo part.

The organ is scored on three staves with registration suggested and dynamics clearly marked.

Godel, Didier (b. 1945)

Sonata da Chiesa pour Trombone et Orgue. Crans-Montana, Switzerland: Editions Marc Reift, 1992.

- Tenor trombone
- Difficulty: Moderate
- Technique: Nothing unusual
- Mutes: None

  I. Moderato

Godel, a Swiss composer, conductor and flutist, received his formal musical training at the University of Geneva. After graduation, he was hired to teach music education at the same institution. From 1972 to 1995, he led the brass ensemble, the Camerata Gabrieli, in Geneva.

Part of the Collection Branimir Slokar, *Sonata da Chiesa* is a seven-minute, single-movement work composed in 1980. The opening, marked "moderato," has a light quality, written in a French style. Meditative, yet chromatic, the composer creates musical interest by blending the colors of the two instruments. The middle section is more rhythmic and builds to a climax. The composer has scored thick textures, which are balanced by the trombone playing chant-like motives alone. The piece ends quietly with a return to the opening material. This work is suited to a recital and a liturgical setting.

The organ part is on three staves with some registration indicated and dynamics clearly marked.

This work has been recorded by Branimir Slokar on the CD *Fantasia*. (Marcophon CD 922-2).

Graap, Lothar (b. 1933)

Choralmusik zur Bestattung für Posaune (Fagott/Violoncello) & Orgel/Klavier. Köln, Germany: Wolfgang G. Haas – Musikverlag Köln E.K., 2007.

- Tenor trombone
- Difficulty: Easy
- Technique: Nothing unusual
- Mutes: None

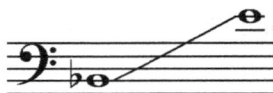

I.	Ich bin ein Gast auf Erden (I am a guest on earth)
II.	O Welt, ich muss dich lassen (O world, I have to leave you)
III.	Ich wollt, dass ich daheime wär (I wish I were at home)
IV.	Wenn mein Stündlein vorhanden ist (When my time has come)
V.	Ach wie flüchtig, ach wie nichtig (Oh how unimportant)
VI.	Christus, der ist mein Leben (Christ, he is my life)
VII.	Jerusalem, du hochgebaute Stadt (Jerusalem, you highly elevated city)
VIII.	Valet will ich dir geben (I want to give to you)
IX.	Mitten wir im Leben sind (In the middle of life we are)
X.	Jesus, meine Zuversicht (Jesus, my confidence)

XI.   Wer weiss, wie nahe mir mein Ende (Who knows, how near my end is)

Graap, a German composer and keyboardist, began his musical training at the age of twelve. He studied composition with Paul Hindemith and Eberhard Wenzel; their influence can be heard in his music. His compositions are deeply rooted in church music. [21]

This collection of eleven movements was composed in 2004. The subtitles, "Choral Music for a Funeral, GWV 504," and "When My Last Hour Has Arrived" (also the title of the fourth movement) both portray the pensive, dark quality expected from funeral music. All eleven movements are short, the longest of which is approximately forty measures. The work is constructed with simple chorale melodies. The complete collection is not intended to be performed in its entirety; it is suited for a recital and a liturgical setting, particularly in a Lenten service. The movements could be used independently, or in combination. Because of the narrow range and simple rhythms of the trombone part, this piece is appropriate for a young trombonist.

The organ part is on two staves with no registration or dynamics indicated.

Graap, Lothar (b. 1933)

Choralpartita zu Advent für Posaune und Orgel. Köln, Germany: Wolfgang G. Haas – Musikverlag Köln E.K., 2003.

- Tenor trombone
- Difficulty: Moderate
- Technique: Nothing unusual

---

[21] Prefatory notes.

- Mutes: None

I.	Introitus
II.	Kleine Toccata
III.	Dialog
IV.	Improvisation
V.	Choral

Choralpartita zu Advent, an eleven-minute, five-movement work was written in 1991 for Sonja Holzapfel. This piece is based on chorale theme, "Die Nacht ist vorgedrungen." The first movement *Introitus,* marked "festlich," begins with a haunting, chant-like theme played by the trombone, shifting between 2/2, 3/2, and 4/2 meter. *Orgelinterludium 1,* a brief organ interlude, is played between the first two movements. The second movement *Kleine Toccata,* marked "lebhaft," is syncopated with ties over the bar-lines. The third movement, *Dialog,* marked "ruhig, verhalten," is a peaceful conversation between the two instruments. The fourth movement, *Improvisation,* begins and ends with reflective, cadenza-like trombone passages. This section begins in 8/4 meter and journeys through 6/4, 7/4, and 10/4 meter. *Orgelinterludium 2,* the second of the two organ interludes, is included between the fourth and final movements. This is a well-placed rest for the trombonist prior to the finale. The fifth and final movement, *Choral,* marked "festlich," is similar to the opening of this work. Chant-like figures are played forte; this intensity remains to the end of the piece. This work is suited for a recital and a liturgical setting.

The organ part is on two staves with no registration indicated and dynamics clearly marked.

Graap, Lothar (b. 1933)

Sonne der Gerechtigkeit, Partita für Posaune und Orgel. Kassel, Germany: Verlag Merseburger, 1995.

- Tenor trombone
- Difficulty: Easy
- Technique: Nothing unusual
- Mutes: None

I.	Festlich, fliessende
II.	Etwas rasch
III.	Straff
IV.	Nicht zu schnell, etwas frei
V.	Lebhaft, nicht hastig
VI.	Choraltempo
VII.	Belebt, festlich

Composed in 1990, *Sonne der Gerechtigkeit* or "Sun of Righteousness," is dedicated to Manfred Rebstadt. This five-minute work is comprised of seven short sketches, the longest of which is twenty-four measures. The movements could be used independently or in combination. The first sketch, *Festlich, Fliessende* (Festive, Flowing) is in 4/2 meter with a stately theme played by the trombone. The second, *etwas rasch* (somewhat fast) features interplay between the trombone and organ, with ties over the bar-lines. The third sketch, *Straff* (Taut), has a march-like quality and ends on a low D (which could be played up the octave in the absence of an F attachment.) The fourth sketch *Nicht zu schnell, etwas frei,* (Not too quickly, somewhat free) returns to 4/2 meter and incorporates quarter-note triplet figures. The fifth sketch, *Lebhaft, nicht hastig,* (Lively, not hastily) is a waltz with simple syncopation. The penultimate movement, *Choraltempo* (Chorale tempo) is simplistic and remains in 4/4 meter. The final sketch, *Belebt, festlich* (Lively, festive) is the longest of the seven sketches and is in 2/2 meter. Due to the narrow range and simplicity, this piece would be excellent for a young trombonist. Furthermore, since the work is in D major, it provides the opportunity to practice the lesser-used positions. This work is suited for a recital and a liturgical setting.

The organ part is on three staves with no registration indicated and dynamics clearly marked.

Graap, Lothar (b. 1933)

Suite für Tuba (Bass Posaune) & Orgel GWV 209. Köln,Germany: Verlag Wolfgang G. Haas, 2003.

- Tuba or Bass Trombone
- Difficulty: Moderate
- Technique: Nothing Unususal
- Mutes: None

I.	Präludium
II.	Improvisation
III.	Cantus
IV.	Toccata
V.	Finale

Composed in 1990, *Suite für Tuba* consists of five short movements. The work is straight forward, however the high tessitura would likely present endurance issues for both tubists and bass trombonists. This work is well-suited for a recital or in a liturgical setting.

The organ part is on two staves with no registrations indicated, and dynamics clearly marked.

Grahl, Kurt (b. 1947)

Eligie und kleine Fuge für Altposaune und Orgel. Köln,Germany: Verlag Christoph Dohr, 2006.

- Alto trombone
- Difficulty: Moderate
- Technique: Nothing unusual
- Mutes: None

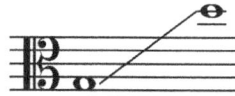

    I.   Eligie
    II.   Kleine "Fuge"

Grahl, a German composer and church musician, received his formal musical training at the Academy of Music in Leipzig, Germany. In 1969, he succeeded his teacher George Trexler as music director at the Catholic parish of St. Trinity in Leipzig. Grahl, an active composer of church music, has published over 600 pieces.

Composed in 2005, this seven-and-a-half minute, two-movement work is composed in the form of a sonata da cheisa. It begins with the slower *Eligie* movement, marked "andante" ♩ = 66. This piece is written in a baroque style and requires a lighter approach than a romantic work. The trombone melody consists of simple sequences played over the organ accompaniment. The second movement, *Kleine "Fuge,"* is marked "Maestoso ♩ = 84." This theme begins with the organ alone. The trombone joins in the last half of the movement with an embellished melody line leading to the coda. This work is suited for a recital and a liturgical setting.

The organ part is on two staves with no registration indicated and dynamics clearly marked. This piece is best suited for a baroque organ.

Graur, Alexander (b. 1952)

Lamentatio Jeremiae Prophetae per trombone e organo. Ancona, Italy: Bèrben Edizioni musicali, 1991.

- Tenor trombone
- Difficulty: Advanced
- Technique: Spoken dialogue,
  Tremolos, Trills, Alternate-notation,
  Flutter tonguing, Vocalization
  through the instrument, Multi-phonics
- Mutes: None

I.   Alla cadenza, moderato espressivo

Graur, a Romanian composer and trombonist, received his Ph.D. in Music Therapy from the Music Academy in Bucharest. He currently works in the field of music therapy, with practices in Italy and the United States.

This ten-minute, modern single-movement work was composed in 1984, and premiered by the composer in October 1985, with organist Massimo Nosetti. Marked "Alla cadenza, moderato espressivo," the piece begins with a technical trombone cadenza which leads to a Largo section in which the trombone is joined by the organ playing dissonant figures, glissandi and difficult double pedaling. The next section is unusual, requiring the trombonist to speak vowels through the instrument. This develops into a spoken dialog performed by the trombonist from Psalm 79: 1-74,4. With the organ playing frantically, these passages would likely have to be shouted. The two instruments build in intensity, leading up to a final trombone cadenza with multi-phonics and another spoken verse from Luke 13: 34-35. The end of the piece is a free-notation, improvised section that is a full-volume glissandi from both instruments. This work is suited for a recital.

The organ part is on three staves with registrations and dynamics indicated.

Graur, Alexander (b. 1952)

Tre Canti Bizantini (di Anton Pann) per trombone e organo. Ancona, Italy: Bèrben Edizioni musicali, 1991.

- Tenor trombone
- Difficulty: Advanced
- Technique: Trills, Grace notes
- Mutes: Straight, Plunger

II.	Stihoavna (Antiphona Virginae)
III.	Chinonic (Laudae)
IV.	Tatal Nostru (Pater Noster)

Composed in 1986, this piece is an adaptation of "Three Byzantine Songs" by the composer Anton Pann (1796-1854). This work has an Eastern European flavor because the themes are borrowed from worship music of the Orthodox Church. The first song, *Stihoavna (Antiphona Virginae)*, marked "Moderato Tranquillo," is primarily a trombone cadenza with long chant-like phrases played out of time over long, organ chords. An organ interlude follows with the section concluding with another trombone cadenza. The second movement, *Chinonic (Laudae)* marked "Maestoso," is without meter and would be best-played from the organ score since no cues are provided in the trombone part. The final movement, *Tatal Nostru (Pater Noster)* marked, "Andante," alternates between organ interludes and trombone cadenzas over held chords. This work is suited for a recital and a liturgical setting.

The organ part is on three staves with registrations indicated and dynamics clearly marked.

Grenager, Lene (b. 1969)

Hver avreise er en hjemkomst (for trombone and organ). Oslo, Norway: Norwegian Music Information Centre, 2002.

- Tenor trombone
- Difficulty: Advanced
- Technique: Half step trills, Glissandi, Alternate notation with F-valve tuning slide removed
- Mutes: Cup mute, Fiber straight mute

      I.   ♩ = 60

Grenager, a Norwegian composer and cellist, studied at the Norwegian State Academy of Music in Oslo. She was awarded the Lindeman Prize for young composers in 2002. As a member of the Norwegian Society of Composers, many of her works have been performed in Europe. She maintains a busy performance schedule as a member of the improvisational ensemble *SPUNK.*

Hver avreise er en hjemkomst (Each Departure is a Return) was commissioned by Inger Lise Ulsrud and Aline Nistad and financed through the Norwegian Composer Fund. This modern eleven-and-a-half-minute, single-movement work was premiered in January 2008. This piece is unusual, requiring the trombonist to partially remove the F-attachment tuning slide, thus creating interesting effects. The first passage with the tuning slide removed has the trombone in a cup mute, playing short, comical interjections from the F-side of the trombone. Later, an entire passage is played through the open tuning slide. The style remains uniformly detached with the exception of short legato sections near the beginning and end. With the use of multi-meter and repetitive sixteenth-note passages, this section resembles an etude or technique study.

The organ part is on three staves with registrations indicated and dynamics clearly marked. This work is suited for a recital and requires a large organ.

Gross, Eric (1926-2011)

Slides and Pistons for Tenor Trombone and Organ op.265. Sydney, Australia: Australian Music Centre, 2002.

- Tenor trombone
- Difficulty: Moderate
- Technique: Tremolo
- Mutes: Hand over Bell

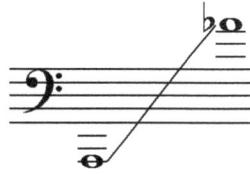

    I.   Con Brio

Gross, an Australian composer and pianist, received his formal musical training in London. After graduation, he worked as a composer of film scores and as a jazz pianist in night clubs and dance bands. Most of his career was spent teaching at the University of Sydney. Upon his retirement, he was made a member of the Order of Australia for his musical contribution to the continent.

Slides and Pistons, a three-and-a-half-minute, single-movement intermezzo was composed in 2002, for Greg van der Struik, principal trombonist with the Australian Opera and Ballet Orchestra in Sydney. He also premiered the work in 2003, at the St. Gallus Church in Wekzheim, near Stuttgart, Germany.

Mr. Gross writes:

Slides and Pistons is stylistically in the manner of an intermezzo. The melodic and rhythmic idiom employed allows for a considerable amount of creative input by the performers. I have used idiomatic trombone figurations and, bearing in mind problems of articulation and time-lag which arise when other instruments perform with organs, I have allowed for the performers to adjust and vary the performance speeds. Being intended as an Intermezzo, the form of the work is deliberately vague, in binary and or ternary form. Both instruments have their own specific motivic fragments but there is also a considerable amount of thematic intertwining and melodic relationship to be found in the material allocated to both instruments. The tempo should be lively and the rhythmic impulses should help in creating a positive and optimistic atmosphere, especially when the work nears its end.[22]

The organ part is on three staves with registration indicated and dynamics clearly marked. The organ registration is done by Dr. Wilbur Hughes.

Gunsenheimer, Gustav (b. 1934)

Alles Ist An Gottes Segen, Choralpartita für Posaune (Trompete) und Orgel. Munich, Germany: Strube Verlag, 1993.

- Tenor trombone
- Difficulty: Easy
- Technique: Nothing unusaul
- Mutes: None

I.	Intrada
II.	Choral 1
III.	Kanon 1
IV.	Choral 2
V.	Kanon 2
VI.	Rezitativ

---

[22] Eric Gross, personal E-mail, November 3, 2008.

VII.   Finale

Gunsenheimer, a composer, cantor and choir director, was born in Silesia (now Poland). After World War II, he and his family relocated to Bamberg, Germany. He received his formal musical training at the Mozarteum in Salzburg; while there he became good friends with Carl Orff. After graduation, he became a lecturer at the University in Wurzburg. His compositional output is broad, including choral works as well as many chamber instrumental works.

This ten-minute, six-movement work is in the form of a theme and variation. The piece is not technically demanding and is comprised of simple quarter-and-eighth-note figures with a narrow range. The two movements titled, *Kanon,* feature a canonic interplay between the trombone and organ. These chant-like figures would be impressive in a reverberant setting. *Finale,* is flashy with the trombonist playing long chains of eighth-notes building up to the ending of piece. There are several repeated sections which could be omitted to vary the performance time. In addition to the score, the publisher includes a trombone and a substitute trumpet part. This work is suited for a recital and for use in a liturgical setting.

The organ part is on two staves and would also be effective on piano. No registrations are indicated and dynamics are clearly marked.

Gunsenheimer, Gustav (b. 1934)

Lobe den Herren Suite für Posaune (Trompete) und Orgel Klavier. Munich, Germany: Strube Verlag, 1989.

- Tenor trombone
- Difficulty: Moderate
- Technique: Nothing unusual
- Mutes: None

I.   Intrada

II.   Aria

III.   Menuett

IV.   Finale

Composed in 1987, this five-minute suite consists of four short movements written in a Baroque style. The first movement, *Intrada,* marked " ♩ = 88," is a twenty-two measure fanfare in common meter, with simple scale patterns and sequences in B-flat major. The second movement, *Aria,* in 3/4 meter, marked " ♩ = 80," features a lyrical melody line passed between the trombone and organ. This movement could be shortened with the removal of the repeated sections if needed. The third movement, *Menuett,* is more difficult than the surrounding movement due to the high tessitura, requiring the trombonist to play up to b-flat1. The fourth movement, *Finale,* is similar to the first movement in its sequencing and patterns, however, dotted-eight-sixteenth patterns are also incorporated. This work is suited for a recital and in a liturgical setting.

In addition to the score, the publisher provides parts for both trombone and trumpet.

The organ part is on two staves with the indication "Pedal ad lib." No registration or dynamics are marked.

Guðmundsson, Hugi (b. 1977)

Signing f. básúnu og orgel. Reykjavik, Iceland: Iceland Music Information Center.

- Tenor trombone
- Difficulty: Moderate
- Technique: Nothing unusual
- Mutes: None

I.   Quarter-note = 50

Guðmundsson, an Icelandic composer, received his formal musical training at the Reykjavik College of Music, the Royal Danish Academy of Music in Copenhagen and the Institute of Sonology in the Netherlands. His compositions range from chamber works to full orchestra; many have been performed internationally. In 2008, Gudmundsson was nominated for Iceland's "DV Cultural Award" for his achievements in the field of music.

Signing, a seven-minute, single-movement work was composed in 2001. The score bears an inscription *to Helga Hrafns Jónssonar.* This chromatic work begins softly with legato trombone figures set over a thinly-scored organ accompaniment. As the piece develops, it uses dissonance and dynamics to build in intensity. Multiple trombone phrases swell from mezzo-piano to fortissimo and back to pianissimo in short order. A chain of triplet figures leads to the climax of the work with the trombone playing full volume and the organ playing loud chord-clusters. The piece returns to a meditative tone, ending softly with remaining hints of dissonance. This work is suited for a recital.

The organ part is on three staves with no registration indicated and dynamics clearly marked.

Haegeland, Eilert Magnus (1951-2004)

Fantasia Polaris for trombone og orgel op.31. Oslo, Norway: Norwegian Music Information Centre, 1991.

- Tenor trombone
- Difficulty: Moderate
- Technique: Nothing unusual
- Mutes: None

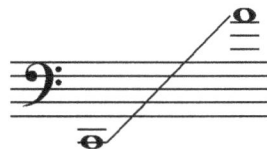

    I.   Moderato rytmico
    II.   Poco vivace

Haegeland, a Norwegian composer and organist, showed interest in music from an early age. He received his formal musical training at the Music Academy in Kristiansand and the College of Music in Oslo. A well-known organist, he began touring in 1975. His compositions are known for their folk-like character.

Fantasia Polaris, an exciting eight-minute, two-movement work begins in common meter. Marked "Moderato Rhythmico," it has a strong sense of pulse throughout. A secondary contrasting section continues with the subdued lyrical character, now in 3/4 meter, however, the conclusion of the movement returns to 6/8 meter. The second movement, marked "Poco Vivace," is playful and technically demanding for the trombonist. Musical interplay between the two instruments leads to a loud dramatic ending. This work is suited for a recital and in a liturgical setting.

The organ part is on three staves with no registrations indicated and ynamics clearly marked.

Hahn, Gunnar (1908-2001)

Himmelriket liknas vid tio jungfrur. Solina, Sweden: Gunnar Hahn Musikförlag,1988.

- Tenor trombone
- Difficulty: Moderate
- Technique: Nothing unusual
- Mutes: None

  I. Andante

Hahn, a Swedish composer, was discovered as a musical prodigy at age three. He studied at the Stockholm Conservatory of Music. After passing the organist examinations in 1930, he chose a career as a concert pianist. Hahn had an interest in folk music, evident in his compositional style. His folk arrangements for orchestra were well-known through a radio program "Gunnar Hahn's Orchestra of Folk Dance," a series which ran between 1957-1963.

Himmelriket liknas vid tio jungfrur (The Kingdom of Heaven Resembles Ten Maidens). Composed in 1979, this five-minute work is primarily in 4/4 meter except for the conclusion in alla breve. This work has a romantic quality with few stylistic changes throughout. Harmonic interest is created through several modulations passing through different pitch centers. There are two trombone cadenzas. This work is suited for a recital and for use in a liturgical setting. The organ part is on three staves with no registrations indicated and dynamics clearly marked.

Haller, William P.

Suite for Trombone and Organ. Unpublished, 1978.

- Tenor trombone
- Difficulty: Moderate
- Technique: Glissandi
- Mutes: None

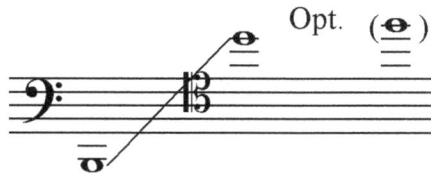

I.   Super Blasto
II.   Enharmonic Nightmare
III.   Tongue and Slur for Pete
IV.   Le Calme

Haller, an American composer and trombonist, studied at the Eastman School of Music. He received his Doctorate in Musical Art from North Texas State University. He is currently a Professor of Organ and Organ Literature at West Virginia Tech University. He maintains a busy performance schedule. Mr. Haller has received international awards and recognition playing at competitions. He is a Fellow of the American Guild of Organists. [23]

Suite for Trombone and Organ, composed in 1978, is a light, eight-minute work in four movements. The piece was written to encourage one of Haller's trombone students who was recovering from a facial injury. The first movement *Super Blasto*, lives up to the title. Marked, "quarter note =104 sometimes faster," this exciting fanfare weaves through many meter changes with the trombone playing sixteenth-note figures. Halfway through the movement, the style changes, becoming legato and mysterious before returning to the opening fanfare material for the conclusion. The second movement, *Enharmonic Nightmare,* marked "lento," is densely-scored with dissonant chords blurring together thus creating a haunting trombone melody. This movement explores the parallel keys of D-flat and C-sharp; reading the numerous double-flats could be challenging. The third movement, *Tongue and Slur for Pete,* (for Pete LaRue) marked "moderato," is written as a waltz. The melody passes sixteenth-note scales and sequences between the instruments, offset with large slurred leaps played by the trombone. The movement is light with a playful character; however, at times seems like an articulation etude. The final movement, *Le Calme,* marked "very slow," is soft and elegant with the trombone and organ voices blending seamlessly and ending peacefully. This work is suited for a recital.

The organ part is on three staves with some registration indicated and dynamics clearly marked.

The original manuscript for this work is available for loan from the International Trombone Association Library located at the University of Arizona Fine Arts Library in Tucson, Arizona. M184. H24.S8.1978. Also available at that location is an unpublished cassette tape recording of this work with trombonist Peter LaRue and William Haller at the organ.

---

[23] http://www.wvu.edu/~music/faculty_staff/whaller.html (accessed August 6, 2008).

Haug, Lukas (b. 1921)

Zwölfteiliges Orgelmosaik. Wilhelmshaven, Germany:
Heinrichshofen Verlag, 1958.

- Tenor trombone
- Difficulty: Easy
- Technique: Nothing unusual
- Mutes: None

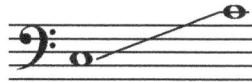

XII.   Aus hartem Weh die Menschheit klagt

Zwölfteiliges Orgelmosaik (Organ mosaic in twelve parts) is
dedicated to Peter Schreiber. An unusual work in twelve movements, the
trombone joins in the final movement playing Bach's chorale theme
"*Aus hartem Weh die Menschheit klagt*" (From strong pain humanity
laments). The score indicates that this section can either be played on
trombone or sung. The movement with trombone is two minutes long.
Due to its simplicity, it would be suited for a young trombonist. This
work is suited for an organ recital and for use in a liturgical setting.

The organ part is on three staves with registrations indicated and
dynamics clearly marked.

Heilmann, Harald (1924-2018)

Fantasia per trombone ed organo. Dusseldorf, Germany: Astoria
Verlag, 1994.

- Tenor trombone
- Difficulty: Moderate
- Technique: Nothing unusual
- Mutes: None

I.   Adagio (stringendo al fine)

Heilmann, a German composer, received his formal musical training at the Hochschule School of Music and Theater in Leipzig and at the Academy of Arts in East Berlin. A pupil of Frank Martin, he is known for composing in a similar French style. After graduation, he was employed as a freelance composer and lecturer at several music schools. He has received numerous awards for his compositions, including the Federal Cross of Merit.

Fantasia per trombone ed organo, a four-minute, single-movement work is dedicated to Armin Rosin. This powerful piece makes use of the full dynamic range of both instruments. Marked "adagio," the work deviates from the opening tempo and style only at a stringendo near the end. The trombone begins with the main motive, built around two quarter-notes, followed by a dotted-eighth-sixteenth. This is a repetitive figure throughout the work. In several sections, the organ leads with the trombone playing an accompanying role. Excitement builds toward the end with the organ playing sixteenth-note runs. The trombone score is notated in bass, tenor and treble clefs. This work is suited for a recital and for use in a liturgical setting.

The organ part is on three staves and requires a large powerful organ. There is no registration indicated and dynamics are clearly marked.

This work has been recorded by Armin Rosin on the CD *Posaune In Unserer Zeit* (FCD 91 407).

Heilmann, Harald (1924-2018)

Poem für Posaune (oder Horn) und Orgel Op. 162. Köln, Germany: Verlag Christoph Dohr, 2006.

- Tenor trombone
- Difficulty: Moderate
- Technique: Nothing unusual
- Mutes: None

I.   Andante

Poem, a simple single-movement, three-and-a-half minute work is structured in ABA form. The opening, marked "andante," features an alternation between two main themes, starting with a legato section in 3/4 meter. The long melodic lines are played by the trombone over an unobtrusive organ accompaniment. The energetic B-theme, marked "Allegretto," is in 2/4 meter, with some syncopation. The piece returns to the opening A-theme, followed by a codetta on B-theme material for a flashy ending.

This work is suited for use in a recital and in a liturgical setting. In addition to the score, the publisher includes trombone and horn parts.

The organ part is on three staves with no registration indicated and dynamics clearly marked.

Heilmann, Harald (1924-2018)

Trauerode für Posaune (Viola, Englisch) und Orgel. Wilhelmshaven, Germany: Heinrichshofen Verlag, 1984.

- Alto trombone
- Difficulty: Easy
- Technique: Nothing unusual
- Mutes: None

I.   Adagio

This haunting four-minute, single-movement work remains primarily in 3/4 meter. *Trauerode,* (ode to grief or mourning) is written in ABA form. The opening, marked "Adagio quarter-note = 54," features a main theme which unfolds with expressive lines played by the trombone. The composer has clearly notated his musical nuance in this section; care should be taken to follow his indications. The contrasting B section is chromatic, written in 5/4 meter. The final section is identical to the opening. This work is notated entirely in alto clef. Because of its relaxed tempo and narrow range, it would be a valuable study for a developing alto trombonist. This work is suited for a recital and for use in a liturgical setting.

The organ part is on three staves with no registration indicated and dynamics clearly marked.

Helmschrott, Robert M. (b. 1938)

Sonata Da Chiesa I, für Posaune und Orgel. Berlin, Germany: Bote & Bock/ New York, NY: Schott Music Corporation, 1986.

- Tenor trombone
- Difficulty: Moderate
- Technique: Slide vibrato, Glissandi, Flutter tounging
- Mutes: Straight

     I.   Elegia

    II.   Laudatio

This twelve-minute, two-movement work is the first piece in a collection of twelve works by the same composer entitled *Sonata Da Chiesa.* The score bears the inscription, "For the town of Ingolstadt," which is where the work was premiered by trombonist Abbie Conant and organist Franz Hauk in June 1984.

The first movement, marked "Andante, ma molto espressivo," begins lyrically, then builds to the climax with repeated figures (d2) played in rapid succession. This is followed by glissandi down to a flutter tongued (Ab). A brief section of contrasting chromaticism with non legato passages creates unrest before a calm ending. The second movement, *Laudatio,* subtitled "Eulogy," and marked "molto vivace," journeys through many styles and tempo changes: toccata-like, then lyrical, returning to a toccata style. The end of the piece slows adding even more drama. This work is suited for a recital and for use in a liturgical setting.

The organ part is on three staves and requires a three manual organ. Registration is indicated and dynamics are clearly marked.

This work has been recorded by trombonist Abbie Conant and organist Schnorr Klemens on the CD *Posaune und Orgel* (Audite 97.410).

Hidas, Frigyes (1928-2007)

Domine, Dona Nobis Pacem für Posaune und Orgel. Crans-Montana, Switzerland: Editions Marc Reift, 1994.

- Tenor trombone
- Difficulty: Moderate
- Technique: Nothing unusual
- Mutes: None

    I.   Moderato

Hidas, a Hungarian composer and conductor, has a large output of music, across a wide range of genres. He received his formal musical training at the Budapest Academy of Music, followed by appointments as music director at the National Theatre and the Municipal Operetta Theatre. He is especially known for his writing for winds, which includes several works for both tenor and bass trombone and piano.

Part of the Collection Branimir Slokar, this four-minute, single-movement work highlights the voice-like, cantabile style of the trombone. The work is composed using simple lyrical lines, with an abundance of quarter-note triplets set against a thinly-textured organ accompaniment. There are no major changes in style and tempo from beginning to end, however, the piece slips briefly into a 5/4 meter section. Because of the high tessitura and slow tempo, with few rests, endurance may be a concern. This work is suited for a recital and for use in a liturgical setting.

The organ part is on three staves with no registration indicated and dynamics clearly marked.

This work has been recoded by trombonist Philip Swanson and organist Barbara Burns on the CD Variations on Veni Creator Spiritus, Music for Trombone and Organ (Classics MS 1137).

Hidman, Aron (b. 1971)

Read My Mind, for trombone and organ. Coventry, England: Warwick Music, 1997.

- Trombone
- Difficulty: Advanced
- Technique: Nothing unusual
- Mutes: None

    I.   ♩ = 76

Born in Uppsala, Sweden, Hidman began his musical journey at the age of ten, playing guitar and writing songs with several bands. After his interest in popular music waned, he began to study classical music and composition. His formal musical studies were at the Piteå School of Music, where he worked with Jan Sandström. Hidman's compositions are primarily orchestral and chamber works. He has received several commissions for European institutions.

Composed in 1995, and dedicated to Daniel Stighäll Framnäs, this five-minute, single-movement contemporary work is a showpiece. The majority of the work is punctuated with accents and syncopated sixteenth-note figures. The trombonist must have a strong command of the instrument becasue several passages have multiple-octave leaps requiring flexibility. The middle section of the piece has a trombone cadenza played over a long pedal point by the organ. *Read My Mind* is suited for an intermediate to advanced trombonist working on rhythmic security. This work is suited for a recital.

The organ part is on three staves with registration indicated and dynamics clearly marked.

Hilfiger, John Jay (b. 1938)

"Christe Sanctorum" Variants. Farmington, NM: Brassworks 4 Publishing, 2007.

- Tenor trombone or Euphonium
- Difficulty: Easy
- Technique: Nothing unusual
- Mutes: None

I.   Moderato

Hilfiger, an American composer, educator, and French-hornist, received his formal musical training at the Eastman School of Music. After graduation, he continued his studies in psychology and biostatistics before completing a Masters of Music at Binghamton University and a Ph.D. in music from the University of Iowa. Hilfiger has been a professor of music at several institutions and has performed with various professional ensembles. His works are published by nine publishing houses.

This four-minute work is composed as a theme with three variations. The original theme marked "moderato," remains in E-flat major. The composer writes in the performance notes:

The tune 'Christe Sanctorum' comes from the Paris *Antiphoner* of 1681. It is well-known in Protestant and Catholic hymnals as 'Father, We Praise You,' 'Father Most Holy,' 'Praise and Thanksgiving,' 'Lord of the Living,' or 'Christ Is the World's Light.'

The first variation is stately with a fanfare-like quality. The second variation, marked "slower," is legato and somber. Written in six flats, a young player may find it helpful to write in a few positions in the part. The final variation marked "joyfully," concludes in an upbeat fashion. With simple rhythms and only a few notes above the staff, this piece is appropriate for a young trombonist. This work is suited for a recital and in a liturgical setting. A French horn edition is also available from the same publisher.

The Organ part is on two staves with registration indicated and dynamics clearly marked.

Hillborg, Anders (b. 1954)

U-TANGIA-NA for alto-trombone and organ. Stockholm, Sweden: Swedish Music Information Center, 1991.

- Alto trombone and organ (or tape)
- Difficulty: Advanced
- Technique: Approximate and indefinite pitch notation
- Mutes: None

    I.   ♩ = 132

Hillborg, a Swedish composer, studied at the Royal College of Music in Stockholm. After a brief appointment as Professor of Composition, he became a freelance composer. His compositions include a wide range of styles from traditional choral works to popular music, including several film scores. He was awarded Swedish Composer of the Year.

U-TANGIA-NA, commissioned in 1991 by Radio Sweden for Christian Lindberg to showcase Conn's 36H alto trombone. This ultra-modern five-and-a-half minute, single-movement work is highly-charged with an array of multiple tonguing and glissandi. The rhythms played by the trombone spell out a coded message from the composer delivered in Morse code. The rapid delivery of these sixteenth-note figures are incredibly demanding for the trombonist. Endurance is also an issue; one section has a stream of sixteenth-notes (d2) played 32 times. There are several ensemble challenges including quintuplet and sextuplet figures played by the alto trombone set against duple patterns on the organ. The piece requires virtuosic skills on both instruments. Because of the low range, this piece requires an alto trombone with a B-flat attachment. This work is also available with a tape accompaniment from the same publisher. This work is suited for a recital.

The organ part is notated on one, two or threes staves as needed. The trombone part is in full-score format.

This work has been recorded by trombonist Christian Lindberg and organist Gunnar Idenstam on the CD *The Sacred Trombone* (BIS CD-488).

Hoag, Charles (b. 1931)

Dark Tango for trombone and organ.

- Tenor trombone

Hoag, an American composer and bassist, received his formal musical training at the University of Iowa and the University of Redlands. After graduation, he was employed as a bassist with the New Orleans Philharmonic and the Oklahoma City Symphony. He served as a Professor of Theory and Composition at the University of Kansas for nearly thirty years before his recent retirement.

Dark Tango was premiered by trombonist Mitch Kaufman at the University of Kansas in 1993. A copy of this work was unobtainable at the time of this writing.

Dark Tango was reviewed by Michael Hall in the ITAJ Volume 30 no. 4. October 2002.

Hogg, Merle E. (1922-2017)

Contrasts for Alto Trombone and Organ. Newton, IA: TAP Music Sales, 2000.

- Alto trombone
- Difficulty: Moderate
- Technique: Nothing unusual
- Mutes: None

I.	Maestoso
II.	Allegro Moderato
III.	"Rhenish" Interlude: Sostenuto
IV.	Alla waltz

Hogg, a trombonist, composer, and music educator, received his formal musical training at Emporia State University and the University of Iowa. He further studied with Nadia Boulanger at the American Conservatory in Fontainebleau, France. He is a former member of the San Diego Symphony and a Professor Emeritus at San Diego State University.

Contrasts, a twelve-minute work in four-movements was composed in 1997. The piece was commissioned by and is dedicated to Ron Robinson. The first movement, *Maestoso,* features expressive lyrical lines set over mixed meter. The second movement, *Allegro Moderato,* is more technical than the first movement, exploring the lower register of the alto trombone. The third movement, *"Rhenish" Interlude: Sostenuto,* opens with the alto trombone chorale line from Schumann's Third Symphony. The final movement, *Alla waltz,* completes the work in a light fashion. This work is suited for a recital and for use in a liturgical setting.

The organ part is on three staves with no registration indicated and dynamics clearly marked.

Holst, Gustav (1874-1934)

"Concertante" Duet for Organ and Trombone. Coventry, England: Warwick Music, 1994.

- Tenor trombone
- Difficulty: Moderate
- Technique: Nothing unusual
- Mutes: None

    I.   Andante quasi Adagio
    II.   Allegro giojoso ma maestoso

Holst, an English composer, keyboardist, and trombonist, is best known for his popular orchestral work *The Planets.* He studied to become a concert pianist, but he was forced to abandon this plan after he developed neuritis in his right arm; because of this, and to help with his asthma, he took up trombone. Holst received his formal musical training at the Royal Conservatory of Music in London. In addition to composing, he supported himself playing trombone in the Queen's Hall Orchestra and the Royal Scottish Orchestra.

Concertante, also known as *Duet for Organ and Trombone,* is a ten-minute, two- movement romantic work, likely the best known piece in the repertoire for trombone and organ because of the composer's importance. Holst was twenty years old at the time he composed the work in 1894. The first-documented performance was at the Highway Congregational Church in Holst's home town of Cheltenham, with his father Adolph von Holst at the organ and J. Boyce on trombone.[24]

The piece is in the form of a sonata da chiesa, with a slow section followed by fast. The opening section, marked "Andante quasi Adagio," is mournful. Fragments of the principal theme from the second movement can be heard throughout, beginning in measure 14. The movement ends with a fermata and should be played attacca into the second movement, marked "Allegro giojoso ma maestoso." Here, the theme is played by the trombone while the organ plays sextuplets. A flowing line appears in the reoccurring 6/4 sections. The high tessitura of the trombone part requires an accomplished trombonist with strong endurance. This work is suited for a recital and in a liturgical setting.

The organ part is on three staves with registration and dynamics clearly marked. The organ part requires an accomplished organist.

This work has been recorded by trombonist Niels-Ole Bo Johansen and organist Ulrich Spang-Hanssen on the CD *Holst: Duo Concertante for Trombone & Organ; Works by Elgar, Guilmant, Liszt, Ropartz, Vaughan Williams & Eben.* (Classico CLASSCD 122), and by trombonist Sebastian Krause and organist Gabrielle Wadewitz on the CD *Sonntagsposaunenstück: Romantic music for trombone and organ.* (Raum Klang RK 9805), and by Ian Bousfield on the CD *Virtuosi* (EMI 723435 66389 2 2), and by Alain Trudel on the CD, *The Art of the Trombone* (8.553716). Another recording is available performed by

---

[24] Mitchell, John C. 1990. *Gustav Holst's Duet for Organ and Trombone.* International Trombone Journal (Winter) 22-25.

Steven Mead (euphonium) and Lidia Ksiazkiewicz (organ) on the CD Hosanna (Bocchino Music – BOCC 121).

Hovland, Egil (1924-2013)

Cantus V for Trombone and Organ op.120. Oslo, Norway: Norsk Musikforlag, 1986.

- Tenor trombone
- Difficulty: Moderate
- Technique: Multiphonics
- Mute: Straight

I.   Quarter note = 50

Hovland, a Norwegian composer, received his formal training at the Oslo Conservatory of Music. He served as the organist at the Glemmen Church, in Fredrikstad from 1949 until 1994. His compositional style was influenced by Hindemith, Stravinsky and Bartók. Hovland had the opportunity to study with Copland at Tanglewood. He is best-known for his 150 sacred works.

Cantus V, is an eight-minute, single-movement work. It was written in 1982, commissioned by the Stockholm Philharmonic, and is dedicated to trombonist John Petersen. The main theme is based on a twelve-tone melody. The work begins with a meditative, chant-like section, followed by a slight change in tempo and style. The trombone plays triplet figures over chromatic sixteenth-note passages on the organ manuals. With the trombone playing triplets against the organ's duple figures, the piece is intentionally disjointed at times. A short trombone cadenza features multiphonics, leading to a playful waltz section. Both players have the opportunity to open up a little in the grandioso section before returning the pensive quality of the opening. This piece is suited for a recital and for use in a liturgical setting.

The organ part is on two staves with no registration indicated and dynamics and manuals clearly marked.

This work has been recorded by Gaute Vikdal on the CD *Skygger* with organist Bjørn Andor Drange Euridice (EUCD 001).

Hübler, Klaus. K (b. 1956)

Am Ende des Kanons Musica con(tro)versa für Posaune und Orgel. Wiesbaden, Germany: Breitkopf & Härtel KG, 1985.

- Tenor trombone
- Difficulty: Advanced
- Technique: Alternate Notation, Grace notes, Glissandi, Wide vibrato
- Mutes: Straight

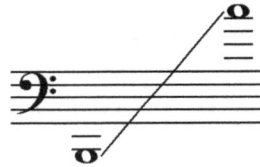

I.   Canonis Jussu
II.   Cercar

Hübler, a German composer studied composition at the University of Munich. After graduation he worked as a freelance composer. Known for his contemporary works, many of his compositions have received international recognition. He has also authored numerous new-music articles.

AM ENDE DES KANONS (At the end of the canon) written in 1983, is an extremely difficult modern two-movement work. The first movement, *Canonis Jussu*, marked sixteenth note = 32 is filled with complex rhythms and played in unusual meters including 15/16, 20/8 and 35/16. This leads to an extended organ interlude best described as "sheets of sound," which covers the entire range of the organ. The second movement, *Cercar,* begins with a trombone cadenza and leads to numerous sections of non-traditional notation, creating many unusual musical effects. This piece requires virtuosic performers. The trombonist must play from an oversized score. This work is suited to a recital.

The organ part is on three staves with registration indicated and dynamics clearly marked. This work requires a three manual organ.

Hutcheson, Jere (b. 1938)

PATTERNS for Trombone and Organ. New York, NY: Seesaw Music, 1976.

- Tenor trombone
- Difficulty: Moderate
- Technique: Glissandi, Grace notes,
- Mutes: Straight

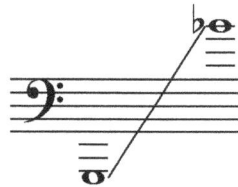

     I.   Moderato

Hutcheson earned a Doctor of Philosophy degree from Michigan State University where he currently serves as Professor of Composition. He is a recipient of the Composer of the Year award from the National Music Educators Association. He has published two theory textbooks, over one hundred compositions and several articles.[25]

Patterns, a seven-minute, modern work composed in 1976, was commissioned by Jeffery Price. The piece explores the full range of trombone articulation. Mixed meter and ties across the bar-lines softens the pulse producing an open quality. The dialogue established between the trombone and organ builds to a stylistic change at the section marked "energico." Here the organ establishes repeating patterns with the use of the reed stops while the trombone plays short percussive figures through

---

[25] http://www.music.msu.edu/faculty/faculty.php?id=15 (accessed August 29, 2008).

the range of the instrument. The trombone part requires flexibility and accuracy since the rhythms and pitches are difficult. The conclusion is similar to the beginning, ending softly with the trombone sliding down to the note (FF). This work is suited to a recital.

The organ part is on three staves with registration indicated and dynamics clearly marked.

Irik, Michiel W. (b. 1953)

The Seventh Seal for Trombone and Organ, Granville, Australia: Trombonis Australis Editions, 2006.

- Tenor trombone
- Difficulty: Moderate
- Technique: Glissandi, Grace notes
- Mutes: None

     I.   Maestoso ♩ = 96

Irik, an Australian composer, conductor and music educator, received his formal musical training at Sydney University. He later studied traditional Chinese instrumental music at the Central Conservatory of Music in Beijing. He served as the conductor for the Armidale Symphony Orchestra and as Vice-President of the Fellowship of Australian Composers.

Composed in 1998, this single-movement, three-minute work was dedicated to Gregory van der Struik. The piece maintains a similar style and tempo throughout, with the exception of a stringendo section near the end. *The Seventh Seal* begins powerfully with a broad organ introduction answered by horn-call figures played by the trombone. Although not technically demanding, the work is dramatic with rapidly changing dynamics and sforzandos. The piece builds to a recitative section in which the trombone plays cadenza-like figures over long-held organ chords. In the following section, marked "liberamente," the trombone plays a two-measure solo passage with glissandi and grace notes prior to returning to material similar to the opening. This piece is suited for a recital and for use in a liturgical setting.

The organ part is on three staves with no registrations indicated and dynamics clearly marked.

Jahn, Thomas (b. 1940)

Lachrimae XCIV Paraphrase über Dowlands "Seven Tears" für Posaune und Orgel. Hamburg, Germany: Peermusic Classical, 1995.

- Tenor trombone
- Difficulty: Moderate
- Technique: Nothing unusual
- Mutes: Straight

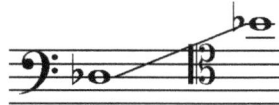

    I.   Grave

Jahn, a German composer, received his formal musical training at the Hochschule für Musik and the Städtisches Konservatorium in Berlin. He also studied at the Hochschule für Musik und darstellende Kunst in Hamburg. Currently, Jahn is a music teacher and freelance composer.

Lachrimae XCIV Paraphrase über Dowlands "Seven Tears," was composed in 1994, premiering the same year by the composer with organist Wolfgang Knuth. A single-movement, three-minute work, this piece is borrowed from a section of the ballet *John Falstaff*, written by the composer. In this section of the ballet, the composer quotes John Dowland's "Lachrimae Tristes" from the collection "Lachrimae or seven tears..."(1605), originally written as seven pavans in five parts for violins and lute. The trombone part depicts the lamentations of the title character after battle.[26]

The opening, marked "grave," is in 4/2 meter. Close harmony and tone clusters by the organ create a sense of grief. The sorrowful trombone melody remains legato throughout creating interest with shaping and dynamics. A figure like a heartbeat is played by the organ, and ending abruptly, conveying death. The conclusion of the work has the trombone playing a motive which is reminiscent of taps before fading away. This piece is suited for a recital and for use in a liturgical setting.

The organ part is on three staves with no registration indicated and dynamics marked below the trombone part.

Janca, Jan (b. 1933)

Suite in 7 movements for trombone and organ. 1996.

A copy of this work was unobtainable at the time of this writing.

This work has been recorded by trombonist Mike Svoboda and organist Ludger Lohmann on the CD *Jan Janca Works for Trombone and Organ* (MDG 606 1462-2).

Janca, Jan (b. 1933)

Tripartita uber Christ ist erstanden for trombone and organ. Munich, Germany: Strube Verlag GmbH. 1991.

---

[26] Thomas Jahn, Personal E-mail, August 27, 2008.

- Tenor trombone
- Difficulty: Moderate
- Technique: Nothing unusual
- Mutes: None

I.   Andante con moto
II.   Larghetto
III.   Maestoso

Janca is a Polish composer and organist. This three-movement, four-minute work is dedicated to, and premiered by Armin Rosin in 1991. The first movement *Andante con moto* features the trombonist playing the theme over triplet figures on the manuals. The second movement, *Larghetto* has lyrical passages over long sustained figures played by the organist. The final movement begins slowly and leads to an allegro section with a mix of 3/4 and 5/4 meters. There is a short trombone cadenza and several ossia sections for the trombone, avoiding the high range.

The organ part is on two staves with registrations indicated and dynamics clearly marked.

This work has been recorded by trombonist Mike Svoboda and organist Ludger Lohmann on the CD *Jan Janca Works for Trombone and Organ* (MDG 606 1462-2).

Jirásek, Jan (b. 1955)

Viribus Unitis. Prague, Czech Republic: Český rozhlas, 2006.

- Tuba
- Difficulty: Moderate
- Technique: Trills
- Mutes: None

Jirásek, a Czech composer, graduated from the Janacek Academy of Musical Art in Brno. After the fall of the Iron Curtain his music was widely performed at festivals across Europe.

With United Forces was commissioned for the Festival Voor de Vind in Amsterdam, Netherlands, and was premiered in 2003. The works title describes the cooperation of the two instruments. The five-minute, single-movement work has many meter, tempo, and key changes throughout. This work is well-suited for a recital or for a liturgical setting.

The organ part is on three staves with no registrations indicated, and dynamics clearly marked. The tuba part is unusually scored beneath the pedal part in the organ score.

Johnsen, Hallvard (1916-2003)

Preludium: for Euphonium in C and Organ Op. 79. Norsk Musikforlag A/S. Oslo, 1985.

- Euphonium
- Difficulty: Easy
- Technique: Nothing unusual
- Mutes: None

Johnsen, a Norwegian composer and flutist, studied at the Oslo Music Conservatory.

Preludium is a single-movement, four-minute work which was composed in 1979. The piece is lyrical and expressive, written in common meter with a brief 6/8 middle section. The high tessitura presents a challenge for the performer. This work is well-suited for a recital or a liturgical setting.

The organ part is on two staves with no registrations indicated, and dynamics clearly marked.

Kameke, Ernst-Ulrich von (1926-2019)

Sonate über Spirituals für Posaune und Orgel. Munich, Germany: Strube Verlag GmbH.

- Tenor trombone
- Difficulty: Moderate
- Technique: Nothing unusual
- Mutes: Straight

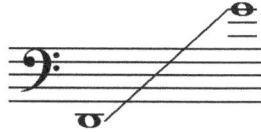

I.	Stand in the need of a prayer
II.	I got a home in a Dat Rock
III.	Deep River
IV.	Ride on, King Jesus

Kameke, a German composer, cantor, and organist, received his formal musical training in Berlin and Heidelberg. After graduation, he played the carillon at the Garnison Church, followed by appointments as cantor and organist at several German churches. In the later part of his career, he became a Professor of Music at the Hochschule für Musik in Hamburg.

This five-and-a-half minute collection of African-American spirituals is in four movements. The first setting, *Stand in the need of a prayer,* marked "allegro," features light syncopation weaving through several meter changes. The scale patterns and triadic sequences, constructed with triplets and sixteenth-notes are technically demanding. The second movement, *I got a home in a Dat Rock,* marked "Moderato," opens with an organ interlude which has a walking bass line in the pedal. The trombone enters, creating a call and response pattern between the two instruments. The third setting is based on the well-known theme "*Deep River.*" In this movement, marked "lento," the trombonist plays expressively over syncopated organ figures. The final movement *Ride on, King Jesus,* is marked "allegro." An upbeat jazz feel is set over another walking bass line in the organ pedal. This movement builds in intensity to a dramatic ending. This piece is suited for a recital and for use in a liturgical setting. Any of the movements could function independently. The organ part is on three staves with no registration indicated and dynamics clearly marked.

Kempton, Jeremy Niles

A Christmas Couplet for Trombone and Organ or Piano. Teaneck, NJ: Puna Music Company, 1999.

- Tenor trombone
- Difficulty: Easy
- Technique: Nothing unusual
- Mutes: None

I.   Moderately, lyrically

Kempton, a composer, conductor, and trombonist, received his formal musical training at the Eastman School of Music where he studied with Emory Remington. He later studied at the University of Illinois with Robert Gray. He holds the solo trombone position with the Tehran National Symphony Orchestra. Kempton conducts music for operas and musical theatre in New York City. He is the founder and conductor of the Island Chamber Symphony on Long Island, New York.

A Christmas Couplet is a six-minute, single-movement setting of two Christmas carols: "Holly and the Ivy," and "What Child is This." Marked "moderately, lyrically," the trombone begins playing the opening theme alone. The trombone part is scored in a high tessitura with soft delicate phrases, which requires endurance. This work would be suited for a December recital or a Christmas service. This work is also available from the publisher as a trombone quartet.

The organ part is on two staves with a few pedal notes on the bottom of the bass clef staff. It could easily be played on piano. No registration is indicated and dynamics are clearly marked.

Kempton, Jeremy Niles

Lament for Trombone and Organ or Piano. Teaneck, NJ: Puna Music Company, 1999.

- Tenor trombone
- Difficulty: Moderate
- Technique: Grace notes
- Mutes: None

     I.   Adagio

Lament, a five-minute, single-movement romantic work, bears the inscription "In remembrance of Helen Manheim." Marked "Adagio ♩ = 60, sempre legato e cantabile," the opening features an organ interlude which establishes the character of the piece. The trombone plays long expressive lines which are passed to the organ. The piece maintains an even style from beginning to end, despite meter and key changes throughout. The long legato phrases require good breath control and a developed slide technique for smooth lines. This work is suited for a recital and for use in a liturgical setting.

The organ part is on two staves with no registration indicated and dynamics clearly marked.

Kingsland, Chappell (b. 1980)

Kung Pao for euphonium (or trombone) and pipe organ. Tuba Euphonium Press/Cimarron Music Press. 2003.

- Euphonium or Trombone
- Difficulty: Advanced
- Technique: Unpitched notation, grace notes, fluttery noises, clapping, spoken words
- Mutes: None

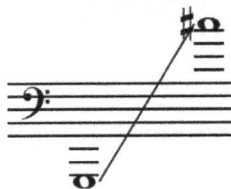

    I.   Gentle, molto rubato

Kingsland, an American composer and organist, studied composition at the Eastman School of Music (BM) and Indiana University's Jacobs School of Music (MM, DM). His compositions have won first-place awards from the Percussive Arts Society, the Jacobs School of Music, and the International Tuba-Euphonium Association, among others. He teaches Music Theory and Piano Class at the University of Denver's Lamont School of Music and plays for Eurhythmy classes at the Denver Waldorf School.

Kung Pao was premiered by Cody Coyne (euphonium) and Chappell Kingsland (organ) in Rochester, NY on October 4, 2003.

The composer writes: "A melding of fiery and delicious material, by turns bluesy, robotic, funky, and danceable. Kung Pao—spicy hot!"

A challenging avant-garde work. The single-movement work includes sections marked: *Aggressive, Bluesy, A Robotic Groove, Expansive, Strict, and Groovin'*. This piece is suited for a recital. In addition to the score, the piece can also be played on trombone with differentiating parts for each instrument in the score.

The organ part is on three staves with registration indications and dynamics clearly marked.

Koch, Erland von (1910-2009)

Trombonia. Stockholm, Sweden: Swedish Music Information Center, 1984.

- Tenor trombone
- Difficulty: Advanced
- Technique: Half and whole step trills, Glissandi
- Mutes: None

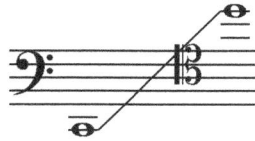

> I.   Moderato

Erland von Koch is the son of the well-known Swedish composer, Sigurd von Koch (1879–1919). Erland received his early musical education from his father. His formal musical training continued at the Stockholm Conservatory with post graduation studies in mainland Europe. He returned to Sweden as a Professor at the Stockholm Musikhögskolan. Koch's music has a folk-like quality and is often viewed as being nationalistic.

Originally orchestrated for trombone and string orchestra, this ten-minute, single-movement adaptation for trombone and organ was written in 1983. It was premiered by trombonist Christer Torgé with composer and organist Torsten Nilsson in Fagersta, Sweden in March 1984. Marked "moderato," the piece begins in 2/2 meter, with the first section of this piece demonstrating the expressive qualities of both instruments. After this lyrical section, the piece becomes more rhythmic with a shift to 3/4 meter. A trombone cadenza leads to the nimble final section marked "allegro vivace," written in 6/8 meter. This piece is suited to a recital.

The organ part is on three staves with no registration indicated and dynamics clearly marked.

Koetsier, Jan (1911-2006)

Choralpartita "Die Tageszeiten" op. 151. Crans-Montana, Switzerland: Editions Marc Reift, 1998.

- Alto or Tenor trombone
- Difficulty: Advanced
- Technique: Nothing unusual
- Mutes: Cup

I.	Morgen
II.	Mittag
III.	Abend

Koetsier was born in Amsterdam in 1911. He received his formal musical training at the Berlin College of Music. After graduation he became the conductor of the Bavarian Radio Symphony Orchestra, and a professor at the Munich College of Music. Influenced by Hindemith and the neo-classical style of Stravinsky, many of his later works feature jazz elements.

Choralpartita "Die Tageszeiten" is a nine-minute work in three-movements, dedicated to Ulrich Leykam. The first movement, *Morgen,* is based on the tune "Aus meines Herzens Grunde," marked "allegretto." The trombone plays a subtle chant-like cantus firmus line over organ passages. The prefatory notes describe this section as representing monks being called to early morning vespers. The second movement, *Mittag,* is based on a theme dating back to 1601, "Gesegn'uns, Herr, die Gaben dein." Featuring the trombone's technical abilities, this movement is more energetic. The fanfares and sixteenth-note passages are mostly unaccompanied. The final movement, *Abend*, is based on the theme "Der Mond ist aufgegangen" by J.A. Peter Schulz, from 1790. This section marked, "adagio" returns to a meditative lyrical style similar to the first movement. The musical motive is passed between the organ and trombone. This piece is suited for a recital and for use in a liturgical setting. In addition to the score, the publisher also includes trombone parts in alto and bass clef.

The organ part is on three staves with no registration indications and dynamics clearly marked.

Koetsier, Jan (1911-2006)

Partita für Posaune und Orgel ("Wachet auf"). Stittgart,Germany: Hänssler-Verlag, 1977.

- Tenor trombone
- Difficulty: Advanced
- Technique: Lip trills
- Mutes: None

I.	Allegro assai
II.	Larghetto
III.	Vivace
IV.	Moderato
V.	Andante maestoso

Partita is a challenging fifteen-minute work in five movements based on Bach's familiar "Wachet auf" theme. This work is not a traditional theme and variation because the theme is not presented in its entirety until the final movement. The piece begins with a small fragment of the theme, developed by the trombone with many technical passages and syncopation lines. The second movement, *Larghetto*, is lyrical and solemn, with the two instruments interweaving melodic lines. The theme is again suggested in a short somber trombone cadenza. The light and dance-like third movement, *Vivace,* is more secular with the organ playing sixteenth-note runs reminiscent of a circus calliope. The final two movements are a homage to Bach. A fuguetta builds to the final movement in 3/2 with the main theme leading to a dramatic ending. This piece is suited for a recital and for use in a liturgical setting. This partita is the third of a set of three for winds and organ, the first two are for English horn and trumpet.

The organ part requires an accomplished organist. It is notated on three staves with no registration indicated and dynamics clearly marked.

This work has been recorded by Armin Rosin on the CD *Posaune In Unserer Zeit* (FCD 91 497), and by trombonist Gabor Hegedüs with organist Hermann Harrassowitz on the CD *Posaune-Orgel-Chor Ein Konzert in St. Lorenz/Nürnberg* (Motette CD50661).

Koetsier, Jan (1911-2006)

Partita für Posaune und Orgel ("Wachet auf"). Crans-Montana, Switzerland: Editions Marc Reift, 1998.

- Tenor trombone
- Difficulty: Advanced
- Technique: Lip trills
- Mutes: None

I.	Allegro assai
II.	Larghetto
III.	Vivace
IV.	Moderato
V.	Andante maestoso

This is the same work as the one listed above from a different publisher. In addition to the score, the publisher includes trombone parts in both bass and tenor clef.

Konowalski, Benedykt (b. 1928)

Victoria Regis, partita na puzon i organy. Warsaw, Poland: Agencja Autorska, 1984.

- Tenor trombone
- Difficulty: Advanced
- Technique: Alternate notation, Glissandi, Flutter tonguing
- Mutes: None

I.	Na Odsiecz Wiednia
II.	Noc Przed Bitwa
III.	Bitwa
IV.	Modlitwa Za Umarlych
V.	Apoteoza

Konowalski, a Polish composer, studied music and law at Warsaw University. Since 1965, he has been employed as a Professor of Music at the State School of Music in Warsaw, and has won numerous awards for his compositions.[27]

Victoria Regis, a twenty-two minute modern work was composed in 1984. The first movement, *Na Odsiecz Wiednia,* (The relief of Vienna) begins with a heroic fanfare which develops dramatically throughout the movement. The second movement, *Noc Przed Bitwa,* (The night before the battle) is reflective, written as a slow 6/8 adagio. The third movement, *Bitwa,* (Battle) makes use of many of the trombones extended techniques including flutter tonguing and alternate notation. It is at times aggressive with the musical depiction of a battle. The fourth

---

[27] Prefatory notes.

movement, *Modlitwa Za Umarlych* (Prayer of Umarlych), is a funeral march in 2/2 meter. The piece ends with a lively finale, *Apoteoza* (The Apotheosis), and includes a rapid organ pedal line. This theme is passed to the trombone. There are several challenging passages for both trombone and organ in this work and may require extensive rehearsal time. The manuscript can be difficult to read since meter is notated above the staff. This piece is suited for a recital.

The organ part is on three staves and requires a large, powerful instrument. No registration is indicated and dynamics are only notated under the trombone part in the organ score.

Kraus, Eberhard (1931-2003)

Hymnus "Verbum Supernum" für Posaune & Orgel. Crans-Montana, Switzerland: Editions Marc Reift, 1995.

- Tenor trombone
- Difficulty: Advanced
- Technique: Half-step trill, Ad libitum sections
- Mutes: Straight

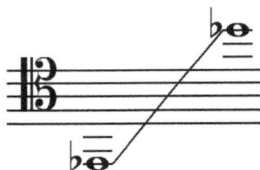

I.	Recitativo
II.	Aria
III.	Duo
IV.	Canzona
V.	Preghiera
VI.	Toccata

Kraus was born in Regensburg, Germany in 1931. He received early musical instruction from his father, the cathedral organist; the same position the younger Kraus would later occupy. The composer received his formal musical training at the Staatliche Hochschule in Munich. His first appointment was organist and director of the Sunday organ concerts at the Regensburger Domspatzen. Kraus was devoted to music education and taught at the Catholic Academy for Church Music at Regensburg University. He has received numerous awards, including the order "Pro Ecclesia et Pontifice" from Pope John Paul II in 1996.

Hymnus "Verbum Supernum" was composed in 1980, premiered the same year by trombonist Armin Rosin with the composer at the organ. This ten-minute, six-movement work is based on a twelfth-century hymn "Verbum supernum," by St. Thomas of Aquino. This piece is written using a twelve-tone series. In addition to the score and parts, the publisher includes notes pertaining to the hymn verses and how they correspond with the movements. The first movement, *Recitativo,* marked "Verbum supernum," begins with a lengthy "ad-libitum" section. The mood is set with trombone alone, later joined by the organ providing thinly scored open harmonies. The second movement, *Aria,* marked "In mortem," has both instruments collaborating in a delicate, expressive style. The third movement, *Duo,* marked "Quibus sub bina specie," is simple, written in a Baroque style. The fourth movement, *Canzona,* marked "Se nascens dedit," is more contemporary than the surrounding movements due to the chromaticism and meter, written in 5/4. There are several instances where the trombone plays ad-libitum chant phrases over tone clusters in the organ. The fifth movement, *Preghiera,* marked "O salutaris hostia," is a return to an expressive style, requiring careful attention to phrasing. The final movement, *Toccata,* is energetic. Marked "Uni trinoque Domino," this section features a chant-like style which leads to a dramatic ending. In addition to the score, the publisher includes trombone parts in both bass and tenor clef. This piece is suited for a recital and for use in a liturgical setting.

The organ part is on three staves with registration and dynamics clearly marked.

Kraus, Eberhard (1931-2003)

Sechs Choralbearbeitungen für Posaune oder andere Melodienstrumente und Orgel. Crans-Montana, Switzerland: Editions Marc Reift, 1995.

- Tenor trombone
- Difficulty: Moderate
- Technique: Flutter tonguing, Glissandi
- Mutes: Straight

I.	Unüberwindlich starker Held, St. Michael
II.	O Traurigkeit, o Herzeleid
III.	Christ ist erstanden
IV.	Nun bitten wir den heiligen Geist
V.	Mein Zuflucht alleine
VI.	Grosser Gott wir loben dich

Sechs Choralbearbeitungen was composed for trombonist Armin Rosin in 1974. Rosin premiered the work the same year at Regensburg Cathedral with the composer at the organ. This chorale setting is constructed using a twelve-tone row, presented in all inversions and retrogrades. The first setting, *Unüberwindlich starker Held, St. Michael* (Invincibly strong hero, Saint Michael), is marked "Mächtig," (Mighty). This movement is powerful and assertive. On two occasions the trombone is required to play (CC) while flutter tonguing, which may be difficult for some trombonists. The second setting, *O Traurigkeit, o Herzeleid* (O sadness, O heartbreak), is brief, consisting of only nine measures. Marked "sotto voce," a slow moving trombone chorale is played above an intricate organ part. The third setting, *Christ ist erstanden* (Christ has risen), is a moving fanfare. The fourth setting, *Nun bitten wir den heiligen Geist* (Now we appeal to the Holy Ghost), is written in a slow and cantabile style. The penultimate movement, *Mein Zuflucht alleine* (My shelter alone), is marked "confidently." This fugue-like movement is in the style of a jig beginning with trombone alone. The final setting, *Grosser Gott wir loben dich* (Great God we praise you), concludes with a weighty German chorale which includes trombone glissandi in a dramatic ending. There are several sections of the trombone part notated in treble clef. This piece is suited for a recital and for use in a liturgical setting. As the title suggest, this work could be played on any solo instrument.

The organ part is on three staves with registration indicated and dynamics clearly marked.

Krol, Bernhard (1920-2013)

Choralpartita "Nun, danket alle Gott" für Posaune & Orgel op. 174. Köln, Germany: Wolfgang G. Haas – Musikverlag Köln E.K., 2004.

- Tenor trombone
- Difficulty: Moderate
- Technique: Nothing unusual
- Mutes: None

    I.   Lento
    II.   Andante con moto
    III.   Tranquillo

Krol, a German French hornist and composer, received his formal musical training in Berlin and Vienna. His best known compositions are for brass instruments, and his style is often compared to Hindemith and Reger. A career orchestral player, he has been a member of the Berlin Philharmonic and the Stuttgart Radio Symphony.

Choralpartita "Nun, danket alle Gott," (Let's all thank God) a seven-minute work in three-movements, is dedicated to "Sebastian." All three movements are in a similar style and tempo. The first movement, *Lento,* features a dialogue between the trombone and organ in 3/4 meter. There is a misprint in this edition; measure 47 and 48 should be in tenor clef. The second movement, *Andante con moto,* continues in 3/4 meter and showcases both the richness and delicacy of the trombone. The final movement, *Tranquillo,* begins in common meter, becoming more technical with eighth-note runs in 3/2 meter. This piece is suited for a recital and for use in a liturgical setting.

The first two movements of the organ score are notated on two staves and the third on three. No registration is indicated and dynamics are clearly marked.

Krol, Bernhard (1920-2013)

Sinfonia sacra for trombone and organ (positive), op. 56. Berlin, Germany: Bote & Bock, 1973.

- Tenor trombone
- Difficulty: Moderate
- Technique: Nothing unusual
- Mute: None

Sinfonia sacra is a nine-minute, single-movement work based on Bach's "Jesu, meine Freude" theme. The piece alternates between somber reflection and joyfulness. The first section has an open feeling, scored with a relatively thin texture. Several sections feature the trombone alone, with cadenza-like interjections. Throughout the work, the organ plays a secondary role to the trombone, simply adding color and harmonic interest. This piece is suited for a recital and for use in a liturgical setting.

The organ part is written on two staves.

This work has been recorded by Alain Trudel on the CD *The Art of the Trombone* (8.553716), and by Armin Rosin on the CD *Posaune & Orgel* (Teldec 6.42164AW).

Kulesha, Gary (b. 1954)

Sonata for Tuba and Organ. Toronto, Canada: Counterpoint Music Library Services Inc., 2009.

- Tuba
- Difficulty: Moderate
- Technique: Nothing unusual
- Mute: None

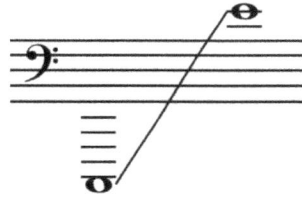

I.	Dotted quarter		note
	= 60		
II.	♩ = 132		
III.	♩ = 66		

Garu Kulesha is a Canadian composer, pianist, conductor, and educator. He is currently a faculty member at the University of Toronto.

Sonata for Tuba and Organ is a ten-minute work composed in 1976 for Scott Irvine. The first movement in 6/8 meter is flowing and lyrical. The middle movement is strong and assertive. The final movement is slightly more playful without technical demand. This piece is suited for a recital and for use in a liturgical setting.

The organ part is on three staves with no registration indicated and dynamics clearly marked.

Lindberg, Oskar Frederik (1887-1955)

Choralvorspiel über: "Denk, wenn einmal der Nebel verschwunden ist" für Posaune/Fagott/Viloncello & Orgel. Köln, Germany:Wolfgang G. Haas – Musikverlag Köln E.K., 2000.

- Tenor trombone
- Difficulty: Easy
- Technique: Trill
- Mutes: None

     I.   Adagio

Lindberg, a Swedish composer, organist and educator, received his formal musical training at the Music Conservatory in Stockholm. He later was employed there as a Professor of Music. His music is known to be lyrical with a nationalistic flavor.[28]

This four-minute, single-movement work begins with an introduction marked, "ad libitum." This is followed by a more-structured section marked, "Choraltempo," beginning in measure fourteen. The composer is specific regarding phrasing and articulation; therefore the trombonist should pay careful attention to the nuance indicated. The third section, marked "risoluto," has many meter changes. The work builds with both instruments playing fortissimo, dissipating towards the conclusion. The final three measures, marked "lento," end with a soft dynamic level. In addition to the score, the publisher includes trombone parts in C (bass clef) and B-flat treble clef. Due to the narrow range and simple nature, this piece would be ideal for a young trombonist, if the trill is omitted. c

---

[28] Prefatory notes.

Linke, Norbert (b. 1933)

Prozession für Posaune und Orgel. Leipzig, Germany: Friedrich Hofmeister Musikverlag, 1999.

- Tenor trombone
- Difficulty: Moderate
- Technique: Nothing unusual
- Mutes: None

    I.   Majestätisch

Linke was born in Steinau, a town in lower Silesia (now Germany). He received his formal musical training at the Hochschule Für Musik, in Hamburg, where he studied with Professor Ernst Gernot Klussmann. His compositional interests are primarily in the genre of new-music. Linke has held academic positions at the Free Academy of Music in Hamburg, and currently is a Professor of Music at the Gerhard-Mercator University in Duisburg.[29]

Prozession, a single-movement, six-minute work begins with the trombone playing assertive figures in the low register of the instrument set over a thinly scored organ part. This introduction, marked "Majestätisch," (Majestically) ends with a fermata, leading to the next section, marked "Etwas schneller" (Somewhat faster). Here, a dialogue is carried on between the trombone and organ, with both marcato and lyrical phrases. The work concludes with a section marked "Chorale-like." Accented phrases give way to soft lyricism and the work concludes softly. This piece is suited for a recital and for use in a liturgical setting.

---

[29] Prefatory note.

The organ part is on two staves with no registration indicated and dynamics clearly marked.

Lingenberg, Wilfried (b. 1969)

Elegie for Tuba (or Euphonium) and Organ. IMSLP, 2017.

- Tuba or Euphonium
- Difficulty: Moderate
- Technique: Nothing unusual
- Mute: None

Lingenberg is a German mathematician and composer who has written a small number of pieces. *Elegie for Tuba and Organ* is a revised publication of *Intermezzo for Tuba (or Horn) and Organ* with a new title. Please see the piece below for more information.

Lingenberg, Wilfried (b. 1969)

Intermezzo for Tuba (or Horn) and Organ. Kleve, Germany: Copy-us, 2006.

- Tuba
- Difficulty: Moderate
- Technique: Nothing unusual
- Mute: None

Intermezzo is a single movement work that was commissioned by Han Martin Corrinth in 2002. The piece is marked Adagio and begins lyrically in both instruments, followed by a section that is more technical. At measure 47, the organ part switches to four staves, one for each hand and foot. Long-held chords develop, first in the left foot, then right, followed by punctuations in the left and right hands. This builds in intensity with the tubist playing in a high tessitura. The piece closes with a return to the lyrical thematic material from the beginning.

The organ part is on three and four staves with some registration indicated and dynamics clearly marked.

Linkenbach, Klaus (1932-2000)

Es kommt ein Schiff, Partita für Posaune und Orgel. Stittgart, Germany: Hänssler-Verlag, 1986.

- Tenor trombone
- Difficulty: Easy
- Technique: Nothing unusual
- Mutes: None

I.	Choral
II.	II. to IV. Variations 1-8

Linkenbach, a German composer, organist and educator began studying music at a young age, receiving instruction from his father. Later, he studied sacred music at the Evangelical Church Musikschule Schlüchtern in Hesse. After graduation, he received a posting at the Evangelical Church in Eschweiler, retiring in 1997.[30]

Composed in 1961, *Es kommt ein Schiff* (A ship is coming), is an eight-minute work consisting of a chorale followed by a set of eight variations. The piece, dedicated to Jürgen Primnitz, is based on a short chorale theme played at the beginning and end of the work. All of the variations are similar in length to the chorale. They are intended to be played without pause. The work is primarily in 6/4 meter with a few

---

[30] http://www.dohr.de/autor/linkenbach.htm (accessed December 27, 2008).

meter changes throughout. Due to the simple rhythms and narrow range, this work would be ideal for a young trombonist. This piece is suited for a recital and for use in a liturgical setting.

The organ part is on two staves with some registration indicated and dynamics clearly marked.

Liszt, Franz (1811-1886)

Hosannah für Bassposaune und Orgel. New York, NY: Schott Music Corporation, 1983.

- Bass trombone
- Difficulty: Easy
- Technique: Nothing unusual
- Mutes: None

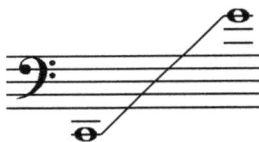

I.   Largo maestoso

Liszt, a Hungarian composer, pianist and music teacher, is renowned as a leader of the Romantic Movement, and one of the greatest piano virtuosos of his time. As a composer, he is credited with the creation of the symphonic poem.

Hosannah, a six-minute, single-movement work, was composed in 1862. Marked "Largo Maestoso," it begins with a series of held organ chords. The bass trombone plays an opening motive doubled with the organ pedal leading to the main section of the work set over a recurring triplet figure on the organ. The bass trombone part is broad, written primarily with quarter and half-notes. The work remains in common meter with a consistant tempo and style throughout and frequent key changes. This work is appropriate for a young bass trombonist. This piece is suited for a recital and for use in a liturgical setting.

The organ part is on three staves with no registrations indicated and dynamics clearly marked.

This work has been recorded by bass trombonist Yves Bauer on the CD *Hommage du baroque au gospel* (FBR 120/1. 2003), and by trombonist Niels-Ole Bo Johansen and organist Ulrich Spang-Hanssen on the CD *Holst: Duo Concertante for Trombone & Organ; Works by Elgar, Gilmanton, Liszt, Ropartz, Vaughan Williams & Eben* (Classico CLASSCD 122), and by trombonist Sebastian Krause and organist Gabrielle Wadewitz on the CD *Sonntagsposaunenstück: Romantic music for trombone and organ.* (Raum Klang RK 9805), and by trombonist Christian Lindberg and organist Gunnar Idenstam on the CD *The Sacred Trombone* (BIS CD-488); and by trombonist Alain Trudel on his recording *The Art of the Trombone* (8.553716), and by trombonist Gabor Hegedüs and organist Hermann Harrassowitz on the CD *Posaune-Orgel-Chor Ein Konzert in St. Lorenz/Nürnberg* (Motette CD50661). Another recording is available performed by Steven Mead (euphonium) and Lidia Ksiazkiewicz (organ) on the CD Hosanna (Bocchino Music – BOCC 121).

Lorentzen, Bent (1935-2018)

Alpha and Omega for Trombone and Organ. Copenhagen, Denmark: Engstrom & Sodring, 1989.

- Tenor trombone

Lorentzen, a Danish composer, received his formal musical training at the University in Aarhus and at the Royal Danish Academy of Music in Copenhagen. After graduation, he taught at the Academy of Music in Aarhus. He has composed a wide range of styles including several instrumental concerti with orchestra, chamber works, fourteen operas and several electronic works.

Alpha and Omega is an eighteen-and-a-half-minute work. A copy of this work was unobtainable at the time of this writing.

This work has been recorded by trombonist Niels-Ole Bo Johansen and organist Ulrich Spang-Hanssen, on the CD *Alpha and Omega* (Paula PACD 87).

Madsen, Jesper (1958-1999)

Intrada per Trombone & Organo. Copenhagen K, Denmark: SNYK, the Secretariat for Contemporary Music, 1999.

Intrada is a two-minute work. A copy of this work was unobtainable at the time of this writing.

Marchand, Todd

Adoro te Devote (Humbly I Adore Thee) for trombone and organ. Dallas, Fort Worth, Texas: Con Spirito Music, 2008.

- Tenor trombone
- Difficulty: Easy
- Technique: Nothing unusual
- Mutes: None

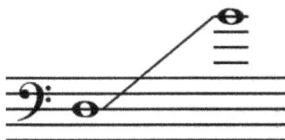

    I.   Freely

Todd Marchand is a trombonist, composer, and educator in the Dallas-Fort Worth area. He is the creator of Con Spirito Music, which offers unique works for soloists and ensemble to church, school, community, and professional musicians.

Adoro te Devote is a two-and-a-half-minute, single-movement work. This piece is suited for a recital and for use in a liturgical setting. A preview of the score with midi sample can be found at the Con Spirito Music website.

The composer writes: "Adoro te Devote" ("Humbly I Adore Thee") is a eucharistic, or communion, hymn with text by St. Thomas Aquinas (1225-1274)."

The origin of the melody is unclear. In some places it is simply described as a Gregorian chant; in others as a 13th-century Benedictine plainsong; in others as a French church melody published in the Paris *Processionale* (hymnal or liturgical manual) of 1697. Regardless, it is a lovely, flowing tune well-suited for the trombone's legato "singing" capabilities.

In this arrangement, the trombone plays the tune through on the first verse in D major, adds a descant over the organ in the second verse and, following a short modulation, recapitulates the tune in the concluding key of G major.

Marchand, Todd

Crusaders Hymn "Fairest Lord Jesus"/"Beautiful Savior" for trombone and organ. Dallas, Fort Worth, Texas: Con Spirito Music, 2013.

- Tenor trombone
- Difficulty: Easy
- Techniques: Nothing Unusual
- Mutes: None

I.   Quarter note = 96

Crusaders Hymn is a four-minute, single-movement work suited for a recital and for use in a liturgical setting. A preview of the score with midi sample can be found at the Con Spirito Music website.

The composer writes: "The Crusaders Hymn is a folk melody from Silesia, a historical region of Central Europe located mostly in modern-day Poland. The tune was published in the *Schlesische Volkslieder* (*Silesian Folk Songs*), 1842; and the text, "Schönster Herr Jesus," by German Jesuits, was published in the *Münster Gesangbuch* (*Münster Hymnal*) in 1677. The Crusaders Hymn is so named due to the legend that it was sung by German Crusaders on their way to the Holy Land. It is perhaps more well-known as "Fairest Lord Jesus" or "Beautiful Savior" from two popular texts with which it is associated. In this arrangement for trombone and organ, the tune is presented by the soloist in verse 1 and by organ with countermelody by soloist in verse 2. Following a brief modulation, the tune is presented ½ step higher by soloist and organ."

Marchand, Todd

"In the Bleak Midwinter" Hymn tune "Cranham" by G. Holst for trombone and organ. Dallas, Fort Worth, Texas: Con Spirito Music, 2010.

- Tenor trombone
- Difficulty: Easy
- Technique: Nothing unusual
- Mutes: None

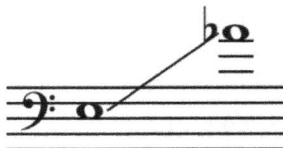

I.   Quarter note = 84

In the Bleak Midwinter is a two-minute, single-movement work suited for a recital and for use in a liturgical setting. A preview of the score with midi sample can be found at the Con Spirito Music website.

The composer writes: "English poet Christina Rossetti (1830-1894) wrote "In the Bleak Midwinter" in response to a request for a Christmas poem by the American magazine *Scribner's Monthly* in 1872. It was published posthumously in her *Poetic Works* in 1904 and became a popular Christmas carol after its inclusion in *The English Hymnal* (1906) in a setting with music by Gustav Holst. The tune was named 'Cranham' after the village in Gloucestershire that was home to Holst's grandparents and mother, and where it is said (though no definitive proof exists) that he wrote the music."

Marchand, Todd

"Let Us Break Bread Together" African-American Spiritual for trombone and organ. Dallas, Fort Worth, Texas: Con Spirito Music, 2013.

- Tenor trombone
- Difficulty: Easy
- Technique: Nothing unusual
- Mutes: None

I.   Quarter note = 88

Let Us Break Bread Together is a three-minute, single-movement work suited for use in a liturgical setting. A preview of the score with midi sample can be found at the Con Spirito Music website.

The composer writes:

"Let Us Break Bread Together is a well-loved spiritual that in three verses expresses worshippers' intent at Holy Communion: 'Let us break bread together on our knees;' Let us drink wine together on our knees;' 'Let us praise God together on our knees.' Each verse is followed by the refrain, 'When I fall on my knees with my face to the rising sun, O Lord, have mercy on me.' The words may date to the eighteenth century,

possibly first sung by slaves in Virginia's Episcopal churches for whom the experience of taking Communion would have involved kneeling toward the rising sun at an early morning service of worship. The tune became widely known after publication in *The Second Book of Negro Spirituals* (1926), compiled by brothers James Weldon Johnson and Rosamond Johnson, and it grew in popularity with its inclusion in many 20th century hymnals and through various choral arrangements. In this arrangement, trombone and organ each take a turn at the verse and refrain, then join together after a modulation up one step on verse, refrain and conclusion."

Marchand, Todd

Meditation on "Wondrous Love" for trombone and organ. Dallas, Fort Worth, Texas: Con Spirito Music, 2015.

- Tenor trombone
- Difficulty: Easy
- Technique: Nothing unusual
- Mutes: None

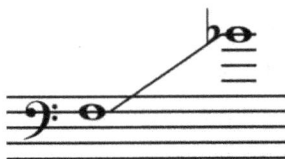

I.   Half note = 56

Meditation is a four-minute, single-movement work suited for a recital and for use in a liturgical setting. A preview of the score with midi sample can be found at the Con Spirito Music website.

The composer writes:

"*Wondrous Love* is the hymn tune name for a folk melody that was published in the 1840 shape-note hymnal, *Southern Harmony*, to accompany a text by an anonymous author that expresses his awe at the wondrous love of Christ, who 'laid aside his crown' to suffer death and rise again to save humanity from the eternal consequences of sin and death. It was later published in the other great 19th-century shape-note hymnal, *The Sacred Harp*, and since the mid-20th century has become widely known through its publication in the hymnals of many Christian denominations. The melody is said to be based on a popular 1701 English song, the 'Ballad of Captain Kidd,' and it is likely it predates that by a century or more. It employs a hexatonic scale of six tones with no major or minor third, comprising 1, 2, 4, 5, 6, and 7 (e.g., G, A, C, D, E, F). The English clergyman and hymn scholar Erik Routley (1817-1982) described the tune as 'incomparably beautiful.' In this arrangement, an improvisatory statement precedes the presentation of the tune by trombone in verse 1 and organ in verse 2, and returns prior to a modulation into the final verse."

The organ part is on three staves with some registration indicated and dynamics clearly marked.

Marchand, Todd

"Processional" for trombone and organ. Dallas, Fort Worth, Texas: Con Spirito Music, 2013.

- Tenor trombone
- Difficulty: Easy
- Technique: Nothing unusual
- Mutes: None

    I.   Majestically Half note = 54

Processional is a three-minute, single-movement work suited for a recital and for use in a liturgical setting. A preview of the score with midi sample can be found at the Con Spirito Music website.

The composer writes:

"*Processional* is a short composition, based on a simple motif that is repeated and inverted in various keys, that is suitable for use as a prelude or postlude to a service of worship"

Downloadable digital sheet music includes bass clef and Bb treble clef solo parts for performance by trombone or, alternatively, Bb treble clef euphonium or Bb trumpet.

Marchand, Todd

"*Rejoice! Rejoice, Believers*" Welsh hymn tune "*Llangloffan*" for *trombone and organ.* Dallas, Fort Worth, Texas: Con Spirito Music, 2013.

- Tenor trombone
- Difficulty: Easy
- Technique: Nothing unusual
- Mutes: None

I.   Andante Quarter note = 54

"*Rejoice! Rejoice, Believers*" is a three-minute, single-movement work suited for a recital and for use in a liturgical setting. A preview of the score with midi sample can be found at the Con Spirito Music website.

The composer writes:

"*Rejoice! Rejoice, Believers* ("Ermuntert euch, ihr Frommen") is a hymn by Laurentius Laurenti (1660–1722) that was published in his 1700 collection, *Evangelica Melodica*. It was translated from German to English by Sarah B. Findlater (1823–1907) and published in her collection, *Hymns from the Land of Luther*, in 1854. The Welsh hymn tune 'Llangloffan,' which often accompanies the text, is the basis for this arrangement. Verse 1 is presented by trombone with light accompaniment by organ; verse 2 features a countermelody in the organ accompaniment; and after a brief modulation, verse 3 and its countermelody are presented in the relative major of the tune's initial minor key."

Marchand, Todd

"Rise Up, Shepherds, and Follow" African-American spiritual for trombone and organ. Dallas, Fort Worth, Texas: Con Spirito Music, 2012.

- Tenor trombone
- Difficulty: Easy
- Technique: Nothing unusual
- Mutes: None

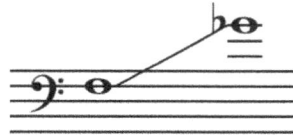

I.   Quarter note = 92

Rise Up, Shepherds, and Follow is a three-minute, single-movement work suited for a recital and for use in a liturgical setting. A preview of the score with midi sample can be found at the Con Spirito Music website.

The composer writes:

"*Rise Up, Shepherd, and Follow* is an African-American spiritual first published in *Slave Songs of the United States* (1867). Its lyrics are based on the nativity account in the gospel of St. Luke, and in particular, chapter 2, verses 8-9: 'There were shepherds living out in the fields nearby, keeping watch over their flocks at night. An angel of the Lord appeared to them, and the glory of the Lord shone around them.' Throughout, the lyrics urge the listener to leave behind one's work and to rise up and follow the star of Bethlehem — perhaps an allusion to rising up and following a path to freedom from slavery as well as a direct exhortation to follow Jesus the Savior. Those familiar with the tune will recognize that it has been altered and adapted for this arrangement, while maintaining the pentatonic scale (plus a flatted seventh) that give the tune its characteristic folk flavor."

Marthinsen, Niels (b. 1963)

Concerto for trombone and organ. Copenhagen, Denmark: Society for Publication of Danish Music (Samfundet), 1992.

- Tenor trombone
- Difficulty: Advanced
- Technique: Multi-phonics, Alternate notation, Pitch bending, Lip trills, Grace notes, Glissandi
- Mutes: Harmon, Cup

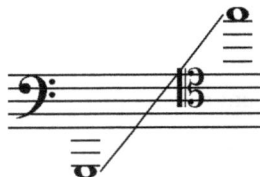

    I.   Genesis
    II.   Noah
    III.   Leviathan

Marthinsen, a Danish composer, received his formal musical training at the Royal Academy Musikkonservatorium in Aarhus. He is best known for his new-music, and is recognized as Denmark's most technically based composer. Marthinsen has written a wide range of works, including several symphonies, three operas and many chamber works. He also teaches music theory and composition in Denmark.

Composed in 1992, this twenty-eight minute concerto is dedicated to Niels-Ole Bo Johansen. It was funded by the Danish Arts Council's music committee.

Marthinsen writes,

Genesis conjuring up a scenario of creation and gradual proliferation- a representation of a Great Birthing. The second movement, Noah, is the psychological mirror image of the first water and emptiness everywhere, after the flood, and only little life left to remember the abundance of the past and to hope for, and perhaps eventually find, comfort on dry land. With the third movement, Leviathan, I have created a monster, a huge awe inspiring sea snake that roams and rules the oceans it inhabits, until, to rephrase the prophet Esajah, the Lord strikes it down on the ultimate day. Together the three movements form a gradual and often labyrinthine loss of momentum – a running out, a freezing down. Little by little energy and tension is petering out, what is left begin to coagulate into a series of loosely connected fragments (or fossils, if you like) until, at the end, again there is light.

An extremely complex modern work, this piece requires virtuosic performers. The prefatory notes indicate that each movement can function as an independent work. This work is suited for a recital.

The organ part is on three staves and requires a large instrument. No registration is indicated and dynamics are clearly marked.

This work has been recorded by trombonist Niels-Ole Bo Johansen and organist Ulrich Spang-Hanssen on the CD *Alpha and Omega* (Paula PACD 87).

Meyer, Hannes (b. 1939)

Sonate C-Moll Für Posaune und Orgel/Klavier nach Motiven von G.B. Pergolesi. Crans-Montana, Switzerland: Editions Marc Reift, 1986.

- Alto trombone
- Difficulty: Moderate
- Technique: Grace notes
- Mute: None

    I.   Adagio
    II.   "Ninetta" Largo Lacrimante
    III.   Marcia dei pifferai

Part of the Collection Branimir Slokar, *Sonate C-Moll* is an eleven-minute work in four movements. This piece, written in a baroque style, is based on themes by Pergolesi, but does not form a typical Baroque suite. The first movement, *adagio*, features a floating cantabile melody played by the trombone set over sixteenth-note arpeggiated figures performed on the organ. The second movement, *allegro*, is more virtuosic, requiring a considerable amount of slide technique to play the sixteenth-note figures. The third movement, *Largo*, is subtitled "Ninetta." The trombone plays mournful phrases set over a sparse organ part. The final movement, *Marcia dei pifferai,* is a jubilant march. Because of the high tessitura of this work, it should be programmed with endurance considerations. In addition to the score, the publisher includes trombone parts in both alto and tenor clef. This piece is suited for a recital and for use in a liturgical setting.

The organ part is on two staves and would be best suited for a baroque organ. No registration is indicated and dynamics are clearly marked.

This work has been recorded by Branimir Slokar on the CD *Barocke Music Für Posaune und Orgel* (Claves D 902) and (Marcophon CD 922-2), and by trombonist Ronald Barron on the CD *The Return of the Alto* (Boston Brass Series BB-1008CD), and by trombonist Thomas Horch and organist Ruth Vollet on the CD *Baroque-Bolero* (Audite 95.437), and by trombonist Branimir Slokar on the CD, *Fantasia* (Marcophon CD 922-2).

Meyer, Hannes (b. 1939)

Suite für Posaune und Orgel "Das Liebesspiel."

Suite für Posaune und Orgel "Das Liebesspiel," is a fourteen-minute, five-movement work. A copy of this work was unobtainable at the time of this writing.

The work has been recorded by trombonist Thomas Horch and organist Ruth Vollet on the CD *Baroque-Bolero* (Audite 95.437), and by trombonist Sebastian Krause and organist Gabrielle Wadewitz on the CD *Sonntagsposaunenstück: Romantic music for trombone and organ* (Raum Klang RK 9805).

Michel, Jean-François (1957)

Kyrie für Posaune und Orgel. Crans-Montana, Switzerland: Editions Marc Reift, 1994.

- Tenor trombone
- Difficulty: Moderate
- Technique: Flutter tonguing, Grace notes, Wide slide vibrato, Glissandi
- Mutes: None

I.   Kadenz lento dramatico

Michel, a Swiss composer and trumpeter, received his formal musical training at the Conservatory in Fribourg. An accomplished performer, he won the position of solo trumpet with the Munich Philharmonic at the age of eighteen. He has toured internationally and recorded several CDs. Michel currently is a Professor of Music, teaching trumpet at the Fribourg Conservatory.[31]

Part of the Collection Branimir Slokar, *Kyrie*, a seven-minute modern work opens with a dramatic trombone cadenza. After the introduction, the piece follows a loosely based ABA form. The B section, "Christe eleison," is faster and livelier than the "Kyrie eleison" sections which

---

[31] Prefatory notes.

bookend the piece. At times the piece has a dark and foreboding quality with dissonance. To create effects, the composer uses glissandi and flutter tonguing played by the trombone and tone clusters on the organ.

The prefatory notes state:

The form is borrowed from the liturgical Kyrie where the pity of God is entreated three times. The three prayers follow one another directly; I have simply replaced the works by musical atmospheres. The first prayer repeatedly asks for God's help in the age of human frailty. The trombone cries out in desperation whilst the organ expresses the monotony of suffering. Christie eleison: Why does God who has assumed human form not revolt? Must one defend oneself by means of aggression? Kyrie eleison: This movement was inspired by a quotation from the writer and traveler Moitessier: *"Forgiveness will always triumph"* The music seeks to express inward peace and the road to hope. This composition is dedicated to all those who stand up for common sense and true moral values.[32]

Kyrie demands a strong upper register and substantial endurance. This work is suited for a recital.

The organ part is on three staves with no registration indicated and dynamics clearly marked.

Michel, Johannes M. (b. 1962)

*Dialog: Sonate für Posaune und Orgel.*Munich, Germany: Strube Verlag, 2007.

---

[32] Prefatory notes.

- Tenor trombone
- Difficulty: Moderate
- Technique: Glissandi, Lip trills
- Mutes: Straight

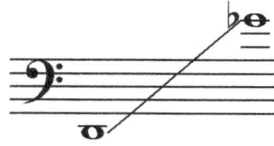

I.	Vivace
II.	Con Calma
III.	Dialog
IV.	Agitato

Michel, a German organist and composer, was influenced by his father Josef Michel, also a composer and church musician. Johannes received his formal musical training in Heidelberg and Frankfurt with an advanced degree in organ at the Musikhochschule Stuttgart with Professor Ludger Lohmann. He currently teaches organ at the Hochschule für Kirchenmusik in Heidelberg and maintains a busy performance schedule.

Dialog, a nine-minute, four-movement work was composed in 2004. The opening movement, *Vivace,* is a duet for trombone and organ pedal. The tempo and technical difficulty requires flexibility on the trombone and agility on the organ pedal. The second movement, *Con Calma,* is expressive, featuring the upper range of the trombone in lyrical passages. *Dialog,* the shortest of the movements, is also the most contemporary, featuring a conversation between the two instruments, beginning with an argument and concluding with remorse. The final movement, *Agitato*, a cut time march, ends dramatically in full voice. This piece is suited for a recital and for use in a liturgical setting.

The organ part is on three staves with no registration indicated and dynamics clearly marked.

Miller, Michael R. (b. 1932)

Play of Sun and Clouds for Trombone and Organ. Toronto, Ontario: Canadian Music Centre, 1989.

- Tenor Trombone
- Difficulty: Moderate
- Technique: Grace notes, Slurs over the harmonic series
- Mutes: Straight

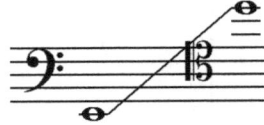

I.   Grave Maestoso

Miller, a Portuguese composer, received his formal musical training in the United States at New York University. He later earned a Ph.D. from the Eastman School of Music. After graduation, Miller emigrated to Canada, becoming a Professor of Music at the Mount Allison University in Sackville, New Brunswick. He retired in 1999, and now lives in Fredericton, New Brunswick. Miller's compositional repertoire includes two operas and many works for band, orchestra, vocal and chamber groups. His music is said to blend the old and new, using melodies and counterpoint often combined with polytonality and serialism.

Composed in 1998, *Play of Sun and Clouds,* is a modern eight-minute piece commissioned by trombonist James Montgomery. He premiered the work with organist Willis Noble. The piece presents contrasting styles, tempos, and meters through the single movement. The opening, marked "Grave Maestoso," begins with a stately fanfare in 3/4 meter. This leads to an energetic trombone cadenza, demonstrating technique and flexibility with slurs over the harmonic series and rapid multiple tonguing. The piece changes character in a delicate lyrical section, using the whole-tone scale. This leads to a playful section marked, "Allegretto giocoso." The remainder of the piece alternates between the two styles, depicting the interaction of the sun and clouds. This piece is suited for a recital and for use in a liturgical setting. Although unpublished, the piece is available for loan from the Mount Allison University Music Library, Sackville, New Brunswick, Canada. Call number: M184 M58 P55 1989.

The organ part is on three staves with some registration indicated and dynamics clearly marked.

Miserendino, Joe (1932-2010)

Canzona della notte scura. Farmington, NM: Brassworks 4 Publishing, 2006.

- Tuba
- Difficulty: Easy
- Technique: Grace notes
- Mutes: None

Miserendino has several works written for tuba and euphonium.

Canzona della notte scura (Song of the Dark Night) is a three-minute lyrical piece. The work begins with solo tuba before the organ enters with a soft, soothing accompaniment. This short piece is well-suited for a recital or for a liturgical setting. The high tessitura for the tuba, would be comfortably played on the euphonium.

The organ part is on three staves with no registrations indicated, and dynamics clearly marked.

Miserendino, Joe (1932-2010)

Canzone di notte dei sogni agrodolci. Farmington, NM: Brassworks 4 Publishing, 2006.

- Euphonium
- Difficulty: Moderate
- Technique: Nothing unusual
- Mutes: None

The title of this work translates to: *Song of a Night of Bittersweet Dreams*. The piece remains in 3/4 meter and alternates between sections marked quarter-note = 70 and 120. There are few technical challenges, however, endurance might be an issue due to the long phrases in a high tessitura, with only a few measures of rest for the euphonium player.

In addition to the score, the publisher provides a bass clef, and B-flat treble clef euphonium parts. This work is well-suited for a recital and for a liturgical setting.

The organ part is on three staves with no registrations indicated, and dynamics clearly marked.

Möckl, Franz (b. 1925)

Intrade für Tenorposaune und Orgel. Köln, German: Wolfgang G. Haas – Musikverlag Köln E.K.,2003.

- Tenor (bass) trombone
- Difficulty: Moderate
- Technique: Nothing unusual
- Mutes: None

I.   Andante commodo

Möckl, a composer and music educator, was born in the Western Bohemian town of Bernau. He received his formal musical training at the Institute for Teacher Training in Coburg. He served as the Director of the Teachers Training College for Primary and Elementary Schools until his retirement in 1988.[33]

Intrade, a four-minute, single movement work is dedicated to Professor Armin Rosin. This piece can be performed on either tenor or bass trombone. The work is non legato in character, featuring sequenced phrases with no change in style and tempo from beginning to end. This piece is suited for a recital and for use in a liturgical setting.

The organ part is on three staves with no registration indicated and dynamics clearly marked.

Moland, Erik

"Once Again!" for Trombone & Orgel. Oslo, Norway: Norwegian Music Information Centre, 1992.

- Alto trombone
- Difficulty: Advanced
- Technique: Improvised sections
- Mutes: Straight

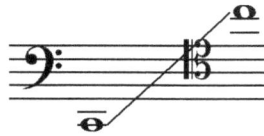

I.	Once
II.	Another One
III.	Again

Moland, a Norwegian composer, received his formal musical training at the Norwegian State Academy of Music. After graduation, he moved to Denmark, where he is currently employed as a music educator and freelance composer.

"Once Again!" a sixteen-and-a-half minute modern work in three movements was composed and published in 1992. The first movement,

---

[33] Prefatory notes.

Once, begins with the trombone playing a pedal Bb and organ playing a glissando. This is followed by a minimalist section where the trombone and organ alternate playing long-held notes using only the pitch "C" for nearly twenty measures. At this point, the instruments venture away from the single-pitch center. The trombone figures throughout the work are highly rhythmic and form repeated patterns that tend to remain on the same pitch. In the second movement, *Another One,* the composer suggests pitches to be improvised by both instruments. As the movement progresses, it becomes more structured, eventually evolving into a traditionally notated part. The final movement, *Again,* begins similarly to the first. The conclusion of the work features an unexpected change to a funk style. This work is suited for a recital. The organ part is on three staves with registration and dynamics clearly indicated.

Mortimer, John Glenesk (b. 1951)

Fantasia for Trombone and Organ. Crans-Montana, Switzerland: Editions Marc Reift, 1992.

- Tenor trombone
- Difficulty: Advanced
- Technique: Flutter tonguing
- Mutes: None

    I.   Maestoso ♩. = ca 54

Mortimer, a Scottish composer, violist and conductor, received his formal musical training at the Royal College of Music in London. After graduation he was employed as an orchestral violist and later moved to Switzerland to teach at the Conservatoires of Neuchâtel and La Chaux-de-Fonds. Mortimer's works for trombone include two concerti, *Prelude and Dance, Suite Parisienne* for trombone quartet and *Divertimento Concertante* for two trombones and orchestra.[34]

Part of the Collection Branimir Slokar, this single-movement, eight-and-a-half-minute work includes several stylistic changes. Romantic in nature, the piece begins with a dramatic introduction, marked "maestoso." A playful section, marked, "allegro moderato" features the organ reed stops in contrast to the mellow lyrical lines of the trombone. A waltz interlude, marked "lento," develops into a technically demanding cut time "allegro moderato" section. The conclusion is similar to the beginning. This piece is suited for a recital and for use in a liturgical setting.

The organ part is on three staves with registration indicated and dynamics clearly marked.

This work has been recorded by trombonist Branimir Slokar on the CD *Fantasia* (Marcophon CD 922-2).

Muller, Johann Immanuel (1640-1670) arr. Allen Ostrander

Praeludium, Chorale, Variations, Fugue for Bass Trombone and Organ. Botsford, CT: Edition Musicus, 1959.

- Bass trombone
- Difficulty: Moderate
- Technique: Nothing unusual
- Mutes: None

    I.   Praeludium
    II.   Chorale
    III.   Variations

---

[34] Prefatory notes

>   IV.   Fugue

Praeludium, Chorale, Variations, Fugue for Bass Trombone is a five-minute work in four movements. The score bears the inscription "From manuscript dated 1839," but no further information is given. The first movement, *Praeludium,* is thirty-five measures long and sets the tone for the piece. The trombone melody is intricately embellished with mordents and trills played by the organ. The second movement, *Chorale*, marked "♩ = 80," features trombone phrases set over a sparse organ accompaniment. The third movement, *Variations*, is divided into three sections. The first is built on the chorale theme, played almost entirely by the organ. The second, scored with large leaps, requires flexibility on the trombone. The third variation, in 6/8 meter, segues directly into the final movement, *Fugue,* building in intensity to the end of the piece. This piece is suited for a recital and for use in a liturgical setting and could be played on the tenor trombone.

The organ part is on two staves with no registration indicated and dynamics clearly marked.

Muller, Johann Immanuel (1640-1670)
arr. Allen Ostrander

Praeludium, Chorale, Variations, Fugue for Bass Trombone and Organ. Botsford, CT: Edition Musicus, 1959.

- Tuba
- Difficulty: Moderate
- Technique: Nothing unusual
- Mutes: None

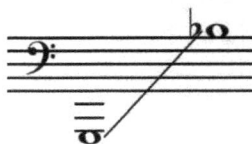

>   I.   Praeludium
>   II.   Chorale

III.   Variations
IV.   Fugue

This is the tuba version of the piece above. Although the organ score is identical to the score printed for the trombone version, there have been alterations for the range of the tuba part, which are not indicated in the organ part.

Näther, Gisbert (b. 1948)

Duo für Tuba und Orgel Op. 69. Freidrich Hofmeister, 1998.

- Tuba
- Difficulty: Easy
- Technique: Nothing unusual
- Mutes: None

Näther, a German composer and hornist, studied at the Academy of Music in Dresden. He has an extensive list of works for ensembles of all sizes, and has won several awards for his works.

Duo is a single-movement, four-minute work in two main sections. The first, *maestoso,* is in 3/2 meter, which is followed by *larghetto* which is set in common time. This piece would be accessible by a young tubist, and is well-suited for a recital or a liturgical setting.

The organ part is on three staves with no registrations indicated, and dynamics clearly marked.

Nelhybel, Vaclav (1919-1996)

Prelude and Chorale on SVATÝ VÁCLAVE. Fish Creek, WI: Alliance Publications, 1999.

- Tenor trombone
- Difficulty: Easy
- Technique: Nothing unusual
- Mutes: None

I.   Moderato

Nelhybel, a Czech composer and conductor, received his formal musical training at Prague Conservatory and Fribourg University in Switzerland. He immigrated to the United States, receiving citizenship in 1962. He taught at the University of Lowell in Massachusetts and the University of Scranton in Pennsylvania. He is best known for his wind and band works for young performers with some difficult compositions. His pieces are often filled with vigorous rhythmic patterns borrowed from Czech tradition.

Prelude and Chorale is based on an ancient twelfth-century chant.

The performance notes include:

This venerated tune takes the form of a Kyrielle, each verse, after invoking the intercession of St. Václav (Wenceslas-Prince of the Czech lands in the 10th century) on behalf of his people, ends with the Kyrie eleison. Further verses, in litany form, call upon the other Czech patron saints, eg. Ludmilla, Prokop John Nepomuk, Agnes. It also became a famous ceremonial song bonding the people together. [35]

This four-minute, single-movement work, commissioned by the Czech Music Alliance was written for and dedicated to Joel Blanik in 1988. The original chant with translation is printed in the back of the score. With narrow range and simple rhythmic figures, this piece would be well-suited to a young trombonist. Scores are available from the publisher for eighteen different instruments and brass quintet parts in lieu

---

[35] Prefatory notes.

of organ. This piece is suited for a recital and for use in a liturgical setting.

The organ part is on two staves with no registration indicted and dynamics clearly marked.

Nelhybel, Vaclav (1919-1996)

Sonata da Chiesa No. 3 Variants on "Our God Almighty" for Trombone(s) (Bassoons, Oboe) and Organ or Harpsichord. Hackensack, NJ: Joseph Boonin, 1977.

- Tenor trombone
- Difficulty: Easy
- Technique: Nothing unusual
- Mutes: None

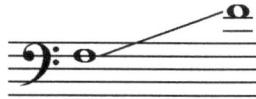

I.   ♩ = 60

S*onata da Cheisa No. 3* is a three-minute work in the form of a theme and variation. Based on the tune *"Our God Almighty,"* the work begins with a four-measure organ introduction, followed by the statement of the main theme played by the trombone (lyrics provided allow this theme to be sung). The variations are simple, alternating between 4/4 and 3/4 meter. This piece is well-suited to a young trombonist because of its narrow range and simple rhythms. In addition to the score and trombone part, the publisher includes an optional second trombone part and a solo oboe part.

This piece is suited for a recital and for use in a liturgical setting.

The organ part is scored on two staves with no registration indicated and dynamics clearly marked.

Nilsson, Torsten (b. 1920)

Concertino for Bronslur in E-flat, or Alto Trombone and Organ, Op.105B. Bromma, Sweden: Edition Reimers, 1983.

- Alto trombone
- Difficulty: Easy
- Technique: Nothing unusual
- Mutes: None

   I. Moderato

Concertino for Bronslur, a curious single-movement, three-minute work, is written for a *bronslur,* an S-shaped Scandinavian wind instrument from the Bronze Age.[36] The work can be performed on an alto trombone. The piece relies solely on the overtone series since the bronslur is without valves, much like a bugle. The composer has written two versions of this work: Opus 105A, for brass quartet, and Opus 105B for organ. Both are available from the same publisher. This work is suited for a recital.

The organ part is on three staves with no registration indicated and dynamics clearly marked.

Nilsson, Torsten (b. 1920)

Concertino per trombone ed organo op.81. Bromma, Sweden: Edition Reimers, 1985.

---

[36] Prefatory notes.

- Tenor trombone
- Difficulty: Advanced
- Technique: Alternate notation, Improvised sections, Flutter tounging
- Mutes: Straight

I.   Vigorosa ♩ -76

Nilsson, a Swedish church musician and composer, received his formal musical training in Stockholm and Vienna, later holding several teaching and playing positions with European colleges and churches. In his compositions, he attempts to break the barrier between sacred and secular music.

Composed in 1978, *Concertino per trombone ed organo op.81* is a nine-minute, single-movement modern work dedicated to trombonist Christer Torgé. He premiered the piece with the composer at the organ in February 1979. The beginning of the work, marked "vigorosa," presents the commanding principal theme. The piece progresses through many style and meter changes, including a lyrical section, a dance-like scherzando and a trombone cadenza leading to a dramatic ending. Nilsson creates a wide variety of color and timbral changes through the manipulation of organ stops. Both trombone and organ parts require accomplished performers. The piece is suited for a recital.

The organ part is scored on three staves and features an improvised section. Registration is indicated and dynamics are clearly marked.

This work has been recoded by trombonist Christer Torgé and organist Hans Fagius on the CD *NILSSON: Nox Angvstiae / Trombone and Organ Concertino* (BIS-CD-138).

Nilsson, Torsten (b. 1920)

Concertino per trombone ed organo op.93. Bromma, Sweden: Edition Reimers, 1986.

- Alto trombone
- Difficulty: Moderate
- Technique: Nothing unusual
- Mutes: Straight

     I.   Dolce

Concertino op 83 was composed between 1981 and 1985. This single-movement, four-and-a-half minute work is dedicated to Christer Torgé. The piece is dissonant with complex harmonies and tone clusters. It has few tempo or stylistic changes but many changes in meter. The work begins with solo trombone and includes a short trombone cadenza near the conclusion. This piece is suited for a recital and for use in a liturgical setting.

The organ part is on three staves with registrations indicated and dynamics clearly marked.

Nordhagen, Stig (b. 1966)

Macchia Nera Di polvere Per Trombone E Organo. Oslo, Norway: Norwegian Music Information Centre, 2004.

- Tenor trombone
- Difficulty: Advanced
- Technique: Glissandi, Wide slide vibrato
- Mutes: None

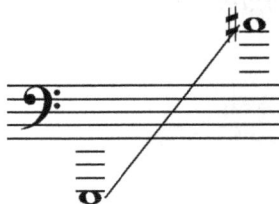

I.   In Modo Barbaro

Nordhagen, a Norwegian clarinetist and composer, received his formal musical training at the Music Conservatory in Oslo, followed by an advanced degree in clarinet at the Rotterdam Music Conservatory. He has been a freelance composer and a member of the Kristinsand Symphony Orchestra.

Composed in 2004, and dedicated to Marius Hesby, *Macchia Nera Di polvere* is a three-minute, single-movement modern piece. The piece opens abruptly, with the organist playing hand clusters at a dynamic of *fortissimo.* Marked "In Modo Barbaro," the trombone joins assertively at full-volume in a figure which plays up to (f #2), then leaps down to (EE). The work is highly rhythmic and requires excellent multiple tonguing and extreme range. This work is suited for a recital.

The organ part is on three staves with no registration indicated and dynamics clearly marked.

Norontaus, Veikko (b. 1930)

Psalmi 42 op.6 nro 5 for trombone and organ/piano. Helsinki, Finland: Finnish Music Information Centre, 1991.

- Tenor Trombone
- Difficulty: Moderate
- Technique: Nothing unusual
- Mutes: None

I.   Andante cantabile

Psalmi 42, a four-minute, single-movement work was composed in 1969. Marked "Andante cantabile," the organ plays a short introduction and is joined by the trombone playing the main theme. At the section marked, "Largo," the trombone plays a soft cadenza-like passage leading to a conspicuously dissonant section in alternating 3/4 and 2/4 meters. The composer may have written this dissonance to portray God's vengeance, however anger is not expressed in the verses of Psalm 42. The work ends much like it begins. This piece is suited for a recital and for use in a liturgical setting.

The organ part is on two staves with no registration indicated and dynamics clearly marked.

Österberg, Sven (b. 1933)

I Praise your name, O Lord. Kariskrona, Sweden: Libitum, 2007.

- Tenor trombone
- Difficulty: Easy
- Technique: Nothing unusual
- Mutes: None

       I.   ♩ =76

Österberg, a Swedish composer, received his formal musical training at the Royal College of Music in Stockholm, where he studied organ, horn, and voice. He has a compositional repertoire of over 250 works. [37]

I Praise your name, O Lord is a four-minute, single-movement work composed in 2007. With manageable keys and simple rhythms at a slower tempo, this work is appropriate to a young trombonist with a strong upper range. This piece is suited for a recital and for use in a liturgical setting.

The organ part is on three staves with no registrations indicated and dynamics clearly marked.

---

[37] Prefatory notes.

Perlongo, Daniel (b. 1942)

Novella for trombone and organ. New York, NY: American Composer Alliance, 1998.

- Tenor trombone
- Difficulty: Advanced
- Technique: Alternate notation
- Mutes: Straight

     I.   Lento

Perlongo, an American composer, received his formal musical training at the University of Michigan and in Rome on a Fulbright scholarship. Several of his works have earned international recognition and awards. He currently teaches Composition and Music Theory at Indiana University of Pennsylvania.

Novella, was commissioned by and written for trombonist Christian Dickinson. He premiered the work with organist Carol Teti at Indiana University of Pennsylvania in 1998. [38] This twenty-five minute piece is divided into thirty-two numbered sections. Several of these sections are for solo organ, intended to give the trombonist a rest during such a long work. Almost all the sections are separated by a moment of silence notated with a rest under a fermata. The piece is notated without meter, however, the composer does indicate tempo changes. The work unfolds as a musical journey beginning with distant chant-like motives which are later developed in the faster technical sections. Several have a recitative quality. The work builds in intensity and concludes with a heroic cadenza. Novella is demanding for both instrumentalists. This piece is suited for a recital.

---

[38] Daniel Perlongo, personal E-mail, March, 14 2008.

The organ part is on three staves with registration indicated and dynamics clearly marked.

Peters, Max (1849-1927)

Elegie für Posaune und Orgel op.9. Winterthur, Switzerland: Bernhard Päuler Amadeus Verlag, 2000.

- Tenor trombone
- Difficulty: Easy
- Technique: Nothing unusual
- Mutes: None

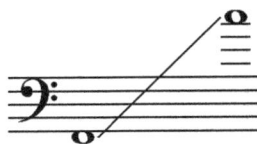

    I.   Maestoso

Peters, a German composer and organist, held the position of city music director for the Baltic town of Pernow, Estonia. He later served as an organist and choir director in Moscow and Berlin. His compositional repertoire includes operettas, numerous choral pieces and several instrumental works. [39]

Composed in 1892, *Elegie,* a five-minute work, is dedicated to the Imperial Russian trombone virtuoso, Rudolf Ziebarth. The opening, marked "maestoso," is meditative and requires expressive lyrical playing; this leads to a contrasting '*con energia,*' section, which is more technical with rapid sixteenth-note patterns and strong marcato feel. The piece ends softly, similarly to the opening. This piece is suited for a recital and for use in a liturgical setting.

The organ part is on two staves with registration and dynamics clearly indicated.

[39] Prefatory notes.

This work has been recorded by trombonist Carsten Svanberg with organist Birgit Marcussen on the CD *Trombone Organ and Piano* (EMI MOAK 37).

Petersen, Lynn L. (1923-2006)

Spiritual Sounds for Trombone and Organ. St. Louis, MO: Concordia Publishing House, 2000.

- Tenor trombone
- Difficulty: Easy
- Technique: Nothing unusual
- Mutes: Straight

I.	I Want Jesus to Walk with Me
II.	Were You There
III.	There Is a Balm in Gilead

Petersen, an American composer, received her Bachelor of Elementary Education from the Dr. Martin Luther College, a Master of Church Music degree from Concordia College-River Forest, and a Ph.D. in Music Theory and Composition from the University of Minnesota. Since graduation, she has served on the faculty of several American colleges including St. Olaf College and Gustavus Adolphus College.

Spiritual Sounds, a five-minute work, is a collection of three traditional African American spirituals. All are simple, written in common meter with a few changes in key. *I Want Jesus to Walk with Me* is marked "Soulfully ♩ = 104." *Were You There* is marked "Somberly ♩ = 92." The final setting, *There Is a Balm in Gilead,* is marked "Moderately slow ♩ = 84." This movement is slightly more difficult with eighth-note sequences and range up to (bb1). This piece is suited for a recital and for use in a liturgical setting. In addition to the score, the publisher includes parts for trombone, trumpet B-flat and instrument in C.

The organ part is on three staves with registration indicated and dynamics clearly marked.

Pezel, Johann (1639-1694)
arr. Kurt Sturzenegger

Suite de Danses pour trombone & orgue. Edition Marc Reift, 1983.

- Trombone
- Difficulty: Easy
- Technique: Nothing unusual
- Mutes: None

I.	Intrada
II.	Allemande
III.	Sarabande
IV.	Bal

Pezel, a German violinist, trumpeter and composer, lived and worked in Leipzig before entering the monastery in Prague in 1672. He wrote many instrumental pieces, and is considered to be influential in the evolution of instrumental forms and styles of orchestral writing.

Due to the narrow range and simple rhythms, this suite of dances would be quite accessible to any trombone or euphonist who can read tenor clef. Each movement is quite short (aprox.12 – 24 measures), and could played separately. In addition to the trombone part in tenor clef, a b-flat treble clef part is included with the organ score. This work is well-suited for a recital or for a liturgical setting.

The organ part is on two staves with no registrations indicated, and dynamics clearly marked.

Pinkham, Daniel (1923-2006)

Dragons and Deeps for Bass Tuba in F and Organ. Boston, MA: ECS Publishing, 2008.

- Bass Tuba in F
- Difficulty: Moderate
- Technique: Nothing unusual
- Mutes: None

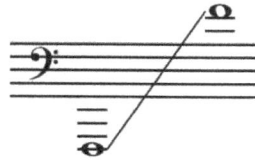

> I.   Andante

Pinkham, an American composer, studied composition with Copland, Hindemith, Barber and Nadia Boulanger. He served as a faculty member at the Boston Conservatory of Music, University of Boston, New England Conservatory of Music and Harvard. A prolific composer, renowned for his music for brass instruments, he wrote in a wide variety of styles and genres.

Written for and premiered by Randall Montgomery in 2001, this five-minute work bears the inscription by the composer:

> Praise the LORD form the earth,
>
> ye dragons and all deeps;
>
> fire and hail, snow and ice,
>
> gales of wind obeying his voice!
>
> > Psalm 148: 7, 8.

Composed as a single-movement piece, there are four distinct sections. The first, *Andante* is reflective and lyrical. The second section, *Piu mosso* weaves and passes a melody line back and forth between the two instruments in what could be described as a conversation. The third section, *con moto* has the fastest tempo of the four. Written in 12/8 for the organ and has staccato quarter notes in 4/4 meter for the tuba. This section builds in intensity towards the climax, before ending with material which is similar to the opening. This work is suited for a recital.

The organ part is primarily on two staves with some double pedaling. No registration is indicated and dynamics are clearly marked.

This work has been recorded by tubist Randall Montgomery on the CD *Daniel Pinkham Music for Brass and Brass & Organ* (ARSIS CD143).

Pinkham, Daniel (1923-2006)

Gifts and Graces for trombone and organ. Boston, MA: ECS Publishing, 1978.

- Tenor trombone
- Difficulty: Moderate
- Technique: Harmonic glissandi
- Mutes: Straight

  I.   Allegro ballando

Gifts and Graces, a single-movement, eight-minute work was commissioned by Jeffrey Price. The piece is meditative and lyrical, allowing expression from both performers. The work features numerous meter and tempo changes with a few instances where the trombone and organ parts are written asymmetrically. The piece concludes with a dramatic finish, employing use of 5/8 and 10/8 meter and ending with a harmonic glissando. This piece is suited for a recital and for use in a liturgical setting.

The organ part is on three staves with no registrations indicated and dynamics clearly marked.

Pinkham, Daniel (1923-2006)

Solemnities for Trombone & Organ. Boston, MA: Ione Press, 2002.

- Tenor trombone
- Difficulty: Moderate
- Technique: Glissandi, Notes played as natural (untempered) 7th harmonic
- Mutes: Straight

I.	Dramatic ♩ = 120
II.	Lyrical ♩ = 80
III.	Joyous ♩ = 144

Solemnities, a seven-minute work in three-movements, was composed in 2000. Dedicated to trombonist Bron Wright, he premiered the piece in February 2002, with the composer at the organ. The piece is based on Isaiah 30:29, the verses inscribed in the score and parts. The first movement, marked "dramatic," is twenty-two measures long. It consists of a solo trombone fanfare punctuated with short organ interludes. Near the end of this movement, the trombone plays the note (a1). The composer indicates that the notes should be played as a natural (untempered) 7th harmonic. In the second movement, marked "lyrical," the trombone plays long melodic lines, sometimes chromatic and dissonant. The final movement, marked "joyous," begins with a fanfare and develops into an exuberant 5/8 jig. This piece is suited for a recital and for use in a liturgical setting.

The organ part alternates between two and three staves as needed. No registration is indicated and dynamics are clearly marked.

This work has been recorded by trombonist Bron Wright on the CD *Daniel Pinkham Music for Brass and Brass & Organ* (ARSIS CD143).

Plog, Anthony (b. 1947)

Sonare for Trombone and Organ. Vuarmarens, Switzerland: Édition Bim, 2011.

- Trombone
- Difficulty: Advanced
- Technique: Nothing unusual
- Mutes: None

Plog is a well-known American trumpeter and composer. He had a successful international career as a soloist. His works have been recorded by groups such as the Canadian Brass, Summit Brass, and the St. Louis Brass Quintet. Since 1993, Plog has worked as Professor of Music at the Musikhochule in Freiburg Germany.

Sonare, an eight-minute, single-movement work is dedicated to Joe Alessi. In the prefatory notes the composer writes:

"Sonare is a work that explores some of the sonic possibilities for the combination of these two beautifully sounding instruments. But instead of just exploring the loud and sonorous possibilities of the trombone and organ, it also concerns itself with soft and intimate textures as well as allegro and staccato styles of playing. The form of the piece alternates between slow/lyrical and fast energetic sections."

The piece is challenging for both instrumentalists, requiring strong technical abilities. This work is well-suited for a recital.

The organ part is on three staves with no registrations indicated, and dynamics clearly marked.

Purser, John (b. 1942)

SKYELINES, for Tenor Trombone and Organ. Coventry, England: Warwick Music, 1997.

- Tenor trombone
- Difficulty: Advanced
- Technique: Glissandi, Slide vibrato,
- Mutes: Straight

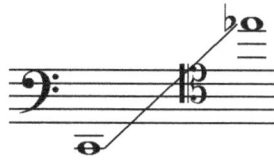

I.   SKYELINES I
II.   SKYELINES II

Purser, a Scottish composer, poet, playwright and musicologist, was born in Glasgow. His book, *Scotland's Music* is an historical account of Scottish music dating back to the Stone Age. His interest in early music led to the reconstruction of the deskford carnyx, a bugle-like instrument which existed in the Iron Age.

SKYELINES, a seven-minute, two-movement work, was composed for trombonists John Kenny and John Kitchen. The first movement begins with the marking "Largo Sostenuto ♩ = 45." This introduction is quiet and recitative. The movement gains momentum at the "Poco piu Andante" section, but remains dream-like for the rest of the movement. Due to the high tessitura and slow tempo, the trombonist must have a solid high register. *SKYELINES II* is fast and lively, marked "vivace e animato ♩. = 55." This section features technical trombone passages punctuated with glissandi and sforztandos. The last section of the piece slows, marked, "largo maestoso." This conclusion scores the trombone playing a chorale melody set over organ chords played at full volume. The ending abruptly changes style, becoming soft with muted trombone playing rising triplet figures before fading. This piece is suited for a recital and for use in a liturgical setting.

The organ part is on three staves with registration and dynamics clearly marked.

This work has been recorded by trombonist John Kenny on the CD *The Voice of the Carnyx,* British Music Label (CD 016).

Raue, Reinhard (1953-2006)

Drie Pastelle für Altposaune und Orgel. Crans-Montana, Switzerland: Editions Marc Reift, 1999.

- Alto trombone
- Difficulty: Advanced
- Technique: Trills, Alternate notation, Glissandi
- Mutes: Straight

> I.   Andante moderato
> II.   Listesso tempo
> III. A piacere (largamente)

Raue, a German church musician and organist, received his formal musical training at the Robert Schumann University in Düsseldorf. After graduation, he served as organist and music director at the Evangelical Church of the Rhineland.[40]

Drie Pastelle is a six-minute work in three movements. The first movement, marked "Andante moderato," features the organ with the trombone playing a secondary accompanying role. This section has many meter changes, including an unusual section with the organ playing six over five over two. The second movement, marked "Listesso tempo," begins with the trombone playing indefinite pitches and creating vocalizations through the trombone. Upon the return of standard notation, the section begins building in intensity with the trombone playing marcato lines and the organ playing reoccurring sextuplet patterns. The final movement, "A piacere (largamente)," is lively with flashy trombone figures. Ensemble balance must be observed in the loud

---

[40] Prefatory notes.

conclusion so that the organ does not overpower the alto trombone. This piece is suited for a recital.

The organ part is notated on three staves with registration indicated and dynamics clearly marked.

Read, Gardner (1913-2005)

Invocation for Trombone and Organ Op.135. North Easton, MA: Robert King, 1978.

- Tenor trombone
- Difficulty: Advanced
- Technique: Nothing unusual
- Mutes: Straight, Cup, Whisper

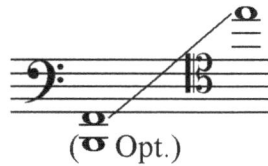

(𝇋 Opt.)

I.   Boldly, with force

Read, an American composer from Evanston, Illinois, studied at Northwestern University while in high school. After high school graduation, he studied composition at the Eastman School of Music. He won several student composition competitions and his works have been performed by the Chicago Symphony Orchestra and the New York Philharmonic. After graduation, he taught composition at the St. Louis Institute of Music, the Kansas City Conservatory, and the Cleveland Institute of Music. Many of his 150 works appear in multiple versions, often re-arranged for different instruments.

Invocation, a dramatic nine-minute, single-movement work, was composed in 1977, commissioned by Gordon College for Jeffrey Price. The piece journeys through many stylistic and emotional changes. Marked, "boldly, with force," the piece requires the trombonist to play up to and hold an (e-flat2) in the first phrase. A cadenza-like dialogue between the two instruments is established, with use of close harmonies and dissonance. The second section returns briefly to the opening material. This is followed by another lyrical passage marked, "*musingly*," which leads to a dramatic ending. This piece is suited for a recital and for use in a liturgical setting and requires virtuosic performers.

The organ part is on three staves with registration indicated and dynamics marked.

This work has been recorded by trombonist Christian Lindberg and organist Gunnar Idenstam on the CD *The Sacred Trombone* (BIS CD-488). Another recording is available performed by Steven Mead (euphonium) and Lidia Ksiazkiewicz (organ) on the CD Hosanna (Bocchino Music – BOCC 121).

Risher, Tim (b. 1957)

Hymns and Strophes. Winter Park, FL: Wehr's Music House, 1997.

- Trombone with F attachment
- Difficulty: Moderate
- Technique: Nothing unusual
- Mutes: Plunger

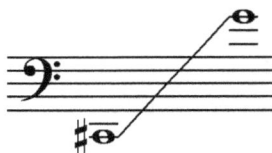

I.	Cloud
II.	Flash of Lightning
III.	Dream

Risher, an American composer and trombonist, received his formal training at the University of Central Florida and Florida State University. He is currently employed as a producer for *Radio Diffusions,* a new-music program on National Public Radio. Risher maintains an active performance schedule with the group Tentoe, an electronic quartet based in Hamburg, Germany.[41]

Hymns and Strophes was composed in 1995, revised in 1997. The piece is dedicated to Jamie Wehr, who premiered it at Seminole Community College in September, 2002. The work expresses life's journey from birth to death. The composer found inspiration for the work from this passage:

"Diamond Sutra" –

As stars, a lamp, a fault of vision,

As dewdrops or a bubble,

A cloud, a flash of lightning, a dream.

Thus we should look upon the world.

From "The Pocket Buddha Reader," edited by Anne Bancroft, 2001.

The composer states:

I was attempting to embody the idea of each of these, not particularly a Buddhist vision of these, but simply looking at the objects and writing about them. The world can be seen as this, or this, or this, but they are all the same. All three movements interlock as one vast structure, as a series of minimalistic variations, all revolving around a set of specific keys or notes.[42]

The first movement, *Cloud*, marked "Gracefully," is hymn-like and meditative at first, but soon becomes authoritative. The second movement, *Flash of Lighting,* marked "quarter note=100," is primarily in compound meter, beginning with a repeating figure played by the trombone using a plunger mute. An up-tempo section follows with the trombone playing above eighth-note figures in the organ. The movement concludes with a short organ solo prior to a flashy ending. The final movement, *Dream,* marked "Adagio Legato," serves as a peaceful,

---

[41] Prefatory notes.

[42] Tim Risher, personal E-mail, June, 1 2008.

reflective conclusion. This piece is suited for a recital and for use in a liturgical setting.

The organ part is on three staves with no registration indicated and dynamics clearly marked.

Rønnes, Robert (b. 1959)

Lento for Bass Trombone and Organ. Oslo, Norway: Norwegian Music Information Centre, 1998.

- Bass trombone
- Difficulty: Moderate
- Technique: Nothing unusual
- Mutes: None

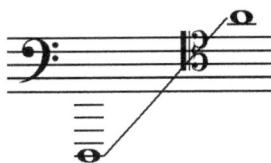

> I.   Lento ♩ = 60

Rønnes, a Norwegian composer, studied bassoon at the Norwegian State Academy of Music and the Conservatory of Music in Geneva, Switzerland. He has held positions in the Stockholm Philharmonic Orchestra and the Stavanger Symphony Orchestra. Rønnes is renowned in the field of contemporary music. His works have been performed in Europe, Russia, and the USA.

Lento, a ten-minute, single-movement work, is an adaptation of the second movement of the composer's *Concerto for Bass Trombone and Orchestra,* written in 1985. The piece is romantic and features the warmth and color of the lower register of the bass trombone. Marked "Lento ♩ =60," the piece remains subdued throughout, the bass trombone part never exceeding a dynamic level of mezzo-forte. A trombone cadenza near the end of the work concludes softly and solemnly. This piece is suited for a recital and for use in a liturgical setting.

The organ part is on three staves with no registration indicated and dynamics clearly marked.

This work has been recorded by trombonist Gaute Vikdal on the CD *Skybrudd* (EUCD 007).

Rosell, Lars-Erik (1944-2005)

Reflections. Bromma, Sweden: Edition Reimers,1979.

- Tenor trombone

Reflections, a fifteen-minute work, was premiered by trombonist John Petersen and organist Gustaf Vasa Kyrka in Stockholm, Sweden in March 1979. The score could not be obtained at the time of this writing.

Ruders, Poul (b. 1949)

Double Entry: Fanfare for Trombone and Organ. Copenhagen, Denmark: Edition Wilhelm Hansen, 2011.

- Trombone
- Difficulty: Advanced
- Technique: Glissandi, Lip Trills, Flutter Tonguing.
- Mutes: None

Ruders, a Danish organist and composer, has written works for choir, chamber ensemble, and solo instruments.

Double Entry is a one-minute, single-movement fanfare written for Niels-Ole Bo Johansen on the occasion of his 50th birthday. The piece is energetic with glissandi, flutter tonguing, and triplet-sixteenth flourishes.

This work is well-suited for a recital. The organ part is on two staves with registrations indicated, and dynamics clearly marked.

Runbäck, Albert (1894-1974)

Basun och Orgel. Slite, Sweden: Wessmans Musikförlag.

- Tenor trombone
- Difficulty: Easy
- Technique: Nothing unusual
- Mutes: None

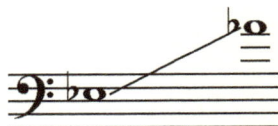

I.	Gör porten hög
II.	Glädjens dag
III.	Tre julmelodier
IV.	Preludio dolente
V.	Krist är uppstånden
VI.	Pingstkoral
VII.	Säg mig den vägen
VIII.	Ditt ljus jag vägen finne
IX.	Min själ skall lova Herran

Basun och Orgel, a nine-movement collection, was composed between 1960 and 1970. Many of the movements are based on hymn tunes. Both the trombone and organ parts are simple and repetitive, the majority of which are approximately thirty measures long.

This collection is suited for use in a liturgical setting, not to be performed in its entirety.

The organ part is on two staves with pedal notes on the bottom of the bass clef staff. Neither registration nor dynamics are indicated.

Sanders, Bernard Wayne (b. 1957)

Rhapsodie für Posaune (Fagott) und Orgel. Köln, Germany: Verlag Christoph Dohr, 1995.

- Tenor trombone
- Difficulty: Easy
- Technique: Nothing unusual
- Mutes: None

    I.   Moderato ♩ = 104

Sanders, an American composer and organist, was born in De Pere, Wisconsin. He received his formal musical training at St. Norbert College, Wichita State University and the Hocshule für Musik in Hamburg, Germany. He currently resides in Tuttlingen, Germany, where he is a church music director and free-lance composer.

Rhapsodie, a seven-minute, single-movement work, was composed in 1995. The beginning, marked "Moderato ♩ = 104," is written in a cantabile style. The middle section changes to compound meter. This section is brisk and transitions to the opening material. This piece is suited for a recital and for use in a liturgical setting.

The organ part is written on three staves. Neither registration nor dynamics is indicated.

Sandström, Jan (b. 1954)

Lacrimae Lacrimae for Trombone and Organ. Stockholm, Sweden: Edition Tarrodi, 1991.

- Alto or tenor trombone
- Difficulty: Moderate
- Technique: Nothing unusual
- Mute: None
- (Organ part available on CD)

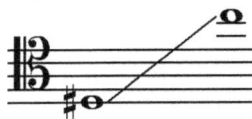

I. $\downarrow$ = 92

Sandström, a Swedish composer, received his formal musical training at the Royal Academy of Music in Stockholm; and the University School of Music in Piteå, where he later became a Professor of Composition. Sandström's compositions cover a broad range of ideals including minimalism, Eastern philosophy and serialism. His *Motorbike Concerto* for trombone and orchestra is one of the most well known Swedish orchestral works, with over 600 performances since its premiere in 1989.

Lacrimae Lacrimae, an eight-and-a-half minute, single movement piece was composed in 1991, for Christian Lindberg to showcase the newly constructed Conn 36H alto trombone. The beginning of the work is marked " $\downarrow$ = 92," and requires expressive playing. A chant-like alto trombone melody floats over a foundation of pedal points and textural effects with a blend of shifting colors and contrasting staccato responses from the organ.

Sandström writes:

The title 'tears, tears' was not connected to any special event as I recall. What I can say is that the activity of bringing out tears seems often present in my composing, unconsciously. Pull out the tears, push away the darkness—and let the joy and light remain.[43]

A tenor trombone version of this work is also available from the same publisher. This piece is suited for a recital and for use in a liturgical setting.

---

[43] Jan Sandström, personal E-mail, March, 5 2008.

The organ part is on three staves with registration indicated and dynamics clearly marked.

This work has been recorded by trombonist Christian Lindberg and organist Gunnar Idenstam on the CD *The Sacred Trombone* (BIS CD-488). Another recording is available performed by Steven Mead (euphonium) and Lidia Ksiazkiewicz (organ) on the CD Hosanna (Bocchino Music – BOCC 121).

Sark, Einar Traerup (1921-2005)

Introduction and Carillon op 42. København, Denmark: SNYK, the Secretariat for Contemporary Music, 1990.

- Tenor trombone

Introduction and Carillon, an eight-minute work, was premiered by trombonist Carsten Svanberg and organist Valeria Zanini in Søyst, Denmark in December 1990. This work is available by rental only, but could not be obtained at the time of this writing.

Schibler, Armin (1920-1986)

"Audiens exaudieris" Fantasie für Posaune und Orgel. Edition Eulenburg, (See C.F. Peters Corporation for Distribution), 1977.

- Tenor trombone
- Difficulty: Advanced
- Technique: Glissandi, Half and whole step trills, Flutter tonguing, Quasi improvised section
- Mutes: Cup, Spitz

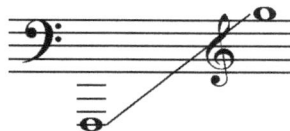

I.   Lento

Schibler, a Swiss composer, studied in Switzerland and England. He later taught public school in Zürich. In the 1950s, he infused his compositions with twelve-tone techniques, influenced by Stravinsky. Schibler's late works blend atonality and jazz elements.

Audiens exaudieris is a nine-minute, single-movement, avant-garde work. The piece showcases the extreme registers of the trombone, beginning with a pianissimo (BB flat) played in a cup mute, descending to (FF). After three measures, (without the mute) the passage reaches (g2). Much of the expressive lyrical playing in this piece is set over a sequence of tone clusters from the organ. A short trombone cadenza develops into passages which include: lip trills, flutter tonguing and a quasi-improvised section. This work is suited for a recital.

The organ part is primarily on two staves with some double pedaling. No registration is indicated and dynamics are clearly marked.

Schiffmann, Ernst (1901-1980)

Intermezzo für Posaune und Orgel Op.53. New York, NY: Schott Music Corporation, 1954.

- Tenor trombone
- Difficulty: Moderate
- Technique: Nothing unusual
- Mutes: None

I.   Ruhig flissend

Intermezzo für Posaune und Orgel is a dramatic nine-minute, single-movement romantic work. The piece alternates between two contrasting sections of thematic material. The opening, marked "Ruhig flissend,"

(Quiet flowing) features an expressive chant-like theme. The contrasting section is angular, using double-dotted figures in 4/2 meter. Even though this section remains in a slow tempo, the phrases build in intensity and power. The conclusion returns to the subdued opening material. There are many large leaps requiring the trombonist to have good breath control in order to sustain the notes. This piece is suited for a recital and for use in a liturgical setting. Shiffmann also has a work for trombone and piano "Concert Piece op.67," available through Schott Music.

The organ part is written on three staves with no registration indicated and dynamics clearly marked. There are several passages with slurred ascending octave figures.

This work has been recorded by Joachim Elser on the CD *Posaune und Orgel* (Mitra CD 16228. 1990.), and by trombonist Alain Trudel on his recording *The Art of the Trombone* (8.553716).

Schilling, Hans Ludwig (b. 1927)

Vier Choralvorspiele. Stittgart, Germany: Hänssler-Verlag, 1976.

- Tenor trombone
- Difficulty: Moderate
- Technique: Lip Trill, Grace notes
- Mutes: Straight

I.	Wie schön leuchtet der Morgenstern
II.	Allein Gott in der Höh sei Ehr
III.	Nun bitten wir den Heiligen Geist
IV.	Im Frieden dein-Ricercar

Schilling, a German composer, studied with Hindemith and Genzmer at the University of Zürich and the University of Freiburg. After graduation, he served as a professor of composition at several universities. His early works are traditional; his later compositions from the 1960s have jazz elements.

Vier Choralvorspiele, a twelve-minute work in four-movements, was written for Armin Rosin. The first movement, *Wie schön leuchtet der Morgenstern,* (How beautifully shines the morning star) is marked "Ruhige Halbe." The trombone plays the principal melody line for most of the movement, with the organ functioning in a supporting role. The second movement, *Allein Gott in der Höh sei Ehr,* (Honor to God in the Highest) marked "Lento," features many tempo and meter changes. The trombone melody is constructed with quarter-note triplets. The third movement, *Nun bitten wir den Heiligen Geist,* (Now we appeal to the Holy Ghost) marked, "Auf breite Ganze – etwas frei," (Brightly, somewhat free) begins with an organ introduction notated without meter. The trombone enters with a simple chant-like figure. The final movement, *Im Frieden dein-Ricercar,*(In thy peace – Ricercar) marked "Ruhige Halbe," is strophic. These four verses, separated with fermati, are more technically demanding than the other movements, due to the changes in meter and the ornamentation for the trombone. This work is suited for a recital.

The organ part is on three staves with registration indicated and dynamics clearly marked.

This work has been recorded by trombonist Armin Rosin on the recording *Posaune & Orgel* (Teldec 6.42164AW 1986/1997).

Schmidt, Siegmund (1874-1939)

Fünf Choralvorspiele für Posaune und Orgel. Munich, Germany: Strube Verlag, 1986.

- Tenor trombone
- Difficulty: Moderate
- Technique: Nothing unusual
- Mutes: None

I.   Erhalt uns, Herr, bei deinem Wort
II.   Sonne der Gerechtigkeit
III.   O gläubig Herz
IV.   Wach auf, wach auf, deutsches Land
V.   Die Sonn hat sich mit ihrem Glanz gewendet

Schmidt, an Austrian composer, pedagogue and cellist, studied composition with Bruckner, and cello with Hellmesberger, at the Conservatory in Vienna. After graduation, he was employed as a cellist with the Vienna Court Opera. He was awarded an Honorary Doctorate from the University of Vienna. His compositions are considered rich in Viennese Romanticism.

These five chorale preludes form a nine-minute work, intended to be played as a complete set; however, each movement could function independently. The first movement, *Erhalt uns, Herr, bei deinem Wort,* (Preserve us, Lord, by thy word) marked "Ruhig," is soft, with the dynamics never rising above the level of mezzo forte. Following an organ introduction, the trombone plays a haunting solo response. The second movement, *Sonne der Gerechtigkeit,* (Sun of Justice) marked "zügig im choraltempo," begins with trombone alone. The third movement, *O gläubig Herz,* (Oh faithful heart) marked "ruhig flissend," is similar to the previous movement, but slightly more lyrical. This section begins and ends softly. The fourth movement, *Wach auf, wach auf, deutsches Land,* (Wake up, Wake up, German land) marked "Frisch choraltempo," is based on Bach's familiar "Sleepers Awake" theme. The final movement, *Die Sonn hat sich mit ihrem Glanz gewendet,* (The sun has turned its luster) is marked "Ruhige Halbe," and features the trombone playing a cantus firmus part. This piece is suited for a recital and for use in a liturgical setting.

The organ part is on three staves with registration indicated and dynamics clearly marked.

Schneider, Enjott (b. 1950)

Golgatha for Trombone and Organ. New York, NY: Schott Music Corporation, 2009.

- Trombone
- Difficulty: Advanced
- Technique: Wide Slide Vibrato, Glissandi, Auxiliary percussion parts to be performed by trombonist.
- Mutes: None

Schneider is a German composer, musicologist, and music educator. As a composer he is best known for his film work, having won the Bavarian Film Award for best film score in 1990.

Golgatha is an eleven-minute, single-movement work which was premiered in 2009 by Stefan Geiger, solo trombonist of the NDR Hamburg symphony orchestra, and Josef Still, cathedral organist in Trier. Schneider wrote in the prefatory notes:

"The mystery of Golgatha is a central element of Christian religion. The cruelty and burden of the Passion can be heard in the introduction. A bell-like C-sharp can be heard 7 times in the middle movement 'Adagio Doloroso' and flows into the chaconne in 7/8 time. The chaconne with its rotating harmony pattern is a symbol of the recurring rituals of transformation. The 7/8 time coupled with puzzlingly floating emphasis is a symbol of mystery. The sound of the trombone awakes in us the ultimate belief that judgement day is the destination of all beings."

There are several technically challenging sections, which include having the trombonist play on a pipe bell or triangle while playing the trombone. This piece is well-suited for a recital.

The organ part is on three staves with no registrations indicated, and dynamics clearly marked.

Schneider, Julius (1805-1885)

Choralvariationen für Bass-Posaune und Orgel op.16. Stittgart, Germany: Hänssler-Verlag, 1988.

- Bass trombone
- Difficulty: Moderate
- Technique: Turns, Trills
- Mutes: None

    I.   Jesus, meine Zuversicht

    II.   Was Gott tut, das ist Wohlgetan

Schneider, a German organist and composer, was music director at the Friedrichswerder Church. He taught organ, voice and composition, at the Royal Institute for Church Music in Berlin. A prolific writer, he composed two operas, two oratorios, a piano concerto, over 200 works for choir and countless pieces for chamber ensembles. Despite this large repertoire, only a few of his compositions have been published.

Choralvariationen, an eight-minute, two-movement work, is a re-release of the original edition published by "Verlags, Kirchen und Schulbuchhandlung Gotth," now out of print. The first movement, *Jesus, meine Zuversicht,* (Jesus, my confidence) is a chorale with four variations. Marked "Andante maestoso," the lyrical melody requires a bass trombonist with a strong upper register. *Variation 1,* marked "Allegro moderato," is more technical with moving eighth-note figures, including turns and trills for the trombonist. *Variation 2,* marked "Piu moderato," is for organ alone, featuring similar ornamentation with sixteenth-note sequences. *Variation 3,* marked "Maestoso," is the shortest variation, constructed with dotted-eighth-sixteenth figures. The final variation, marked "Moderato," is a fugue and chorale. The organ introduces the fugue; then the trombone plays an augmented version of the chorale theme in whole notes. The second movement, *Was Gott tut, das ist Wohlgetan,* (What God does, that is well done) is a chorale and three variations. The first variation, marked "Andante con moto," features flowing eighth-note patterns with a high tessitura. The second variation is an organ interlude, written in 12/8 meter. The third variation is the most technically demanding for the trombonist, building to the end of the work. This piece is suited for a recital and for use in a liturgical setting.

The organ part is on two staves with registration indicated and dynamics clearly marked.

This work has been recorded by trombonist Sebastian Krause and organist Gabrielle Wadewitz on the CD *Sonntagsposaunenstück: Romantic music for trombone and organ* (Raum Klang RK 9805), and by trombonist Helmut Lang on the CD Intradas and Chorale Settings for Organ and Brass (Hänssler 98.544).

Schnittke, Alfred (1934-1998)

Schall und Hall für Posaune und Orgel. Vienna, Austria: Universal Edition, 1983.

- Tenor trombone
- Difficulty: Advanced
- Technique: Glissandi, Alternate notation, Grace notes
- Mutes: Straight

    I.   Lento

Schnittke, a Russian composer, received his formal musical training at the Moscow Conservatory. After graduation, he worked as a freelance composer writing for theater and film, composing sixty-six scores for Soviet film companies. He wrote articles and gave lectures on the importance of contemporary music. He received international recognition for his compositional work. [44]

This eleven-minute, single-movement avant-garde piece was written for trombonist Rudolf Josel and organist Martin Haselböck, who premiered it in Vienna, June 1983. *Schall und Hall,* (Sound and Resound) creates a hypnotic mood with dialogue between the trombone and organ. The opening marked *lento,* begins softly and builds in intensity. The work has an open quality with emphasis placed on how each note reacts to the acoustical surrounding.

The performance notes state:

The two part title "Sound and Resound" suggests the multiplicity of interpretative levels: question and answer in the resonant acoustic of large spaces; two instruments with similar yet fundamentally different tonal properties; the organ as a tonal extension of the syllabic trombone sound; trombone and organ as instruments with pronounced octave harmonics; the tension between a "mensurated" line and freely cadenced suspended sound.

The piece features two short cadenzas. This work could be an excellent introduction to contemporary music for an intermediate trombonist. It is suited for a recital.

The organ part is on three staves with some registration indicated and dynamics clearly marked.

This work has been recorded by trombonist Christian Lindberg and organist Gunnar Idenstam on the CD *The Sacred Trombone* (BIS CD-488), and by trombonist Anatoly Skobelev on the CD *Alfred Schnittke In Memoriam* (CHAN 9466).

---

[44] Ivan Moody and Alexander Ivashkin, "Schnittke, Alfred," in *Grove Music Online. Oxford Music Online*,

http://www.oxfordmusiconline.com/subscriber/article/grove/music/51128 (accessed August 5, 2008).

Schubert, Heino (b. 1928)

Sonata da chiesa sopra Tuba mirum spargens sonum for trombone and organ. Bad Schwalbach, Germany: Edition Gravis, 1992.

- Tenor trombone
- Difficulty: Moderate
- Technique: Glissandi, Grace notes
- Mutes: None

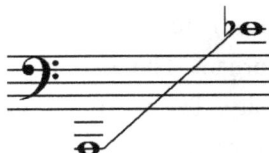

     I.   Con affetto
     II.   Movimento rubato
     III.   Molto espressione
     IV.   Agitato

Schubert, a German composer, organist and cantor was music director at Münsterkirche Essen. He later served as Professor of Organ and Tuning at the Musikhochschule in Köln. In 1978 he was appointed as Professor of Music Theory at the Johannes-Gutenberg-Universität in Mainz. The majority of Schubert's music is intended for young performers, mostly consisting of sacred vocal and instrumental works.

Composed in 1979, *Sonata da chiesa sopra Tuba mirum spargens sonum* is a seventeen-minute modern work in four-movements. The piece begins dramatically with a wide dynamic range and angular figures. The first movement, marked "Con affetto," has several meter changes. The second movement, marked "Movimento rubato," features a blend of soft lyrical figures,mixed with contrasting accented sixteenth-note figures. The third movement, marked "Molto Espressione," has many meter changes and develops ideas using triplet patterns. The final movement "Agitato," remains mostly in 12/4 meter and builds to a dramatic ending.

The organ part is on three staves, no registration indicated and dynamics are clearly marked.

Senon, Gilles (b. 1932)

Prière pour Trombone et Orgue. Paris, France: Gérard Billaudot, 1978.

- Tenor trombone
- Difficulty: Moderate
- Technique: Grace notes
- Mute: None

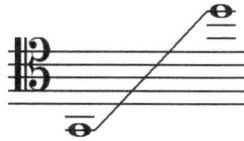

Prière, (prayer) a four-and-a-half minute, single-movement romantic work, features the singing quality of the trombone. The tempo and style of this work remains consistent, with a few animated sections building intensity. Modulating through several less-common keys, it would be good practice for a young trombonist. Endurance considerations must be observed due to the somewhat high tessitura and only a two-measure rest for the trombonist. This piece is suited for a recital and for use in a liturgical setting.

The organ part is on two staves with registration indicated and dynamics clearly marked.

This work has been recorded by Jean Douay on the CD *Trombone et Orgue* (Corelia CC 78030).

Siekmann, Frank H.

Two Powerful Hymns: A Mighty Fortress Is Our God—All Hail the Power of Jesus' Name. Kutztown, PA: Brelmat Music, 2003.

- Tenor trombone
- Difficulty: Moderate
- Technique: Trombonist plays with back to audience

- Mutes: None

    I.   Maestoso, religioso ♩ = 100

Siekmann, a composer, educator, music publisher and performer, remains active in the musical world after a teaching career spanning over forty years. He received his formal musical training at New York University and Columbia University. After graduation, he taught music in the public school system, and later became a Professor of Music at Kutztown University, Kutztown, PA.

This four-minute, two-movement work was performed at the dedication ceremony of the new pipe organ at St. John's Lutheran Church in Kutztown, PA. The piece incorporates two well-known hymn tunes. It begins with the trombone playing the opening phrase of *A Mighty Fortress Is Our God*. On several occasions, the trombone plays a descant part, featuring sixteenth-note figures. Snippets of themes and motives come through the many layers, followed by a subdued chant-like section. The composer notes that this section should be played with the trombonist's back to the audience. Several meter and key changes create a transition to the second hymn tune, *All Hail the Power of Jesus' Name*. A brief quasi-cadenza leads to a grand conclusion, again with the trombone facing away from the audience. This piece is suited for a recital and for use in a liturgical setting. Siekmann's *Coventry for Tenor Trombone, Organ and Timpani* is also available through Brelmat Music.

The organ part is on three staves with registrations indicated and dynamics clearly marked.

Sörenson, Torsten (1908-1992)

...Sonas for trombone och orgel. Stockholm, Sweden: Swedish Music Information Center, 1983.

- Tenor trombone
- Difficulty: Advanced
- Technique: Trills (half and whole step), Flutter tonguing, Quasi improvised sections
- Mutes: Straight

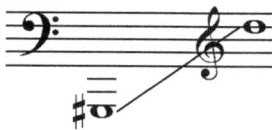

I.   Largo

Sörenson, a Swedish composer and organist, received his formal musical training at the Royal College of Music in Stockholm. He later studied composition with Hilding Rosenberg and Carl Orff. He served as organist at a church in Göteborg.

"…Sonas," a dramatic eight-minute, single-movement work was composed in 1983. The piece was premiered that same year by trombonist Jan Allan Persson with Karl Axel Thunander at the organ in Vaggeryd, Sweden. The piece begins forcefully with densely-scored figures for both instruments. The work builds in intensity before an extended trombone cadenza which leads to a commanding ending. This piece is difficult and requires virtuosic performers on both instruments. It is suited for a recital.

The organ part is on three staves with no registration indicated and dynamics clearly marked.

Spring, Rudi (b. 1962)

Metamorphoses for Trombone and Organ Op 7. Leipzig, Germany: Pfefferkorn Musikverlag, 2010.

- Trombone
- Difficulty: Moderate

- Technique: lip trills, glissandi, grace notes
- Mutes: None

Spring, born in Lindau Germany, is an organist, pianist, composer, and academic. He is best-known for his vocal compositions on texts by poets, his chamber music and his three Chamber Symphonies.

Metamorphoses was composed in 1981, with revisions in 1989. The beginning of this seven-minute, single-movement depicts strife between the organ and trombone. The vocal qualities of the trombone highlight the chorale melody "Christ, who makes us blessed." This leads to an Allegro Moderato section with is more technical for the trombonist. The texture builds in energy before the trombone returns to the chorale theme near the end of the piece. This work is well-suited for a recital.

The organ part is on three staves with registrations indicated, and dynamics clearly marked.

Stamm, Hans-André (b. 1958)

Zwei Suiten für Posaune (Tenorhorn) & Orgel. Leverkusen, Germany: Eufonia Edition Kathrin Stamm, 1999.

- Tenor trombone
- Difficulty: Moderate
- Technique: Nothing unusual
- Mutes: None

Suite Nr. 1

I.	Romanze
II.	Fugato
III.	Suite Nr. 2
IV.	Meditation
V.	Toccata

Stamm, a German composer and organ prodigy, began his performance career at the age of eleven. At sixteen, he performed his first recital at Notre Dame de Paris. He received his formal musical training at the Conservatory of Music in Liege, and at the Robert Schumann University, in Düsseldorf. Scientific studies at the University of Bonn led to the construction of the enharmonic pipe organ, an instrument in the acoustically-pure sentiment with 48 tones per octave. Stamm maintains a busy performance schedule and has numerous recordings. He has composed several works for brass and organ.

Combined, the two suites form a ten-minute work. The first movement in Suite Nr 1, *Romanze,* is marked "Andante ♩ = 66." This section features lyrical melody lines, passed from trombone to the organ. The second movement, *Fugato,* is marked "Allegro, dotted-half-note = 56," and begins with the organ presenting the fugue theme answered by the trombone fifteen measures later. This movement is demanding for both players with rapid technical passages. The first movement of the second suite, *Meditation,* marked "Adagio ♩ = 60," features a relaxing trombone melody set over sixteenth-note patterns in the organ. As the movement develops, it leads to a short cadenza before ending softly. The final movement, *Toccata,* is marked "Allegro maestoso ♩ = 98." This section is written in 2/4 meter, but soon shifts to a fast 7/8 meter, marked "eighth-note = 288." The work concludes with several repeated motives, producing a minimalist feel, before the dramatic ending. This piece is suited for a recital and for use in a liturgical setting. The publisher provides trombone parts in tenor and bass clef along with a Tenor horn in B part.

The organ part is on three staves with registration indicated and dynamics clearly marked.

Stout, Alan (1932-2018)

Solemn Prelude. Leverkusen, Germany: Eufonia Edition Kathrin Stamm, 1953.

At the time of this writing, this work was temporarily out of print.

Stover, Harold (b. 1946)

Scenes from the life of a Saint, Music for Trombone and Organ.
Copyright by Harold Stover, 1986.

- Tenor trombone
- Difficulty: Advanced
- Technique: Grace notes, Alternate notation
- Mutes: None

    I.   Nobilmente a sonore

Stover, an American organist and composer, is a graduate of the Julliard School of Music. He is currently the organist and music director at Woodfords Congregational Church in Portland, Maine. He has played recitals at The Riverside Church in New York, Westminster Abbey in London and many other distinguished venues.

Scenes from the life of a Saint , a seven-minute, single-movement modern work was premiered by trombonist Ronald Barron and organist Leonard Raver at Second Presbyterian Church in New York City in February, 1987.

The prefatory notes state:

In this piece the trombone/saint protagonist encounters a succession of worldly scenes and characters, all enacted by the organ, and reacts to each with kindness, forbearance, or righteous anger as the situation requires.

The work begins with solo trombone playing a recitative chant, followed by a fanfare. The remainder of the piece develops from the opening phrases of the trombone, using a number of twentieth-century compositional techniques including free dissonance, polyrhythm, rhythmic canon and polytonality.[45] The organ joins at the "Maestoso alla Marcia" section which has a jazz flavor with syncopated figures and a walking bass-line in the organ pedal. The "Lento Sostenuto" section has a lyrical cantabile trombone part over florid sequences from the organ. The work journeys through a fast 7/8 "Scherzando" and a bolero with a rhythmically-challenging trombone part before concluding with chant material similar to the opening. This work is suited for a recital. Although the work is unpublished, it is available through Harold Stover's website at www.haroldstover.com.

The organ part is on three staves with registration indicated and dynamics clearly marked.

Struik, Gregory van der

Figtree Fantasy for Trombone and Organ, 2007, Australia: Trombonis Australis Editions, 2007.

- Tenor trombone
- Difficulty: Moderate
- Technique: Nothing unusual
- Mutes: None

I.   Adagio ♩ = 60

Struik, an Australian trombonist and composer, received his formal musical training at the Sydney Conservatorium High School and graduated as an Associate from the State Conservatorium of Music. He

---

[45] Harold Stover, Personal Email, December 5, 2008.

is currently principal trombonist with the Australian Opera and Ballet Orchestra. He initiated the Trombonis Australis Project to develop and present an Australian contribution to the international brass community.

Figtree Fantasy, a six-minute, single-movement piece was premiered by the composer at Saint Mark's Anglican Church in Hunters Hill, Sydney in March 2007. The work depicts the Figtree River located near the church. Programmatic motives can be heard throughout with flowing eighth-note figures and rhythmic embellishments. The piece remains in common meter with the exception of a few measures in 6/4 meter. Although not technically demanding, an extended section written in seven flats can be challenging. This piece is suited for a recital and for use in a liturgical setting.

The organ part is on three staves with registration indicated and dynamics clearly marked.

Struik, Gregory van der

Suite Noëlesque for Trombone and Organ. Granville, Australia: Trombonis Australis Editions, 2003.

- Tenor trombone
- Difficulty: Moderate
- Technique: Grace notes, Trills
- Mutes: None

> I.   In Initio
> II.   Petit Rondeau
> III.   Moto Perpetuo

Suite Noëlesque, a ten-minute, three-movement work was premiered by the composer at St Andrew's Cathedral, Sydney, with Pastór de Lasala at the organ in December 2005.

The program notes from that performance state:

The writing of Gregory's *Suite Noëlesque* came about in the interest of developing a larger contribution by local composers to trombone and organ repertoire. At Pastór's suggestion, Gregory created an original work based on old French Christmas themes. Only a melody and bass line were provided, their source being *Chants des Noëls: Anciens et nouveaux, 1703* by Christophe Ballard. The arrangement and style of the movements are entirely left to the composer. It was intended to use simple structures and to present each melody in a more modern setting as part a larger movement, which would allow the work to be performed throughout the year. An important consideration is the organ registration, which is integral to the dialogue between the two instruments.

The first movement, *In initio,* marked "andante maestoso e mysterioso," features the tune "Une Jeune Pucelle" (A young maid). The movement begins with the main theme played over a pedal point from the organ. It remains in alla breve meter throughout and, with the exception of the high tessitura, presents no challenges. The second movement, *Petit Rondeau* (Little Rondeau) marked "Andante," is based on the theme "À la venue de Noël" (At the arrival of Christmas). Again, written in alla breve, the theme is passed from trombone to the organ in the middle section. The final movement, *Moto Perpetuo* (Perpetual Motion) is a toccata with a reoccurring pentatonic figure. Cross-rhythms in the trombone part add interest to the joyous theme, "Où s'en vont ces gais bergers" (Where are these gay sheperds). At times, the organ and trombone share the theme simultaneously in thirds. This piece is suited for a recital and for use in a liturgical setting.

The organ part is on three staves with registration indicated and dynamics clearly marked.

Struik, Gregory van der

Welzheim Procession for Trombone and Organ. Granville, Australia: Trombonis Australis Editions, 2003.

- Tenor trombone
- Difficulty: Moderate
- Technique: Nothing unusual
- Mutes: None

I.   Maestoso ♩ = 66-72

This single-movement, three-minute work, bears the inscription "For Ulrike Bantleon-Bader and the Town of Welzheim," where the work was premiered by the composer in July 2003.[46] The piece is in ABA form, with the opening marked, "Maestoso ♩ = 66-72." The work remains in a similar style and tempo throughout, beginning with fanfare-like material presented by the trombone using dotted-eighth-sixteenth-notes and triplet figures. The contrasting B section is quiet and lyrical, constructed with mostly quarter and eighth-notes. The opening material returns for a dramatic ending. This piece is suited for a recital and for use in a liturgical setting.

The organ part is easy, notated on three staves with no registration indicated and dynamics clearly marked.

---

[46] Gregory van der Struik, Personal E-mail, January 19, 2009.

Studer, Hans (1911-1984)

Tres Laudes für Alt-Posaune und Orgel. Crans-Montana, Switzerland: Editions Marc Reift, 1988.

- Alto trombone
- Difficulty: Moderate
- Technique: Grace notes
- Mutes: Straight

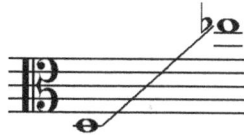

    I.   Etwas freies tempo
    II.   Ruhig
    III.   Freies tempo

Studer, a Swiss composer, organist, conductor, and music educator, taught at the Women Teachers Training College and served as music director and church organist in his hometown of Muri-Gümligen. He worked to encourage a better understanding of the artistic values of music, both past and present. In appreciation of this service, he was awarded the Music Prize of Berne in 1965.[47]

From the Collection Branimir Slokar, this ten-and-a-half minute work in three-movements is dedicated to Branimir Slokar and Heinrich Gurtener.

The prefatory notes state:

The internal structuring remains quite clear and it is generally supported by the alternation between the wind instrument leading melodically and the organ which may be playing in a toccata-like manner or in contrapuntal imitation or else in chordal progressions. It may not

---

[47] Prefatory notes.

be directly heard, but it is clearly to be felt, that all three "Laudes" are developed out of the same musical material [48]

The first movement, marked "Etwas freies tempo," features many shifts in meter while showing off the delicate cantabile abilities of the alto trombone. The second movement, marked "Ruhig Langsam," features a stately melody set over atmospheric patterns from the organ. The final movement, *Laudes,* establishes call and response patterns between the alto trombone and organ. This builds in intensity to the end of work. This piece is suited for a recital and for use in a liturgical setting.

The organ part is on three staves with no registration indicated and dynamics clearly marked.

This work has been recorded by Branimir Slokar on the CD *Fantasia* (Marcophon CD 922-2).

Swanson, Philip (b. 1949)

Variations on Veni Creator Spiritus. Unpublished. 1997.

• Tenor trombone

Swanson, a trombonist, keyboardist, conductor and composer, received his formal musical training at the Eastman School of Music and earned a Doctorate of Musical Arts from the New England Conservatory of Music. He is a Professor of Music at Salem State College, teaching Theory and Composition. He has served as principal trombonist with the Miami Symphony.

Variations on Veni Creator Spiritus, a thirty-minute, five-movement work, is based on the Pentecostal hymn from the Roman Catholic Church. This piece was written as part of the composer's doctoral dissertation. The score could not be obtained at the time of this writing.

---

[48] Ibid.

It is held in archive at the New England Conservatory Spaulding Library Vault. Archives MT4.B7 N385 1997. S9

This work has been recorded by trombonist Philip Swanson and organist Barbara Burns on the CD *Variations on Veni Creator Spiritus, Music for Trombone and Organ* (Classics MS 1137).

Thybo, Leif (1922-2001)

Mouvement Symphonique. 1979.

Mouvement Symphonique is an eleven-minute, single-movement work. A copy of this work was unobtainable at the time of this writing.

This work has been recorded by John Petersen on the CD *Leif Thybo: Vocal and Instrumental Works* (Da Cappo 8.224009).

Thiel, Wolfgang (b. 1947)

Winterballade für Tuba und Orgel. Leipzig, Germany: Friedrich Hofmeister Musikverlag, 2002.

- Tuba
- Difficulty: Moderate
- Technique: Trills
- Mutes: None

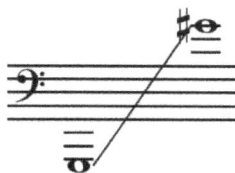

    I.   Energico

Thiel, a German composer, studied at Humboldt University and Academy of Music Hanns Eisler in Berlin. He works as a freelance composer and musicologist specializing in film music.

Winterballade is a six-minute work, composed during the winter of 2000-2001. Written in A-B-A form, the piece begins with an energetic pulsing introduction by the organ, followed by a back-and-forth dialogue between the two instruments. The lyrical B section is marked *tranquillo* and moves through several different keys. A short transition section returns to the tempo primo section to round out the work. This work is well-suited for a recital or for a liturgical setting.

The organ part is on three staves with no registrations indicated, and dynamics clearly marked.

Treherne, Terry (b. 1937)

Infant Holy, Infant Lowly for Euphonium and Organ. Euphonium Collective. 2009.

- Euphonium
- Difficulty: Easy
- Technique: Nothing unusual
- Mutes: None

    I.   Andante pastorale

Treherne, a conductor and composer, has directed several well-known brass bands as well as serving as bandmaster for the Salvation Army bands in Exeter and London. The majority of his musical education came through the Salvation Army. In addition to conducting, Treherne has composed and arranged a number of choral, instrumental and orchestral pieces although the majority of his works have been for brass bands.

Infant Holy, Infant Lowly was written for the British euphonium artist Charley Brighton. The piece is in 3/4 meter and is lyrical throughout. In the brass band tradition, the euphonium part is in b-flat treble clef. In addition to the organ arrangement, a brass band version is available.

The organ part is on three staves with no registrations indicated, and dynamics clearly marked.

Various Composers

Musica Sacra, Church Album for Trombone, Tenorhorn, Baritone, Euphonium and Organ. Rot an der Rot, Germany: Musikverlag Rundel, 1995.

- Trombone, Tenorhorn, Baritone, Euphonium
- Difficulty: Easy
- Technique: Grace notes, Trills
- Mutes: None

I.	Halleluja	Loritz
II.	Christ ist ertannden	Loritz
III.	Agnus Dei	Obrecht
IV.	Recercada	Oritz
V.	Canzon	Frescobaldi
VI.	Allein Gott in der Höh sei Ehr	Hasse/Loritz
VII.	Petite Suite Européenne	Fantini/Purcell/Delalnde
VIII.	Vom Himmel hoch	Zachow/Loritz
IX.	Wie schön leuchtet der Morgenstern	
		Kauffmann
X.	Sonata	Galliard
XI.	Wachet auf! Ruft uns die Stimme	Bach
XII.	Jesus bleibet meine Freude	Bach
XIII.	Adagio	Mozart
XIV.	Larghetto	Haydn
XV.	Nun danket alle Gott	Tag
XVI.	Vater unser im Himmelreich	Mendelssohn
XVII.	O Haupt voll Blut und Wunden	Brahms
XVIII.	Paraphrase über "Trochter Zion"	Loritz

This collection features a wide range of selections covering many musical periods and styles from Obrecht's *Agnus Dei*, to Guilmant's *Morceau Symphonique*. The majority of these selections would be appropriate for a young performer. Along with the organ score, the publisher provides two trombone parts—one in bass clef, the other in b-flat treble clef.

The organ part is on three staves with no registration indicated and dynamics clearly marked.

Vidjeskog, Patrik (b. 1964)

Canzona for Alto Trombone and Organ. Helsinki, Finland: Finnish Music Information Centre, 1999.

- Alto Trombone
- Difficulty: Advanced
- Technique: Flutter tongue, Glissandi
- Mutes: None

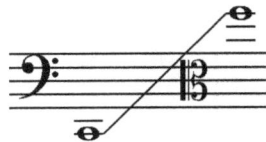

> I.   Adagio

Vidjeskog, a Finnish composer, received his formal musical training at the Sibelius Academy in Helsinki. He is currently working as a freelance composer; his works have been performed around the world.

He has also written a trombone sonata with piano and work for contrabass trombone.[49]

Canzona, an eight-and-a-half-minute, single-movement modern work, was commissioned and premiered by trombonist Patrik Möller, with support from the Madetoja Foundation. The piece is chromatic and the trombone part has an extremely wide range. Because of the low range, an alto trombone with a B-flat attachment is required for this work. The piece remains slow and lyrical throughout, especially at the beginning, marked "Adagio ♩ = 32." This piece is suited for a recital.

The organ part is on three staves with registration indicated and dynamics clearly marked.

Voegelin, Fritz (b. 1943)

MÉDITATION sur B-A-C-H pour trombone et orgue. Vuarmarens, Switzerland: Édition Bim, 1992.

- Tenor trombone
- Difficulty: Moderate
- Technique: Grace note, Alternate positions, Glissandi
- Mutes: straight

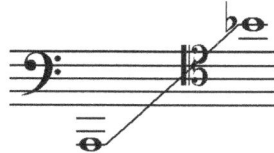

    I.   ♩ = 66

Voegelin, a Swiss composer, violinist and conductor, studied at the Berne Conservatory and at the Basle Musik-Akademie. He became the director of the National Conservatory of Columbia after conducting for several Swiss orchestras. Voegelin has received several awards for his

---

[49] Patrick Vidjeskog, Personal E-mail, March 11, 2008.

compositions. Composed in 1992, and dedicated to the memory of Arthur Honegger, this six-minute, single-movement work, has several changes of tempo and style throughout. The piece begins softly, featuring an angular style. The composer has "senza sord" in measure 20, but does not provide enough time to actually remove the mute. A trombone recitation occurs over an organ tremolo, leading to a change of meter and style: first a 6/8 meter march-like section followed by a waltz. The work concludes similarly to the beginning. This piece is suited for a recital.

The organ part is on three staves with registration indicated and dynamics clearly marked.

Walker, Gwyneth (b. 1947)

Celestial Keys for Tuba and Organ. St. Louis, MO: MMB Music, 2004.

- Tuba
- Difficulty: Moderate
- Technique: trills, glissandi, "tubist may play at organist, or at audience members!" grace notes, flutter tonguing,
- Mutes: None

    I.   Light
    II.   Listening
    III.   Imagination
    IV.   Glory

Dr. Gwyneth Walker is a graduate of Brown University and the Hartt School of Music. She holds B.A., M.M, and D.M.A. Degrees in Music Composition. A former faculty member of Oberlin College

Conservatory, Walker resigned from academic employment in 1982 in order to pursue a career as a full-time composer. She now lives on a dairy farm in Braintree, Vermont.

Celestial Kyes is a fourteen-minute, multi movement work composed for James Hawkinson—Organist, and Jay Hunsberger—Tubist.

The composer writes:

"These four pieces for Tuba and Organ were composed during a Composer Residency by the sea, near Sarasota, Florida. Thus, the reference to 'keys' pertains to the location of composition (Manasota Key Island) and to the keyboard of the Organ. [And to the beautiful tonalities!] Additional island references appear in the movement titles.

'Light' is everywhere on the island—on the sand, in the sunlight bouncing off of the waves. Thus, the opening movement is delicate, perhaps with a bounce. This is a short movement, in the 'bright' key of D Major. The opening is marked 'Grandly, as a church filling up with light.'

When one is by the ocean, one often listens, mostly to the sounds of the waves. And, this second movement is quiet, as if listening to the sea. Wave-patterns are introduced near the middle of the piece. Throughout, there is motivic imitation between the Tuba and Organ, as each listens to, and answers, the other. This becomes an intense movement, perhaps as though listening to the soul of the sea.

'Imagination' is light-hearted, with the musicians playing at one another, perhaps teasing one another, and also teasing the audience! There is a humorous/nautical character to the theme, which is marked 'jaunty,' in the style of a sea chanty.

'Glory' is inspired by the vast beauty of the sea, as well as by the glorious strength of the Organ and Tuba. Thus, the opening theme is marked 'grandly.' There are considerable 'forte' passages in this movement, often using the lowest ranges of the instruments. Brass timbres are predominant in the Organ registration, in strength."

This piece is well-suited for a recital and for use in a liturgical setting.

The organ part is on three staves with some registration indicated and dynamics clearly marked.

Walker, Gwyneth (b. 1947)

Profound Praise for Tuba and Organ. Munich, St. Louis, MO: E.C.S. Schirmer Music Company, 2016.

- Tuba
- Difficulty: Moderate
- Technique: Grace Notes
- Mutes: None

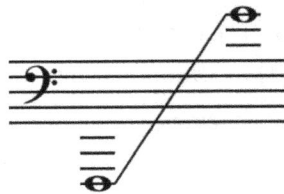

Hymns of Celebration

1. A Mighty Fortress
2. Fairest Lord Jesus
3. Christ is Risen (Easter Hymn)

Three Christmas Carols

1. O Come, O Come, Emmanuel
2. Angels We Have Heard On High!
3. Good Christians Friends Rejoice!

Profound Praise consists of two parts: *Hymns of Celebration* (8 minutes) and *Three Christmas Carols* (7 minutes) dedicated to Jay Hunsberger, Tubist.

The composer writes:

"Hymns of Celebration is a set of three familiar Protestant hymns arranged for tuba and organ. The intent is to provide additional repertoire for these two powerful instruments—forces which can balance and match their magnificent strengths.

The organ writing is mostly in hymn-style (chordal). Meanwhile, the tuba offers commentary, occasionally doubles the bass line and presents newly composed interludes.

The three hymn tunes, favorites of the composer, were selected to offer a variety of styles: 1. *A Mighty Fortress* (power), 2. *Fairest Lord Jesus* (lyricism) and 3. *Christ is Risen* (Easter Hymn) (rhythmic energy).

Three Christmas Carols are reinterpretations of three familiar carols for tuba and organ. Each of the new arrangements features one or more special musical characteristics, or views of the carol, which shapes the music.

O Come, O Come, Emmanuel opens with a sparkling counter- motive, perhaps as the spirit of anticipation, the Holy Spirit, surrounding the melody (plainchant). During the refrains (where the lyrics "Rejoice, O Come Emmanuel" would appear), the accompaniment joins with the tuba in chordal-style affirmation. In contrast, the verses are florid.

Angels We Have Heard on High has a similar counter-motive to *O Come, O Come, Emmanuel* , but it is now bright and energetic, as if fully announcing the coming of the Christ-child. During the refrain, the organ plays chords on the off-beats, as joyful punctuation. This dialogue of off-and-on beats continues throughout the movement. The final refrain overlaps the statements of the theme.

Good Christian Friends Rejoice! is placed in a bouncing 6/8 meter. The expected alternation between tonic and dominant harmonies is presented in the organ pedal, thus allowing the tuba the freedom to play the melody—a pleasant switch of traditional roles. The agile tubist is asked to scamper around the range of the instrument in various playful, scalar passages, all in the spirit of rejoicing!"

This piece is well-suited for a recital and for use in a liturgical setting and would be ideal for a younger tubist.

The organ part is on two staves with some registration indicated and dynamics clearly marked.

Westkemper, Gregor

Drei Stücke für Posaune und Orgel. Munich, Germany: Strube Verlag GmbH, 1988.

- Tenor trombone
- Difficulty: Moderate
- Technique: Nothing unusual
- Mutes: None

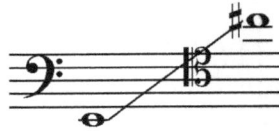

I.	Pfingstquodlibet
II.	Nun bitten wir den Heiligen Geist
III.	Freies Stück

Drei Stücke, a eight-minute, three-movement work, was composed from 1983 to 1984. The first movement, *Pfingstquodlibet,* is dedicated to Herbert Beuerle. Marked "Ruhig, etwas frei," this section features a melancholy chant-like theme, written without meter. The second movement, *Nun bitten wir den Heiligen Geist,* (Now we appeal to the Holy Spirit) is dedicated to trombonist Gudrun Mau. Marked "frei, mit Fantasie," this section, also without meter, is based on Bach's BWV385. The final movement, *Freies Stück*, marked "Sehr ruhig," is lyrical and more structured, written in 6/8 meter with a soft conclusion.

The organ part is mostly on three staves with no registration indicated and dynamics clearly marked.

Wilby, Philip (b. 1949)

RUACH 'Breath of God' for trombone and organ. Coventry, England: Warwick Music, 1998.

- Tenor trombone
- Difficulty: Advanced
- Technique: Multi-phonics,
  Approximate and indefinite pitch
  notation, Flutter tonguing
- Mute: Harmon

I. $\downarrow$ = 100

Wilby, an English composer, received his formal musical training at Oxford where he graduated with a Bachelor of Music in composition and violin performance. He is currently the Principal Lecturer in Composition at the University of Leeds. In addition to his brass and wind band compositions, Wilby is a notable composer in the field of church music.

RUACH 'Breath of God,' a six-and-a-half-minute, single-movement avant-garde work, was commissioned jointly by Elliot Chasanov and the British Trombone Society. The manuscript bears the inscription, "Prophesy, Son of Man: Come, Breath, from the Four Winds, and let these dead live! : Ezekiel 37."

The prefatory notes state:

The trombonist should be placed in clear sight of the audience. In ideal circumstances he requires the use of foot operated electronic reverberation unit. The organist is required to use 3 erasers to sustain certain pitches on an Echo manual.

The work has a thin texture throughout with both instruments creating musical effects. For example, the trombone uses a Harmon mute with the stem in to produce speech-like patterns. In several places, the composer indicates "circular movement with bell." The electronic reverb unit, combined with multi-phonics, produces additional effects. A cadenza played through the reverb unit uses held notes repeatedly swelling from ppp-fff. The work concludes with the trombonist making breathing sounds through the instrument. This piece is suited for a recital.

This organ part is written on three staves with registration indicated and dynamics clearly marked.

Zimmermann, Margrit (b. 1927)

Triptychon für Posaune & Orgel. Op. 58. Crans-Montana, Switzerland: Editions Marc Reift, 1990.

- Tenor trombone
- Difficulty: Moderate
- Technique: Alternate notation, Glissandi, Variable speed wide vibrato, Grace notes
- Mutes: Straight

I.	Prologue
II.	Choral-Meditation
III.	Appasionatta

Zimmermann, a Swiss composer, studied in Berne, Lausanne, Paris, and Milan. She has received many awards for her compositions. She describes her style as "atonal, but traditional."

From the Collection Branimir Slokar, *Triptychon*, a seven-and-a-half-minute, three-movement work, is dedicated to trombonist Pia Bucher. Pointillistic in nature, the work features extremely short phrases lacking shape, focusing instead on sound combinations combined with extended techniques. The three movements are intended to be played without pause. The first movement, *Prologue,* marked "Moderato assai," is in 4/4 meter with a march-like feel. A brief cadenza played by the trombone slows into the second movement, *Chorale-Meditation,* marked "Lento." In this section, lyricism is replaced with a sense of freeness and space due to a lack of meter. Coloration is created with the use of fast organ tremolos and wide trombone vibrato. The final movement,

Appassionatta, marked "poco agitato," returns to material similar to the opening. The work builds dramatically, abruptly changing style with a subdued ending.

This piece is suited for a recital and for use in a liturgical setting.

The organ part is on three staves with no registrations indicated and dynamics clearly marked. The organ requires a fast-sounding tremolo in the manuals with several glissandi in the pedal.

This work has been recorded by Pia Bucher on the CD *Fascination* (Marcophon CD 901).

Solos by Difficulty Level

Tenor Trombone—Easy

Baratto, Paolo (1926-2008) *Andante Cantabile*. Zurich, Switzerland: Musikverlag Paolo Baratto, 1931.

Bartmuss, Richard (1859-1919) *Recitativ und Arioso Op 24*. Ditzingen, Germany: Edition Musica Rinata E. Hofmann, 1994.

Böhler, Friedel W. *In the Upper Room, 15 Spirituals fur Posaune und Orgel*. Munich, Germany: Strube Verlag, 1999.

Burgmann, J. Hartmut *4 Choralvorspiele in traditionellem Stil mit Chorälen für Posaune und Orgel*, Band I. Ingersheim, Germany: Musikverlag Castellano, 1998.

de Haan, Jacob (b. 1959) *Missa Brevis for trombone and Organ*. Heerenveen, Holland: De Haske Publications, 2004.

Graap, Lothar (b. 1933) *Choralmusik zur Bestattung für Posaune (Fagott/Violoncello) & Orgel/Klavier*. Köln, Germany: Wolfgang G. Haas – Musikverlag Köln E.K., 2007.

Graap, Lothar (b. 1933) *Sonne der Gerechtigkeit, Partita für Posaune und Orgel*. Kassel, Germany: Verlag Merseburger, 1995.

Gunsenheimer, Gustav (b. 1934) Alles Ist An Gottes Segen, Choralpartita für Posaune (Trompete) und orgel. Munich, Germany: Strube Verlag, 1993.

Haug, Lukas *Zwölfteiliges Orgelmosaik*. Wilhelmshaven, Germany:Heinrichshofen Verlag, 1958.

Hilfiger, John Jay *"Christe Sanctorum" Variants*. Farmington, NM: Brassworks 4 Publishing, 2007.

Kempton, Jeremy Niles *A Christmas Couplet for Trombone and Organ or Piano*. Teaneck, NJ: Puna Music Company, 1999.

Lindberg, Oskar Frederik (1887-1955) Choralvorspiel über: "Denk, wenn einmal der Nebel verschwunden ist" für Posaune /Fagott /Viloncello & Orgel. Köln, Germany: Wolfgang G. Haas – Musikverlag Köln E.K., 2000.

Linkenbach, Klaus (1932-2000) *Es kommt ein Schiff, Partita für Posaune und Orgel*. Stittgart, Germany: Hänssler-Verlag, 1986.

Marchand, Todd *Adoro te devote (Humbly I Adore Thee) for trombone and organ*. Dallas, Fort Worth, Texas: Con Spirito Music, 2008.

Marchand, Todd Crusaders Hymn "Fairest Lord Jesus"/"Beautiful Savior" for trombone and organ. Dallas, Fort Worth, Texas: Con Spirito Music, 2013.

Marchand, Todd "In the Bleak Midwinter" Hymn tune "Cranham" by G. Holst for trombone and organ. Dallas, Fort Worth, Texas: Con Spirito Music, 2010.

Marchand, Todd "Let Us Break Bread Together" African-American Spritiual for trombone and organ. Dallas, Fort Worth, Texas: Con Spirito Music, 2013.

Marchand, Todd *Meditation on "Wondrous Love" for trombone and organ*. Dallas, Fort Worth, Texas: Con Spirito Music, 2015.

Marchand, Todd *"Processional" for trombone and organ*. Dallas, Fort Worth, Texas: Con Spirito Music, 2013.

Marchand, Todd "Rejoice! Rejoice, Believers" Welsh hymn tune "Llangloffan" for trombone and organ. Dallas, Fort Worth, Texas: Con Spirito Music, 2013.

Marchand, Todd "Rise Up, Shepherds, and Follow" African-American spritual for trombone and organ. Dallas, Fort Worth, Texas: Con Spirito Music, 2012.

Nelhybel, Vaclav (1919-1996) *Prelude and Chorale on SVATÝ VÁCLAVE.* Fish Creek, WI: Alliance Publications, 1999.

Nelhybel, Vaclav (1919-1996) Sonata da Chiesa No. 3 Variants on "Our God Almighty" for Trombone(s) (Bassoons, Oboe) and Organ or Harpsichord. Hackensack, NJ: Joseph Boonin, 1977.

Österberg, Sven (b. 1933) *I Praise your name, O Lord.* Kariskrona, Sweden: Libitum, 2007.

Peters, Max (1849-1927) *Elegie für Posaune und Orgel op.9.* Winterthur, Switzerland: Bernhard Päuler Amadeus Verlag, 2000.

Petersen, Lynn L. (1923-2006) *Spiritual Sounds for Trombone and Organ.* St. Louis, MO: Concordia Publishing House, 2000.

Pezel, Johann (1639-1694) arr. Kurt Sturzenegger *Suite de Danses pour trombone & orgue.* Edition Marc Reift, 1983

Runbäck, Albert (1894-1974) *Basun och Orgel.* Slite, Sweden: Wessmans Musikförlag.

Sanders, Bernard Wayne (b. 1957) *Rhapsodie für Posaune (Fagott) und Orgel.* Köln, Germany: Verlag Christoph Dohr. 1995.

Various Musica Sacra, Church Album for Trombone, Tenorhorn, Baritone, Euphonium and Organ. Rot an der Rot, Germany: Musikverlag Rundel, 1995.

Tenor Trombone—Moderate

Aho, Kalevi (b. 1949) *Epilog für Posaune und Orgel.* Helsinki, Finland: Fennica Gehrman, 2002.

Argast, Felix (b. 1936) *Partita für Posaune in C/B & Orgel.* Köln, Germany: Wolfgang G. Haas – Musikverlag Köln E.K., 2008.

Bendix, Hermann (1859-1935) *Elegie für Posaune und Orgel op. 92 Nr. 2.* Köln, Germany: Verlag Christoph Dohr, 2008.

Beraldo, Primo (1924-2006) *Dialogo per Trombone e Organo.* Horgen, Switzerland: Pizzicato Verlag Helvetia, 1980.

Berg, Fred Jonny (b. 1973) *Paralysing Atmosphere Op.11.* Bodø, Norway: Symbiophonic, 2008.

Beuerle, Herbert (1911-1994) *Kleine Studie für Posaune (Violoncello, Fagott) und Orgel.* Munich, Germany: Strube Verlag, 1986.

Böhler, Friedel W. (b. 1946) *Funf Miniaturen fur Posaune und Orgel.* Munich, Germany: Strube Verlag, 1986.

Breman, Niklas (b. 1966) *Intrata for Organ and Trombone.* Stockholm, Sweden: Swedish Music Information Center, 1995.

Bresgen, Ceaser (1913-1988) *Meditation for Trombone and Organ.* Berlin, Germany: Edition Gravis, 1993.

Brown, Rayner (1912-1999) *Sonata for Trombone and Organ.* Composer's Library, 1985.

Burgmann, J. Hartmut 4 Choralvorspiele in traditionellem Stil mit Chorälen für Posaune und Orgel, Band II. Ingersheim, Germany: Musikverlag Castellano, 1998.

Burgmann, J. Hartmut 5 Choralvorspiele in taditionellem Stil mit Chorälen für Posaune und Orgel, Band III. Ingersheim, Germany: Musikverlag Castellano, 1998.

Burgmann, J. Hartmut *6 Choralvorspiele in traditionellem Stil für Posaune und Orgel, Band IV*. Ingersheim, Germany: Musikverlag Castellano, 1998.

Burgmann, J. Hartmut 7 Choralvorspiele in traditionellem Stil mit Chorälen für Posaune und Orgel, Band V. Ingersheim, Germany: Musikverlag Castellano, 1999.

Burgmann, J. Hartmut Choralvorspiele in taditionellem Stil mit Chorälen für Posaune und Orgel, Band VI. Musikverlag Castellano, 2000.

Burgmann, J. Hartmut 10 Choralvorspiele in taditionellem Stil mit Chorälen für Posaune und Orgel, Band VII. Ingersheim, Germany: Musikverlag Castellano, 2001.

Burgmann, J Hartmut *Die Nacht ist vorgedrungen für Posaune und Orgel*. Ingersheim, Germany: Musikverlag Castellano, 1996.

Burgmann, J. Hartmut *Südtiroler Brugen-Suite für Posaune und Orgel*. Ingersheim, Germany: Musikverlag Castellano, 2003.

Callahan, Charles *Out of the Depths I Cry to You, O Lord,* for trombone, euphonium, or tuba and organ. Fenton, MO: Briamwood Publications, a division of MorningStar Music Publishers a division of E.C.S Schirmer Music Company, 2008.

Cesare, Giovanni Martino (1590-1667) *La Hieronyma from Musicali Melodie*, 1621. Pembroke, MA: Robert King, 1972.

Christensen, Bernhard (1906-2004) *Concerto for trombone and organ.* Copenhagen, Denmark: Society for Publication of Danish Music (Samfundet), 1977.

Cohen, Jules (1835-1901) *Andante pour Trombone et Orgue (Piano)*. Paris, France: Editions Musicales Européenes, 1995.

Diemer, Emma Lou (b. 1927) *Psalm 1 for Bass or Tenor trombone & Organ or Piano*. Ithaca, NY: Ensemble Publications, 2002.

Donati, Guido (b. 1949) …Buccina parva canente per Trombone barocco e Organo (oppure Trombone e Pianoforte). Sondrio, Italy: Animando Edizioni Musicali, 2002.

Eben, Petr (1929-2007) *Two Invocations for Trombone and Organ*, Essex, England: United Music Publishers, 1996.

Eversole, James *ESQUISSES for Trombone and Organ*. Seattle, WA: Ars Nova Press, 2006.

Erdmann-Abele, Veit (b. 1944) *Epilog für Posaune und Orgel*. Reutlingen, Germany: Veit Erdmann-Abele, 1985.

Fischer, Carl August (1829-1892) Fantasie für Solo-Posaune (oder violoncello) und Orgel (oder pianoforte) op.21. Leipzig: C.F. Kahnt. 1978.

Gadsch, Herbert (1913-2011) *Konzert für Posaune und Orgel*. Ditzingen, Germany: Edition Musica Rinata E. Hofmann, 1997.

Gadsch, Herbert (1913-2011) *Spiritual-Suite für Posaune und Orgel*. Ditzingen, Germany: Edition Musica Rinata E. Hofmann, 1997.

Gárdonyi, Zsolt (b. 1946) *Rhapsodie für Posaune und Orgel*, Frankfurt, Germany: Musikverlag Zimmermann, 1982.

Gerlach, Günter (1928-2003) *Introduktion und Choral für Posaune und Orgel*. Köln, Germany: Verlag Christoph Dohr, 1996/2002.

Gerlach, Günter (1928-2003) Sonatine : "Wie schon leucht' uns der Morgenstern" : fur Posaune und Orgel. Glendale, NY: C.F. Peters, 1992.

Glauser, Max (b. 1937) *Trilogie für Posaune & Orgel*. Crans-Montana, Switzerland: Editions Marc Reift, 1992.

Godel, Didier (b. 1945) *Sonata da Chiesa pour Trombone et Orgue*. Crans-Montana, Switzerland: Editions Marc Reift, 1992.

Graap, Lothar (b. 1933) *Choralpartita zu Advent für Posaune und Orgel*. Köln, Germany: Wolfgang G. Haas – Musikverlag Köln E.K., 2003.

Gross, Eric (1926-2011) *Slides and Pistons for Tenor Trombone and Organ op.265*. Sydney, Australia: Australian Music Centre, 2002.

Gunsenheimer, Gustav (b. 1934) *Lobe den Herren Suite für Posaune (Trompete) und orgel Klavier*. Munich, Germany: Strube Verlag, 1989.

Guðmundsson, Hugi (b. 1977) *Signing f. básúnu og orgel*. Reykjavik, Iceland: Iceland Music Information Center.

Haegeland, Eilert Magnus (1951-2004) *Fantasia Polaris for trombone og orgel op.31*. Oslo, Norway: Norwegian Music Information Centre, 1991.

Hahn, Gunnar (1908-2001) *Himmelriket liknas vid tio jungfrur*. Solina, Sweden: Gunnar Hahn Musikförlag, 1988.

Haller, William P. *Suite for Trombone and Organ*. Unpublished, 1978.

Heilmann, Harald (1924-2018) *Fantasia per trombone ed organo*. Dusseldorf, Germany: Astoria Verlag, 1994.

Heilmann, Harald (1924-2018) *Poem für Posaune (oder Horn) und Orgel Op. 162.* Köln,Germany: Verlag Christoph Dohr, 2006.

Helmschrott, Robert M. *Sonata Da Chiesa I, für Posaune und Orgel.* Berlin, Germany: Bote & Bock/ New York, NY: Schott Music Corporation, 1986.

Hidas, Frigyes (1928-2007) *Domine, Dona Nobis Pacem für Posaune und Orgel.* Crans-Montana, Switzerland: Editions Marc Reift, 1994.

Holst, Gustav (1874-1934) *"Concertante" Duet for Organ and Trombone.* Coventry, England: Warwick Music, 1994.

Hovland, Egil (1924-2013) *Cantus V for Trombone and Organ op.120.* Oslo: Norsk Musikforlag, 1986

Hutcheson, Jere (b. 1938) *PATTERNS for Trombone and Organ.*New York, NY: Seesaw Music, 1976.

Irik, Michiel W. (b. 1953) *The Seventh Seal for Trombone and Organ,* Granville, Australia: Trombonis Australis Editions, 2006.

Jahn, Thomas (b. 1940) *Lachrimae XCIV Paraphrase über Dowlands "Seven Tears" für Posaune und Orgel.* Hamburg, Germany: Peermusic Classical, 1995.

Janca, Jan (b. 1933) *Tripartita uber Christ ist erstanden for trombone and organ.* Munich, Germany: Strube Verlag GmbH. 1991.

Kameke, Ernst-Ulrich von (1926-2019) *Sonate über Spirituals für Posaune und Orgel.* Munich, Germany: Strube Verlag GmbH.

Kempton, Jeremy Niles *Lament, for Trombone and Organ or Piano.* Teaneck, NJ: Puna Music Company, 1999.

Kraus, Eberhard (1931-2003) *Sechs Choralbearbeitungen für Posaune oder andere Melodienstrumente und Orgel.* Crans-Montana, Switzerland: Editions Marc Reift, 1995.

Krol, Bernhard (1920-2013) *Choralpartita "Nun, danket alle Gott" für Posaune & Orgel op. 174.* Köln, Germany: Wolfgang G. Haas – Musikverlag Köln E.K., 2004.

Krol, Bernhard (1920-2013) *Sinfonia sacra for trombone and organ (positive), op. 56.* Berlin, Germany: Bote & Bock, 1973.

Laukvik, Jon *Arabesque.* Frederiksberg, Denmark: Edition Svitzer, 2016

Linke, Norbert (b. 1933) *Prozession für Posaune und Orgel.* Leipzig, Germany: Friedrich Hofmeister Musikverlag, 1999.

Michel, Jean-François (1957) *Kyrie für Posaune und Orgel.* Crans-Montana, Switzerland: Editions Marc Reift, 1994.

Michel, Johannes M. (b. 1962) *Dialog: Sonate für Posaune und Orgel.*Munich, Germany: Strube Verlag, 2007.

Miller, Michael R. (b. 1932) *Play of Sun and Clouds for Trombone and Organ.* Toronto, Ontario: Canadian Music Centre, 1989.

Möckl, Franz (b. 1925) *Intrade für Tenorposaune und Orgel.* Köln, German: Wolfgang G. Haas – Musikverlag Köln E.K., 2003.

Norontaus, Veikko (b. 1930) *Psalmi 42 op.6 nro 5 for trombone and organ/piano.* Helsinki, Finland: Finnish Music Information Centre, 1991.

Pinkham, Daniel (1923-2006) *Gifts and Graces for trombone and organ.* Boston, MA: ECS Publishing, 1978.

Pinkham, Daniel (1923-2006) *Solemnities for Trombone & Organ.* Boston, MA: Ione Press, 2002.

Risher, Tim *Hymns and Strophes.* Winter Park, FL: Wehr's Music House, 1997.

Sandström, Jan *Lacrimae Lacrimae for Trombone and Organ.* Stockholm, Sweden: Edition Tarrodi, 1991.

Schiffmann, Ernst (1901-1980) *Intermezzo für Posaune und Orgel Op.53.* New York, NY: Schott Music Corporation, 1954.

Schilling, Hans Ludwig (b. 1927) *Vier Choralvorspiele.* Stittgart,Germany: Hänssler-Verlag, 1976.

Schmidt, Siegmund (1874-1939) *Fünf Choralvorspiele für Posaune und Orgel.* Munich,Germany: Strube Verlag, 1986.

Schubert, Heino (b. 1928) *Sonata da chiesa sopra Tuba mirum spargens sonum for trombone and organ.* Bad Schwalbach, Germany: Edition Gravis, 1992.

Senon, Gilles (b. 1932) *Prière pour Trombone et Orgue.* Paris, France: Gérard Billaudot, 1978.

Siekmann, Frank H. Two Powerful Hymns: A Mighty Fortress Is Our God—All Hail the Power of Jesus' Name. Kutztown, PA: Brelmat Music, 2003.

Spring, Rudi (b. 1962) *Metamorphoses for Trombone and Organ Op 7.* Leipzig, Germany: Pfefferkorn Musikverlag, 2010.

Stamm, Hans-André (b. 1958) *Zwei Suiten für Posaune (Tenorhorn) & Orgel.* Leverkusen, Germany: Eufonia Edition Kathrin Stamm, 1999.

Struik, Gregory van der *Figtree Fantasy for Trombone and Organ,* 2007, Australia: Trombonis Australis Editions, 2007.

Struik, Gregory van der *Suite Noëlesque for Trombone and Organ.* Granville, Australia: Trombonis Australis Editions, 2003.

Struik, Gregory van der *Welzheim Procession for Trombone and Organ.* Granville, Australia: Trombonis Australis Editions, 2003.

Voegelin, Fritz (b. 1943) *MÉDITATION sur B-A-C-H pour trombone et orgue.* Vuarmarens, Switzerland: Édition Bim, 1992.

Westkemper, Gregor *Drei Stücke für Posaune und Orgel.* Munich, Germany: Strube Verlag GmbH, 1988.

Zimmermann, Margrit (b. 1927) *Triptychon für Posaune & Orgel. Op. 58.* Crans-Montana, Switzerland: Editions Marc Reift, 1990.

Tenor Trombone—Advanced

Ayerst, Jonathan (b. 1971) *Victimae Paschali.* Coventry, England: Warwick Music, 2002.

Bausznern, Dietrich von (1928-1980) *Konzert für Posaune und Orgel.* Kassel, Germany: Verlag Merseburger, 1981.

Borg, Kim (1919-2000) *Church Music, for Trombone and Organ, op.26.* Helsinki, Finland: Finnish Music Information Centre, 1991.

Bornefeld, Helmut (1906-1990) *LITUUS für Posaune und Orgel.* Echterdingen, Germany: Carus Verlag.1977

Bottje, Will Gay (b. 1925) *LITTLE SONATA NR.VI for Trombone and Organ.* New York, NY: American Composers Alliance, 1983.

Braun, Peter Michael (b. 1936) Jericho – die fallenden Mauern, Geistliche Musik für Posaune und Orgel. Berlin, Germany: Bote & Bock, 1982.

Callhoff, Herbert (b. 1933) *5 Versetti sopra "VENI SANCTE SPIRITUS" for Trombone and Organ.* Berlin, Germany: Edition Gravis, 2004.

Callhoff, Herbert (b. 1933-2016) *Vier Meditationen für Posaune und Orgel.* Bergisch Gladbach, Germany: Musikverlag Hans Gerig, 1976.

Cresswell, Lyell (b. 1944) *Canzone for trombone and organ.* Wellington, New Zealand: Center for New Zealand Music, 1992.

Eversole, James (b. 1929-2015) *ESQUISSES (Athedra IV for Trombone and Organ).* Missoula, MT: Ars Nova Press, 1994.

Eversole, James (1929-2015) *ESQUISSES for Trombone and Organ*. Missoula, MT: Alpine Sheet Music, 2006.

Foreman, Roger *Resolution for Trombone and Organ*, Unpublished, 2009.

Fork, Gunter (1930-1998) *Kanzone, Fuge, und Madrigal für Posaune und Orgel*. Renningen, Germany C.F. Schmidt, 1992.

Forsyth, Malcolm (1936-2011) *Soliloquy, Epitaph and Allegro for trombone and organ*. Markham, Canada: Counterpoint Musical Services, 1988.

Forsyth, Michael *Welzheim Flourish for Trombone and Organ*. Granville, Australia: Trombonis Australis Editions, 1998.

Genzmer, Harald (b. 1909) *Sonate Für Posaune und Orgel*. New York, NY: Litolff/Peters, 1989.

Glauser, Max (b. 1937) *Canzona Für Posaune und Orgel (Klavier)*. Crans-Montana, Switzerland: Editions Marc Reift, 1992.

Graur, Alexander *Lamentatio Jeremiae Prophetae per trombone e organo*. Ancona, Italy: Bèrben Edizioni musicali, 1991.

Graur, Alexander *Tre Canti Bizantini (di Anton Pann) per trombone e organo*. Ancona, Italy: Bèrben Edizioni musicali, 1991.

Grenager, Lene *Hver avreise er en hjemkomst (for trombone and organ)*. Oslo, Norway: Norwegian Music Information Centre, 2002.

Hidman, Aron (b. 1971) *Read My Mind, for trombone and organ*. Coventry, England: Warwick Music, 1997.

Hübler, Klaus. K (b. 1956) *Am Ende des Kanons Musica con(tro)versa für Posaune und Orgel*. Wiesbaden, Germany: Breitkopf & Härtel KG, 1985.

Koch, Erland von (1910-2009) *Trombonia.* Stockholm, Sweden: Swedish Music Information Center, 1984.

Koetsier, Jan (1911-2006) *Choralpartita "Die Tageszeiten" op. 151.* Crans-Montana, Switzerland: Editions Marc Reift, 1998.

Koetsier, Jan (1911-2006) *Partita für Posaune und Orgel ("Wachet auf").* Stittgart, Germany: Hänssler-Verlag, 1977.

Koetsier, Jan (1911-2006) *Partita für Posaune und Orgel ("Wachet auf").* Crans-Montana, Switzerland: Editions Marc Reift, 1998.

Konowalski, Benedykt (b. 1928) *Victoria Regis, partita na puzon i organy.* Warsaw, Poland: Agencja Autorska, 1984.

Kraus, Eberhard (1931-2003) *Hymnus "Verbum Supernum" für Posaune & Orgel.* Crans-Montana, Switzerland: Editions Marc Reift, 1995.

Marthinsen, Niels (b. 1963) *Concerto for trombone and organ.* Copenhagen, Denmark: Society for Publication of Danish Music (Samfundet), 1992.

Mortimer, John Glenesk (b. 1951) *Fantasia for Trombone and Organ.* Crans-Montana, Switzerland: Editions Marc Reift, 1992.

Nilsson, Torsten (b. 1920) *Concertino per trombone ed organo op.81.* Bromma, Sweden: Edition Reimers, 1985.

Nordhagen, Stig (b. 1966) *Macchia Nera Di polvere Per Trombone E Organo.* Oslo, Norway: Norwegian Music Information Centre, 2004.

Perlongo, Daniel (b. 1942) *Novella for trombone and organ.* New York, NY: American Composer Alliance, 1998.

Plog, Anthony (b. 1947) *Sonare for Trombone and Organ.* Vuarmarens, Switzerland: Édition Bim, 2011.

Purser, John (b. 1942) *SKYELINES, for Tenor Trombone and Organ.* Coventry, England: Warwick Music, 1997.

Read, Gardner (1913-2005) *Invocation for Trombone and Organ Op.135.* North Easton, MA: Robert King, 1978.

Ruders, Poul (b. 1949) *Double Entry: Fanfare for Trombone and Organ.* Copenhagen, Denmark: Edition Wilhelm Hansen, 2011.

Schibler, Armin (1920-1986) *"Audiens exaudieris" Fantasie für Posaune und Orgel.* Edition Eulenburg (See C.F. Peters Corporation for Distribution), 1977.

Schneider, Enjott (b. 1950) *Golgatha for Trombone and Organ.* New York, NY: Schott Music Corporation, 2009.

Schnittke, Alfred (1934-1998) *Schall und Hall für Posaune und Orgel.* Wien, Germany: Universal Edition, 1983.

Sörenson, Torsten (1908-1992) *...Sonas for trombone och orgel.* Stockholm, Sweden: Swedish Music Information Center, 1983.

Stover, Harold (b. 1946) *Scenes from the life of a Saint, Music for Trombone and Organ.* Copyright by Harold Stover, 1986.

Wilby, Philip *RUACH 'Breath of God' for trombone and organ.* Coventry, England: Warwick Music, 1998.

Bass Trombone

Easy

Liszt, Franz (1811-1886) *Hosannah für Bassposaune und Orgel.* New York, NY: Schott Music Corporation, 1983.

Various Musica Sacra, Church Album for Trombone, Tenorhorn, Baritone, Euphonium and Organ. Rot an der Rot, Germany: Musikverlag Rundel, 1995.

Moderate

Callahan, Charles *Out of the Depths I Cry to You, O Lord,* for trombone, euphonium, or tuba and organ. Fenton, MO: Briamwood Publications, a division of MorningStar Music Publishers a division of E.C.S Schirmer Music Company, 2008.

Diemer, Emma Lou (b. 1927) *Psalm 1 for Bass or Tenor trombone & Organ or Piano.* Ithaca, NY: Ensemble Publications, 2002.

Frith, John (b. 1947) *Meditation for bass trombone and organ.* Coventry, England: Warwick Music, 2010.

Graap, Lothar *Suite für Tuba (Bass Posaune) & Orgel GWV 209.* Köln,Germany: Verlag Wolfgang G. Haas, 2003.

Möckl, Franz (b. 1925) *Intrade für Tenorposaune und Orgel.* Köln, German: Wolfgang G. Haas – Musikverlag Köln E.K.,2003.

Muller, Johann Immanuel Praeludium, Chorale, Variations, Fugue for Bass Trombone and Organ. Botsford, CT: Edition Musicus, 1959.

Rønnes, Robert (b. 1959) *Lento for Bass Trombone and Organ.* Oslo, Norway: Norwegian Music Information Centre, 1998.

Schneider, Julius (1805-1888) *Choralvariationen für Bass-Posaune und Orgel op.16.* Stittgart,Germany: Hänssler-Verlag, 1988.

Advanced

Büsing, Otfried (b. 1955) *Nox für Bass-Posaune und Orgel.* Berlin, Germany: Edition Gravis, 2002.

Diemer, Emma Lou (b. 1927) *Psalm 122 for Bass Trombone (Tuba) & Organ (Piano).* Ithaca, NY: Ensemble Publications, 1999.

Fork, Gunter (1930-1998) *Kanzone, Fuge, und Madrigal für Posaune und Orgel.* Renningen, Germany C.F. Schmidt, 1992.

Alto Trombone

Easy

Heilmann, Harald (b. 1924) *Trauerode für Posaune (Viola, Englisch) und Orgel.* Wilhelmshaven, Germany: Heinrichshofen Verlag, 1984.

Heilmann, Harald (b. 1924) *Trauerode für Posaune (Viola, Englisch) und Orgel.* Wilhelmshaven, Germany: Heinrichshofen Verlag, 1984.

Nilsson, Torsten (b. 1920) *Concertino for Bronslur in E-flat, or Alto Trombone and Organ*, Op.105B. Bromma, Sweden: Edition Reimers,1983.

Moderate

Angerer, Paul (1927-2017) *Luctus et Gaudium für Altposaune und Orgel.* Vienna, Austria: Musikverlag Ludwig Doblinger, 1983.

Breimo, Bjørn (b. 1958) *Postludium for alt-trombone og orgel.* Oslo, Norway: Norwegian Music Information Centre, 1983.

Daetwyler, Jean (1907-1994) *Sérénade au Clair de Lune pour Trombone Alto et Orgue.* Crans-Montana, Switzerland: Editions Marc Reift, 1991.

Grahl, Kurt (b. 1947) *Eligie und kleine Fuge für Altposaune und Orgel.* Köln, Germany: Verlag Christoph Dohr, 2006.

Hogg, Merle E. *Contrasts for Alto Trombone and Organ.* Newton, IA: TAP Music Sales, 2000.

Meyer, Hannes (b. 1939) *Sonate C-Moll Für Posaune und Orgel/Klavier nach Motiven* von G.B. Pergolesi. Crans-Montana, Switzerland: Editions Marc Reift, 1986.

Nilsson, Torsten (b. 1920) *Concertino per trombone ed organo op.93.* Bromma, Sweden: Edition Reimers, 1986.

Sandström, Jan *Lacrimae Lacrimae for Trombone and Organ.* Stockholm, Sweden: Edition Tarrodi, 1991.

Studer, Hans (1911-1984) *Tres Laudes für Alt-Posaune und Orgel.* Crans-Montana, Switzerland: Editions Marc Reift, 1988.

Advanced

Hillborg, Anders (b. 1954) *U-TANGIA-NA for alto-trombone and organ.* Stockholm, Sweden: Swedish Music Information Center, 1991.

Koetsier, Jan (1911-2006) *Choralpartita "Die Tageszeiten" op. 151.* Crans-Montana, Switzerland: Editions Marc Reift, 1998.

Moland, Erik *"Once Again!" for Trombone & Orgel.* Oslo, Norway: Norwegian Music Information Centre, 1992.

Raue, Reinhard (1953-2006) *Drie Pastelle für Altposaune und Orgel.* Crans-Montana, Switzerland: Editions Marc Reift, 1999.

Vidjeskog, Patrik (b. 1964) *Canzona for Alto Trombone and Organ.* Helsinki, Finland: Finnish Music Information Centre, 1999.

Euphonium

Easy

Campbell, Bruce (b. 1948) *Meditation for Euphonium and Organ*, San Antonio, TX: Southern Music Company a division of Lauren Keiser Music Publishing, 1990.

Hilfiger, John Jay *"Christe Sanctorum" Variants*. Farmington, NM: Brassworks 4 Publishing, 2007.

Johnsen, Hallvard (1916-2003) *Preludium: for Euphonium in C and Organ Op. 79*. Norsk Musikforlag A/S. Oslo, 1985.

Muller, Johann Immanuel (1640-1670) arr. Allen Ostrander *Praeludium, Chorale, Variations, Fugue for Bass Trombone and Organ*. Botsford, CT: Edition Musicus, 1959.

Näther, Gisbert (b. 1948) *Duo für Tuba und Orgel Op. 69*. Freidrich Hofmeister, 1998.

Treherne, Terry (b. 1937) *Infant Holy, Infant Lowly for Euphonium and Organ*. Euphonium Collective. 2009.

Various Musica Sacra, Church Album for Trombone, Tenorhorn, Baritone, Euphonium and Organ. Rot an der Rot, Germany: Musikverlag Rundel, 1995.

Moderate

Callahan, Charles *Out of the Depths I Cry to You, O Lord,* for trombone, euphonium, or tuba and organ. Fenton, MO: Briamwood Publications, a division of MorningStar Music Publishers a division of E.C.S Schirmer Music Company, 2008.

Lingenberg, Wilfried (b. 1969) *Elegie for Tuba (or Euphonium) and Organ.* IMSLP, 2017.

Miserendino, Joe *Canzone di notte dei sogni agrodolci.* Farmington, NM: Brassworks 4 Publishing, 2006.

Advanced

Kingsland, Chappell *Kung Pao for euphonium (or trombone) and pipe organ.* Tuba Euphonium Press/Cimarron Music Press. 2003.

Tuba

Easy

Akerwall, Martin (b. 1965) *Meditation for tuba and organ*: Just Sheet Music. http://www.justsheetmusic.com, 2001.

Miserendino, Joe (1932-2010) *Canzona della notte scura*. Farmington, NM: Brassworks 4 Publishing, 2006.

Näther, Gisbert (b. 1948) *Duo für Tuba und Orgel Op. 69*. Freidrich Hofmeister, 1998.

Moderate

Callahan, Charles (b. 1951) *In the Beginning, Biblical Poem for Tuba (Cello) and Organ*. St Louis, MO: MorningStar Music Publishers a division of E.C.S Schirmer Music Company, 1994.

Callahan, Charles *Out of the Depths I Cry to You, O Lord,* for trombone, euphonium, or tuba and organ. Fenton, MO: Briamwood Publications, a division of MorningStar Music Publishers a division of E.C.S Schirmer Music Company, 2008.

Ehmann, Heinrich (b. 1938-1998) *Drei Stücke für Tuba und Orgel*. Wolfenbüttel, Germany: Mösler Verlag, 1982.

Goddard, Philip (b. 1942) *The Unknown, Opus 24*, Lagny-sur-Marne, France: Musik Fabrik Music Publishing, 1999.

Graap, Lothar *Suite für Tuba (Bass Posaune) & Orgel GWV 209*. Köln,Germany: Verlag Wolfgang G. Haas, 2003.

Jirásek, Jan (b. 1955) *Viribus Unitis*. Prague, Czech Republic: Český rozhlas, 2006.

Kulesha, Gary *Sonata for Tuba and Organ*. Toronto, Canada: Counterpoint Music Library Services Inc., 2009.

Lingenberg, Wilfried (b. 1969) *Elegie for Tuba (or Euphonium) and Organ*. IMSLP, 2017.

Lingenberg, Wilfried *Intermezzo for Tuba (or Horn) and Organ*. Kleve, Germany: Copy-us, 2006.

Muller, Johann Immanuel (1640-1670) arr. Allen Ostrander *Praeludium, Chorale, Variations, Fugue for Bass Trombone and Organ*. Botsford, CT: Edition Musicus, 1959.

Pinkham, Daniel (1923-2006) *Dragons and Deeps for Bass Tuba in F and Organ*. Boston, MA: ECS Publishing, 2008.

Thiel, Wolfgang (b. 1947) *Winterballade für Tuba und Orgel*. Leipzig, Germany: Friedrich Hofmeister Musikverlag, 2002.

Walker, Gwyneth (b. 1947) *Celestial Keys for Tuba and Organ*. St. Louis, MO: MMB Music, 2004.

Walker, Gwyneth *Profound Praise for Tuba and Organ*. Munich, St. Louis, MO: E.C.S. Schirmer Music Company, 2016.

Advanced

Drude, Matthias (b. 1960) *Solo für Tuba*. Aurich, Germany: ADU Verlag, 2000.

Ungraded *(Works not examined)*

Allers, Hans Gunther (b. 1935) *Pavane Opus 62 für Posaune und Orgel*. Kassel, Germany: Verlag Merseburger, 1995.

Brown, Rayner *Meditation for Trombone and Organ*. Greeley, CO: Western International Music.

Brown, Rayner *Prelude and Fugue for Trombone and Organ*. Greeley, CO: Western International Music.

Cejka, Petr D. *Through for Trombone and Organ*. 1998.

Hoag, Charles *Dark Tango for trombone and organ*.

Janca, Jan *Suite in 7 movements for trombone and organ*. 1996.

Lorentzen, Bent *Alpha and Omega for Trombone and Organ*. Copenhagen, Denmark: Engstrom & Sodring, 1989.

Madsen, Jesper *Intrada per Trombone & Organo*. Copenhagen K, Denmark: SNYK, the Secretariat for Contemporary Music, 1999.

Meyer, Hannes *Suite für Posaune und Orgel "Das Liebesspiel."*

Rosell, Lars-Erik *Reflections*. Bromma, Sweden: Edition Reimers, 1979.

Sark, Einar Traerup (1921-2005) *Introduction and Carillon op 42*. København, Denmark: SNYK, the Secretariat for Contemporary Music,1990.

Stout, Alan (1932-2018) *Solemn Prelude*. Leverkusen, Germany: Eufonia Edition Kathrin Stamm, 1953.

Swanson, Philip (b. 1949) *Variations on Veni Creator Spiritus.*
    Unpublished. 1997.

Thybo, Leif (1922-2001) *Mouvement Symphonique.* 1979.

References

Amann, Jean-Pierre. "Voegelin, Fritz." In *Grove Music Online. Oxford Music Online*, http://www.oxfordmusiconline.com/subscriber/article/grove/music/47380 (accessed July 11, 2008).

"Argast, Felix." http://www.haas-koeln.de/en/komponisten/argast-felix.php (accessed October 10, 2008).

"Ayerst, Jonathan." http://www.warwickmusic.com/composers/a++c/jonathan+ayerst (accessed December 17, 2008).

Baker's Bibliographical Dictionary of Musicians, 7th ed., rev. Nicolas Slonimsky. New York: Schirmer Books, 1990.

"Baratto, Paolo." www.reift.ch/fichiers/pdfcomposers/39.pdf (accessed August 12, 2008).

"Bausznern, Dietrich von." http://www.mic.no/mic.nsf/doc/art200210071456105784433 (accessed August 12, 2008).

"Bendix, Hermann." http://www.dohr.de/autor/bendix.htm (accessed December 17, 2008).

"Berg, Fred Jonny." http://www.mamut.net/fjb/ (accessed: August 29, 2008).

Berg, Wesley. "Forsyth, Malcolm." In *Grove Music Online. Oxford Music Online*, http://www.oxfordmusiconline.com/subscriber/article/grove/music/44087 (accessed August 11, 2008).

"Böhler, Friedel W." http://*www.dohr.de/autor/boehler.htm (accessed December 2, 2008).*

Bone Jr., Lloyd E et al. The *Guide to the Euphonium Repertoire: The Euphonium Source Book.* IN: Indiana University Press, 2007.

Borg, Kim. J.B. Steane. "Borg, Kim." In *Grove Music Online. Oxford Music Online,*
http://www.oxfordmusiconline.com/subscriber/article/grove/music/03583 (accessed July 24, 2008).

"Bornefeld, Helmut." http://www.helmut-bornefeld.de/bio.html (Accessed August 19, 2008).

"Bottje, Will Gay."
http://esm.rochester.edu/sibley/specialc/findaids/display.php?id=117 (accessed August 12, 2008).

"Braun, Peter Michael."
http://www.petermichaelbraun.de/en/index.html (accessed July 8, 2008).

"Breimo, Bjørn."
http://www.mic.no/mic.nsf/doc/art2002100714561057850308 (accessed August 12, 2008).

"Bresgen, Ceaser."
http://www.grainger.de/music/composers/bresgen.html (accessed December 27, 2008).

"Brown, Rayner."
http://www.usc.edu/libraries/archives/arc/libraries/collections/records/300home.html (accessed December 9, 2008).

"Büsing, Otfried." http://www.punctum.com/art/buesing/index.html (accessed February 11, 2009).

Cassaro James P. "Nelhybel, Vaclav." In *Grove Music Online. Oxford Music Online*, http://www.oxfordmusiconline.com/subscriber/article/grove/music/ 19706 (accessed July 11, 2008).

Colin Matthews. "Holst, Gustav." In *Grove Music Online. Oxford Music Online*, http://www.oxfordmusiconline.com/subscriber/article/grove/music/ 13252 (accessed December 9, 2008).

Cresswell, Lyell. Personal E-mail, March 25, 2008.

Crotty, Joel. "Gross, Eric." In *Grove Music Online. Oxford Music Online*, http://www.oxfordmusiconline.com/subscriber/article/grove/music/ 47745 (accessed June 25, 2008).

"Daetwyler, Jean." http://www.naxos.com/composerinfo/bio22581.htm (accessed June 25, 2008).

Dalos, Anna. and Kroó, György. "Hidas, Frigyes." In *Grove Music Online. Oxford Music Online*, http://www.oxfordmusiconline.com/subscriber/article/grove/music/ 12992 (accessed July 11, 2008).

Dodd, Mary Ann. "Read, Gardner." In *Grove Music Online. Oxford Music Online*, http://www.oxfordmusiconline.com/subscriber/article/grove/music/ 22990 (accessed July 11, 2008).

"Donati, Guido." http://www.asporpiemonte.org/curricula/curriculum.Donati.html (accessed December 10, 2008).

"Eben, Petr." http://apimusic.org/composersb.cfm?ln=E (accessed August 13, 2008).

Edwards, J. Michele. "Diemer, Emma." In *Grove Music Online. Oxford Music Online*, http://www.oxfordmusiconline.com/subscriber/article/grove/music/ 45072 (accessed July 11, 2008).

"Erdmann-Abele, Veit." http://www.erdmann-abele.de/biographie.html (accessed December, 10 2008).

"Eversole, James." http://www.arsnovamusic.com/eversole.html (accessed April 24, 2008).

Feisst, Sabine. "Pinkham, Daniel." In *Grove Music Online. Oxford Music Online*, http://www.oxfordmusiconline.com/subscriber/article/grove/music/ 21784 (accessed July 11, 2008).

"Fischer, Carl August." http://www.tribalsmile.com/music/article_169.shtml (accessed, December 16, 2008).

"Gadsch, Herbert." http://www.bach-cantatas.com/Lib/Gadsch-Herbert.htm (accessed December 10, 2008).

"Gárdonyi, Zsolt." http://www.gardonyi.de/english/zsolt/zsolt.html (accessed August 14, 2008).

"Godel, Didier." http://www.musinfo.ch/index.php?content=maske_personen&pers_i d=146 (accessed December 2, 2008).

"Grahl, Kurt." http://www.dohr.de/autor/grahl.htm (accessed December 10, 2008).

"Graur, Alexander." http://medicamu.ipower.com/author.htm (accessed December 10, 2008).

"Grenager, Lene." http://www.grenager.no/index.php?id=abo_eng (accessed December 10, 2008).

Gross, Eric. Personal E-mail, November 3, 2008.

"Guðmundsson, Hugi." http://musmap.com/index.php/hugigu/ (accessed December 13, 2008).

"Gunsenheimer, Gustav." http://www.fsb-online.de/geschichte/komponisten/gunsenheimer.html (accessed December 2, 2008).

"Haegeland, Eilert Magnus." http://www. haegeland.no/bio (accessed December 13, 2008).

Haglund, Rolf. "Hillborg, Anders." In *Grove Music Online*. *Oxford Music Online*, http://www.oxfordmusiconline.com/subscriber/article/grove/music/46505 (accessed July 11, 2008).

Haglund, Rolf. "Koch, Erland von." In *Grove Music Online*. *Oxford Music Online*, http://www.oxfordmusiconline.com/subscriber/article/grove/music/15227 (accessed September 19, 2008).

Haglund, Rolf. "Nilsson, Torsten." In *Grove Music Online*. *Oxford Music Online*, http://www.oxfordmusiconline.com/subscriber/article/grove/music/19970 (accessed July 11, 2008).

"Haller, William P." http://www.wvu.edu/~music/faculty_staff/whaller.html (accessed August 6, 2008).

"Heilmann, Harald." http://d-nb.info/gnd/119139316 (accessed June 12, 2008).

Herbert, Trevor. The Trombone. New Haven, CT: Yale University
    Press, 2006.

Herresthal, Harald. "Hovland, Egil." In *Grove Music Online. Oxford
    Music Online*,
    http://www.oxfordmusiconline.com/subscriber/article/grove/music/
    13424 (accessed July 11, 2008).

"Hidman, Aron." http://www.warwickmusic.com/composers/g+-
    +i/aron+hidman (accessed October 1, 2008).

"Hilfiger, John Jay." http://users.penn.com/~jhilf/ (accessed August 6,
    2008).

"Hoag, Charles." http://www.leonarda.com/composers-
    LE/comp326.html (accessed December 25, 2008).

"Hogg, Merle E." http://music.sdsu.edu/lynn/merle.html (accessed
    February 3, 2009).

"Hübler, Klaus. K." http://www.schallplattenkritik.de/bio/huebler.html
    (accessed December 25, 2008).

Hutcheson, Jere, Personal E-mail, March 11· 2008.

"Hutcheson, Jere."
    http://www.music.msu.edu/faculty/faculty.php?id=15 (accessed
    August 29, 2008).

"Irik, Michiel W." http://www.tops.org.au/members/Irik.htm. (accessed
    January 26, 2009).

Isaacson, Charles. 1996. 20th- Century Music for Trombone and Organ.
    International Trombone Journal (Winter) 24-29.

Jahn, Thomas, Personal E-mail, September 10 2008.

Kagarice, Vern. Solos for the Student Trombonist: An Annotated Bibliography. Nashville, TN: The Brass Press, 1979.

Kameke, Ernst-Urich von." http://www.garnisonkirche.de/download/ (accessed January 28, 2009).

"Kempton, Jeremy Niles." http://punamusic.com/kempton.html (accessed October 10, 2008).

Klein, Rudolf. "Angerer, Paul." In *Grove Music Online. Oxford Music Online*, http://www.oxfordmusiconline.com/subscriber/article/grove/music/ 00927 (accessed August 5, 2008).

"Kraus, Eberhard ." http://www.reift.ch/fichiers/pdfcomposers/9.pdf (Accessed August 4, 2008).

"Krol, Bernhard." http://www.editions-bim.com/index.php?main_page=page&id=200&chapter=1. (accessed December 9, 2008).

Lasala, Pastór de. Program notes December, 2005.

Laster, James H. *Catalogue of Music for Organ and Instruments*. Lanham, MD: Scarecrow Press, 2005.

"Linkenbach, Klaus." http://www.dohr.de/autor/linkenbach.htm (accessed December 27, 2008).

Loomis, George W. "Schilling, Hans Ludwig." In *Grove Music Online. Oxford Music Online*, http://www.oxfordmusiconline.com/subscriber/article/grove/music/ 24862 (accessed July 11, 2008).

"Lorentzen, Bent."
   http://en.ewh.dk/Default.aspx?TabId=2449&State_2955=2&compos
   erId_2955=952 (accessed January 29, 2009).

"Marthinsen, Niels."
   http://www.ewh.dk/Default.aspx?TabId=2449&State_2955=2&com
   poserId_2955=1001 (accessed August 4, 2008).

"Michel, Johannes M." http://www.bach-cantatas.com/Bio/Michel-
   Johannes-Matthias.htm (accessed December 9, 2008).

"Miller, Michael R." http://www.musiccentre.ca/apps/michaelrmiller
   (accessed September 18, 2008).

Mitchell, John C. 1990. Gustav Holst's Duet for Organ and Trombone.
   International Trombone Journal (Winter) 22-25.

"Moland, Erik."
   http://www.mic.no/mic.nsf/doc/art2002100713530323380178
   (accessed December 23, 2008).

Moody, Ivan and Ivashkin Alexander. "Schnittke, Alfred." In *Grove
   Music Online. Oxford Music Online*,
   http://www.oxfordmusiconline.com/subscriber/article/grove/music/
   51128 (accessed August 5, 2008).

Morris, R. Winston and Perantoni, Daniel. The *Guide to Tuba
   Repertoire: The New Tuba Souce Book*. IN: Indiana University
   Press, 1996.

Muggler, Fritz and Walton, Chris. "Schibler, Armin." In *Grove Music
   Online. Oxford Music Online*,
   http://www.oxfordmusiconline.com/subscriber/article/grove/music/
   24837 (accessed July 11, 2008).

"Nordhagen, Stig ." http://www.kso.no/hovedtekst.aspx?m=32&amid=280 (accessed December 12, 2008).

Oramo, Ilkka. "Aho, Kalevi." In *Grove Music Online. Oxford Music Online*, http://www.oxfordmusiconline.com/subscriber/article/grove/music/00337 (accessed August 2, 2008).

"Perlongo, Daniel." http://www.arts.iup.edu/facmus/perlongo/ (accessed December 12, 2008).

Perlongo, Daniel Personal E-mail, March, 14 2008.

"Pinkham, Daniel." http://www.pelicanmusicpublishing.com/composers.htm#Lynn%20 Petersen (accessed December 25, 2008).

"Purser, John." http://www.footstompin.com/artists/john_purser (accessed December 2, 2008).

Riedlbauer, Börg. "Genzmer, Harald." In *Grove Music Online. Oxford Music Online*, http://www.oxfordmusiconline.com/subscriber/article/grove/music/10881 (accessed July 11, 2008).

Risher, Tim. Personal E-mail, June, 1 2008.

"Rønnes, Robert." http://www.mic.no/mic.nsf/doc/art20021007201851 43658503 (accessed September 30, 2008).

"Sanders, Bernard Wayne." http://www.cph.org/cphstore/Author.asp?AI=119 (accessed December 10, 2008).

Sandström, Jan. Personal E-mail, March, 5 2008.

"Sandström, Jan." http://www.jansandstrom.com/theperson.html
(accessed December 24, 2008).

"Schmidt, Siegmund." http://www.bach-cantatas.com/Lib/Schmidt-
Franz.htm. (accessed February 6, 2009).

"Siekmann, Frank H." http://www.brelmatmusic.com/whoisfrank.htm
(accessed September 18, 2008).

"Stamm, Hans-André." http://www.eufonia.de/deutsch/person.php
(accessed December 3, 2008).

"Stover, Harold." http://www.haroldstover.com/biography.html.
(accessed December 9, 2008).

Stover, Harold. Personal Email, December 5, 2008.

"Struik, Gregory van der."
http://www.trombonisaustralis.com/about.htm (accessed January 26,
2009).

Struik, Gregory van der. Personal E-mail, January 19, 2009.

"Swanson, Philip." http://www.msrcd.com/1137/1137.html (accessed
January 29, 2009).

Thompson, J. Mark and Lemke, Jeffrey Jon. *French Music for Low
Brass Instruments: An Annotated Bibliography*. Bloomington, IN:
Indiana University Press, 1994.

Thomson, J.M. "Cresswell, Lyell." In *Grove Music Online. Oxford
Music Online*,
http://www.oxfordmusiconline.com/subscriber/article/grove/music/
40557 (accessed July 11, 2008).

Vidjeskog, Patrik. Personal E-mail, March 11, 2008.

Walker, Alan et al. "Liszt, Franz." In *Grove Music Online. Oxford Music Online*,
   http://www.oxfordmusiconline.com/subscriber/article/grove/music/
   48265pg3 (accessed February 4, 2009).

Wennekes, Emile. "Koetsier, Jan." In *Grove Music Online. Oxford Music Online*,
   http://www.oxfordmusiconline.com/subscriber/article/grove/music/
   15257 (accessed July 11, 2008).

Wiedemann, Erik. "Christensen, Bernhard." In *The New Grove Dictionary of Jazz*, 2nd ed., edited by Barry Kernfeld. *Grove Music Online. Oxford Music Online*,
   http://www.oxfordmusiconline.com/subscriber/article/grove/music/J
   085900 (accessed July 11, 2008).

"Wilby, Philip." http://www.chesternovello.com/wilby.bio (Accessed August 22, 2008).

Winkler, Klaus. 1985. Bibliographie der Kompositionen für Posaune und Orgel.Brass Bulletin, no. 51: 63-66.

Winkler, Klaus. 1986. Posaune und Orgel- Dialog zweier Instrumente.Brass Bulletin, no. 56: 75-89.

Discography

Angerer, Paul. Luctus et Gaudium für Altposaune und Orgel.
Branimir Slokar, Claves D707.

Bartmuss, Richard. Recitative and Arioso, Op. 24.
Sebastian Krause, Raum Klang 9805.

Belcke, Friedrich August. Fantasia for Trombone and Organ, Op. 58.
Sebastian Krause, Raum Klang 9805.
Alain Trudel, Naxos 8.553716.

Bornefeld, Helmut. *LITUUS für Posaune und Orgel*.
Armin Rosin, Teldec 6.42164AW.

Cejka, Petr D. Through for trombone og orgel.
Gaute Vikdal, Euridice EUCD 007.

Christensen, Bernhard. Concerto for trombone and organ.
Niels-Ole Bo Johansen, Paula PACD 87.

Cohen, Jules. *Andante pour Trombone et Orgue*.
Benny Sluchin, ADDA 581247.

Daetwyler, Jan. Sérénade au Clair de Lune pour Trombone Alto et
Orgue.
Branimir Slokar, Macrophon CD922-2.

Diemer, Emma Lou. *Psalm 1 for Bass or Tenor trombone & Organ or
Piano*.
Bryan Anton, RBW Record Company RBWCD015.

Diemer, Emma Lou. Psalm 122 for Bass Trombone (Tuba) & Organ
(Piano).

Bryan Anton, RBW Record Company RBWCD013.
Bryan Anton, RBW Record Company RBWCD015.

Drude, Matthias. Solo für Tuba.
   Markus Hötzen, Audiolis, P2005.

Eben, Petr. Two Invocations.
   Christian Lindberg, BIS CD 488.
   Niels-Ole Bo Johansen, Classico CLASSCD 122. (Invocation #1)
   Kalfus Votava, Supraphone (111438-1231).
   Lars-Göran Carlsson, OPUS 3 (OP9301CD).
   Sebastian Krause, Raum Klang 9805.

Fischer, Carl August. Fantasie für Solo-Posaune
   Sebastian Krause, Raum Klang 9805.

Fork, Gunter. Kanzone, Fuge, und Madrigal für Posaune und Orgel.
   Joachim Elser, Mitra CD 16228.

Gárdonyi, Zsolt. Rhapsodie für Posaune und Orgel.
   Martin Göss, Hännsler Classic 98.945.
   Sándor Hegedüs, Psalmus Records OVA-002.

Genzmer, Harald. Sonate Für Posaune und Orgel.
   Alain Trudel, Naxos 8.553716.
   Armin Rosin, FCD 91 497.

Glauser, Max. Trilogie für Posaune & Orgel.
   Branimir Slokar, Macrophon CD 922-2.

Godel, Didier. Sonata da Chiesa pour Trombone et Orgue.
   Branimir Slokar, Macrophon CD 922-2.

Heilmann, Harald. Fantasia per trombone ed organo.
   Armin Rosin, FCD 91 497.

Helmschrott, Robert. Sonata da Chiesa I.
  Abbie Conant, Audite 368.410.

Hidas, Frigyes. Domine, Dona Bois Pacem für Posaune und Orgel.
  Philip Swanson, Classics MS 1137.

Hillaborg, Anders. U-Tangia-Na.
  Christian Lindberg, BIS CD 488 and BIS CD 638.

Holst, Gustav. Concertante. (Duet for trombone and organ)
  Ian Bousfield, EMI 72435 66289 2 2.
  Alain Trudel, Naxos 8.553716.
  Sebastian Krause, Raum Klang 9805.
  Niels-Ole Bo Johansen, Classico CLASSCD 122.
  Steven Mead (euphonium), Bocchino Music BOCC 121.

Hovland, Egil. Cantus V for Trombone and Organ op.12.
  Gaute Vikdal, Euridice EUCD 001.

Janca, Jan. Suite in 7 movements for trombone and organ.
  Mike Svoboda, MDG 606 1462-2.

Janca, Jan. Tripartita on Christ ist erstanden for trombone and organ.
  Mike Svoboda, MDG 606 1462-2.

Koetsier, Jan. Partita für Posaune und Orgel (Wachet auf, ruft uns die
  Stimme).
  Armin Rosin, FCD 91 497.
  Gabor Hegedüs, Motette CD50661.

Krol, Bernhard. Sinfonia sacra for trombone and organ, op. 56.
  Alain Trudel, Naxos 8.553716.
  Armin Rosin, Teldec 6.42164AW.

Lorentzen, Bent. Alpha and Omega for trombone and organ.
  Niels-Ole Bo Johansen, Paula PACD 87.

Liszt, Franz. Hosannah.
  Christian Lindberg, BIS CD 488.
  Alain Trudel, Naxos 8.553716.
  Yves Bauer, FBR 120/1.
  Niels-Ole Bo Johansen, Classico CLASSCD 122.
  Gabor Hegedüs, Motette CD50661.
  Sebastian Krause, Raum Klang 9805.
  Steven Mead (euphonium), Bocchino Music BOCC 121.

Marthinsen, Niels. Concerto for trombone and organ.
  Niels-Ole Bo Johansen, Paula PACD 87.

Meyer, Hannes. Sonate C-Moll Für Posaune und Orgel.
  Branimir Slokar, Macrophon CD 922-2.
  Thomas Horch, Audite 95.437.
  Ronald Barron, Boston Brass Series -1008CD.

Meyer, Hannes. Suite für Posaune und Orgel "Das Liebesspiel."
  Thomas Horch, Audite 95.437.
  Sebastian Krause, Raum Klang 9805.

Mortimer, John Glenesk. Fantasia.
  Branimir Slokar, Macrophon CD 922-2.

Muller, Bernhard Edvard. Gebet (Prayer) Op.65b.
  Erkki T. Hirsimäki, Jase CD 0019.
  Sebastian Krause, Raum Klang RK 9805.
  Nilsson, Torsten. Concertino per trombone ed organo op.81.
  Christer Torge, BIS-CD-138.

Peters, Max. Elegie für Posaune und Orgel op.9.
  Carsten Svanberg, EMI Moak 37.

Pinkham, Daniel. Solemnities. Dragons and Deeps for Bass Tuba in F
    and Organ.
    Randall Montgomery, ARSIS CD143

Pinkham, Daniel. Solemnities.
    Bron Wright, ARSIS CD 143.

Purser, John. Skylines for Trombone & Organ.
    John Kenny, British Music Label CD 016.

Read, Gardner. Invocation for Trombone and Organ Op.135.
    Christian Lindberg, BIS CD 488.
    Steven Mead (euphonium), Bocchino Music BOCC 121.

Rønnes, Robert. Lento for Bass Trombone and Organ.
    Gaute Vikdal, EUCD 007.

Sandstrom, Jan, Lacrimae, Lacrimae.
    Christian Lindberg, BIS CD 488.
    Steven Mead (euphonium), Bocchino Music BOCC 121.

Schiffmann, Ernst. Intermezzo, Op. 53.
    Alain Trudel, Naxos 8.553716.
    Joachim Elser, Mitra CD 16228.

Schilling, Hans Ludwig. Vier Choralvorspiele.
    Rosin, Armin, Teldec 6.42164AW.

Schneider, Johann Julius. Choralvariationen für Bass-Posaune und
    Orgel op.16.
    Sebastian Krause, Raum Klang 9805.
    Helmut Lang, Hänssler 98.544.

Schnittke, Alfred, Schall und Hall.
    Christian Lindberg, BIS CD 488.
    Anatoly Skobelev, CHAN 9466.

Senon, Gilles, Prière pour trombone et orgue.
    Jean Douay, Corelia CC 78030.

Studer, Hans. Tres Laudes für Alt-Posaune und Orgel.
    Branimir Slokar, Macrophon CD 922-2.

Swanson, Philip. Variations on Veni Creator Spiritus.
    Philip Swanson, Classics MS 1137.

Thybo, Leif. Mouvement Symphonique.
    John Petersen, Da Cappo 8.224009.

Zimmermann, Margrit. Triptychon für Posaune & Orgel. Op. 58.
    Pia Bucher, Marcophone CD 901-2.

Publishers and Contact Information

ADU Verlag. Heerenkamp 34, 26605 Aurich, Tel.: 04941 62623, Fax: 04941 64870. post@adu-verlag.de. *http://www.adu-verlag.de.*

Agencja Autorska, ZAiKS, ul. Hipoteczna 2, 00-950 Warsaw, Poland. 48-22-827 60 61. informatycy@zaiks.org.pl. *http://autorska-agencja.pl*

Alliance Publications. 585 County Road Z, Sinsinawa, WI 53824-0157. (608) 748-4411 X 124. api@apimusic.org *http://apimusic.org.*

American Composers Alliance. PO Box 1108, New York, NY 10040. (212) 568-0036. info@composers.com. *http://composers.com.*

Animando Edizioni Musicali. 23-23100 Sondrio, Italy. +39-0342-191.336. info@animando.com. *http://www.animando.com.*

Ars Nova Press. PO BOX 1985, Seattle, WA 98109. (206) 551-2650. glenn@arsnovamusic.com. *http://www.arsnovamusic.com.*

Astoria Verlag. 19 Hospital Street, 40597 Dusseldorf, Germany. +4921171 79 96. info@astoria-verlag.com. *http://www.astoria-verlag.de.*

Australian Music Centre. P.O. Box N690, Grosvenor Place NSW 1220, The Rocks, Sydney, NSW, Australia. +61 2 9935 7805. info@australianmusiccentre.com.au. *https://www.australianmusiccentre.com.au.*

Bèrben Edizioni Musicali. Via Redipuglia 65, 60122 Ancona, Italy. 71.204428. info@berben.it. *http://www.berben.it.*

Bernhard Päuler Amadeus Verlag. 27a High Street Guard, 8400 Winterthur, Switzerland. 41 052 233 28 66. nfo@amadeusmusic.ch. *http://www.amadeusmusic.ch.*

Bote and Bock, See Schott Music Corporation.

Brassworks 4 Publishing. 9 Road 3787, Farmington, NM 87401. (505) 860-8122. bw4@brassworks4.com. *http://www.brassworks4.com.*

Breitkopf & Härtel KG. Walkmühlstraße 52, 65195 Wiesbaden, Germany. Tel +49 (0) 611-45008 0. *https://www.breitkopf.com.*

Brelmat Music. 241 Kohler's Hill, Kutztown, PA 19530. (610) 756-6324. brelmat@verizon.net. *http://www.brelmatmusic.com.*

C.F. Kahnt, See C.F. Peters Corporation.

C.F. Peters Corporation. 70-30 80th Street, Glendale NY 11385. (718) 416-7800. sales.us@editionpeters.com. *http://www.edition-peters.com.*

C.F. Schmidt Musikverlag. Leonberger Strasse 1, 71272 Renningen. 07159-2969. *http://www.ghv-renningen.de.*

Canadian Music Centre. Chalmers House, 20 St. Joseph Street, Toronto, Ontario M4Y 1J9. 416.961.6601. info@musiccentre.ca. *http://www.musiccentre.ca.*

Carus-Verlag GmbH & Co KG. Sielminger Str. 51, D-70771 Lf.-Echterdingen, Germany. +49 711-797 330-0. info@carus-verlag.com. *http://www.carus-verlag.com.*

Center for New Zealand Music. PO Box 10042, Wellington 6143, Level 1, 39 Cambridge Terrace, Wellington 6011, New Zealand. 64 4 801 8602. info@sounz.org.nz. *http://sounz.org.nz.*

Český rozhlas. Vinohradská 12, 120 99 Praha 2, Czech Republic. tel.: +420 221 551 111. *http://www.rozhlas.cz.*

Composer's Library (no information found).

Concordia Publishing House. 3558 S. Jefferson, St. Louis, MO 63118. (314) 268-1000. order@cph.org. *http://www.cph.org.*

Con Spirito Music. Fort Worth, Texas. mail@conspiritomusic.com. *https://www.conspiritomusic.com.*

Copy-us Internet Music Publishing. D-47533, Kleve, Germany. info@copy-us.com. *www.copy-us.com.*

Counterpoint Musical Services Inc. 39 Riviera Drive, Unit 6, Markham, Ontario, Canada. (800) 690-0515. music@CounterpointMusic.ca. *http://counterpointmusic.ca.*

De Haske International. See Music Shop Europe.

E.C.S Schirmer Music Company. 1727 Larkin Williams Road, St. Louis, Missouri, 63026. (800) 647-2117. *http://www.ecspublishing.com.*

Edition BIM & Brass Press. Route des Echelettes 51 CH-1674 Vuarmarens, Switzerland. +41-(0)21-909 1000. *http://www.editions-bim.ch.*

Edition Eulenburg. See C.F. Peters Corporation.

Edition Gravis. Grabbeallee 15, 13156 Berlin, Germany. +49 (0)30 - 61-69 81 0. info@editiongravis.de. *http://www.editiongravis.de.*

Editions Henry Lemoine. 27 boulevard Beaumarchais, F-75004 PARIS Tél. : 33 (0)1 56 68 86 65. Fax : 33 (0)1 56 68 90 66. info@henry-lemoine.com. *https://www.henry-lemoine.com.*

Edition Musica Rinata E. Hofmann. Leharstr.7, 71254 Ditzingen,
Germany. (07156) 5755. edition@musica-rinata.de.
http://www.musica-rinata.de.

Edition Musicus, Inc. See Ensemble Publications

Edition Reimers. Mårdvägen 44, SE-167 56 Bromma, Sweden. +46-
(0)8-704 02 80. info@editionreimers.se.
http://www.editionreimers.se. For distribution see Theador Presser
Company.

Edition Svitzer. Roarsvej 6, kld. Th, DK-2000 Frederiksberg, Denmark.
+45 25 79 73 71. mail@editionsvitzer.com.
http://www.editionsvitzer.com.

Edition Tarrodi. Valhallavagen 110, S-114 41 Stockholm, Sweden.
info@tarrodi.se. *http://www.tarrodi.se.*

Editions Marc Reift. Case Postale 308, Route du Golf 150, CH-3963,
Crans-Montana, Switzerland. +41 (0) 27 483 12 00. info@reift.ch.
http://www.reift.ch.

Editions Musicales Européenes. See Editions Henry Lemoine

Edition Wilhelm Hansen. Bornholmsgade 1A, 1266 Copenhagen K,
Denmark. +45 33 11 78 88. ewh@ewh.dk.
http://www.musicsalesclassical.com

Engstrom & Sodring. Borgergade 17, DK-1300, Copenhagen K,
Denmark. +45 33 14 32 28.

Ensemble Publications. P.O. Box 32, Ithaca, NY 14851. (607) 592-
1778. Enspub@outlook.com.

Eufonia Edition Kathrin Stamm. Edelrather Weg 192, 51375
Leverkusen. (+49) 214 840 44 24. edition@eufonia.de.
http://www.eufonia.de.

The Euphonium Collective. terencetreherne@btinternet.com.
http://www.euphoniumcollective.co.uk

Fennica Gehrman Oy Ab. PO Box 158, FIN-00121 Helsinki, Finland.
+ 358-40-8370629. info@fennicagehrman.fi.
https://www.fennicagehrman.fi.

Finnish Music Information Center. Lauttasaarentie 1, FIN-00200
Helsinki, Finland. +358 9 6810 1313. info@fimic.fi.
http://www.fimic.fi.

Friedrich Hofmeister Musikverlag. Melscher Strasse 1, D-04299
leipzig, Germany. +49-341 / 9 60 07 50. info@hofmeister-
musikverlag.com. *http://www.friedrich-hofmeister.de.*

Gérard Billaudot Editeur. 14, rue de l'Echiquier, 75010 Paris, France.
(33 1) 47 70 14 46. *http://www.billaudot.com.*

Gunnar Hahn Musikförlag. c/o Kudu Media, Drejargatan 5, SE-113 42,
Stockholm, Sweden. +46 701 555 262. order@gunnarhahnmusik.se.
http://www.gunnarhahnmusik.se.

Hänssler Verlag. Stittgart, Germany. Info@haenssler.de.
http://www.haenssler.de.

Heinrichshofen Verlag. Liebigstraße 16, D-26389 Wilhelmshaven,
Germany. 49 (0) 4421-9267-0. *http://www.heinrichshofen.de.*

Iceland Music Information Centre. Laugavegur 105

IS-105 Reykjavík, Iceland. (354)-5683122. itm@mic.is.
http://www.mic.is.

Ione Press, See ECS Publishing.

International Music Score Library Project (IMSLP). *http://imslp.org.*

Joseph Boonin Publishing. Hackensack, New Jersey.

Just Sheet Music. http://www.justsheetmusic.com

Laured Keiser Music Publishing. 10750 Indian Head Industral Boulevard

St. Louis, MO 63132, USA. 203-560-9436 (phone), 314-270-5305 (fax)

info@laurenkeisermusic.com. http://laurenkeisermusic.com

Libitum Musik, See Norwegian Music Information Centre.

MMB Music Inc., 9051 Watson Rd #161, St. Louis, MO 63126. info@mmbmusic.com. *http://mmbmusic.com.*

Möseler Verlag. V. F. Hoffmann-Str. 8, 38304 Wolfenbüttel, Germany. +49-5331-95970. www.moeseler-verlag.de/

MorningStar Music Publishers, see E.C.S Schirmer Music Company

Music Shop Europe. Music Shop Europe B.V., Postbus 744, Businesspark Friesland-West 15, NL-8440 AS Heerenveen, Netherlands. +32 3 289 29 86 (NL). info@musicshopeurope.com. *https://www.musicshopeurope.com.*

Musik Fabrik Music Publishing. 18, rue Marthe Aureau, 77400 Lagny-sur-Marne, FRANCE. tél/fax (33) 01.73.58.50.59. infoATclassicalmusicnow.com. *http://www.classicalmusicnow.com.*

Musikverlag Castellano. 74379 Ingersheim, Gottlob-Ansel-Strasse 2, Germany. 07142-55812. post@musikverlag-castellano.de. *http://www.musikverlag-castellano.de.*

Musikverlag Hans Gerig. Mailbox 100435, 51404 Bergisch Gladbach, Germany. +49 2204 2003-0. info@greig.de. http://gerig.de

Musikverlag Ludwig Doblinger. Dorotheergasse 10, A-1010, Wien, Austria. +43 1 515 03-0. music@doblinger.co.at. *www.doblinger.at.*

Musikverlag Rundel. 08395-94260. info@rundel.de. http:// www.rundel.de

Musikverlag Zimmermann. Strubbergstraße 80, 60489 Frankfurt am Main, Germany. 069-978286-6. info@zimmermann-frankfurt.de. *http://www.zimmermann-frankfurt.de.*

Norsk Musikforlag. P.O. Box 1499 Vika, N- 0116 Oslo, Norway. (+47) 23 00 20 10, order@musikforlaget.no. *http://www.norskmusikkforlag.no.*

Norwegian Music Information Centre. Oslo, Norway. +47 90175338. info@mic.no. *http://www.mic.no.*

Peermusic Classical. Sierichstraße 39-22301 Hamburg, Germany. + 49/40/278379-0. info@peermusic-classical.de. *http://www.peermusic-classical.de.*

Pfefferkorn Musikverlag. Thiemstraße 8, D-04299 Leipzig, Gemany. +49 (0)341 980 4608. http://www.pfefferkorn-verlag.com.

Pizzicato Verlag Helvetia. Scharachlistrasse 3, CH-8810 Horgen, Switzerland. + 41 (0)44 710 62 52. info@pizzicato.ch. *http://www.pizzicato.ch.*

Puna Music Company. P.O. Box 3004, Teaneck, NY 7666. Jan@punamusic.com._http://www.punamusic.com.

Robert King Music Company. 140 50 Corporate Park Drive, Suite 770, Pembroke, MA 02359. (508) 238 8118. ecommerce@rkingmusic.com. http://www.rkingmusic.com.

Schott Music Corporation. 254 West 31st Street, Floor 15, New York, NY 10001. 212 461 6940. ny@schott-music.com. http://www.schott-music.com.

Seesaw Music Corporation. 60 Depot St., Verona, New Jersey, 10023. 973.857.3440. mail@subitomusic.com. www.subitomusic.com.

SNYK, the Secretariat for Contemporary Music. Gråbrødretorv 16, DK-1154 Copenhagen K, Denmark. + 45 33 93 00 24. snyk@snyk.dk. http://www.snyk.dk.

Society for Publication of Danish Music (Samfundet). Gråbrødrestræde 18.st., DK-1156 Copenhagen K, Denmark. +45 33 13 54 45. sales@samfundet.dk._http://www.samfundet.dk.

Southern Music Company, see Lauren Keiser Music Publishing

Strube Verlag GmbH. Pettenkoferstraße 24, D-80336 Munich, Germany. +9 (0) 89 544 266 11. info@strube.de. http://www.strube.de.

Swedish Music Information Center. Sandhamnsgatan 79, BoX 17092 104 62, Stockholm, Sweden. 08-783 88 00. info@svenskmusik.org. http://www.mic.stim.se.

Symbiophonic AS. c/o Kunnskapsparken Bodø AS, Boks 815, 8001 Bodø, Norway. (Fax) 47 75 69 02 48. info@symbiophonic.as. http://www.symbiophonic.no.

TAP Music Sales. 1992 Hunter Avenue, Newton, IA, 50208. 641-792-0352. tapmusic@tapmusic.com. *http://www.tapmusic.com.*

Trombonis Australis Editions. 5/35 Blaxcell Street Granville, NSW 2142, Australia. +61 2 9682 2002. alltrombone@optusnet.com.au. *http://trombonisaustralis.com.*

Tuba Euphonium Press/Cimarron Music Press. 860-483-8822. *https://www.cimarronmusic.com*

United Music Publishers. 71 Chedburgh Road, Bury St Edmunds, Suffolk, England, IP29 5QU. (0)1992 703110. sales@ump.co.uk. *http://www.ump.co.uk.*

Universal Edition. Karl Platz 6, A-1010 Vienna, Austia. +43 1 337 23 0. office@universaledition.com. *http://www.universaledition.com.*

Veit Erdmann-Abele. Kammweg 48, 72762 Reutlingen, Germany. 07121 22592. veit.erdmann@emailpostamt.de. *http://www.erdmann-abele.de.*

Verlag Christoph Dohr Köln / edition dohr. Kasselberger Sindorfer Straße 19, D-50127 Bergheim, Köln, Germany. +49 / (0) 2271 / 70 72 05. info@dohr.de. *http://www.dohr.de.*

Verlag Merseburger. Naumburger Straße 40, 34127 Kassel, Germany. +49 561 789809-11. order@merseburger.de. *www.merseburger.de.*

Warwick Music. Dot Com House, Broomfield Road, Coventry, England, CV5 6 GY. +44 (0)24 7671 2081. sales@warwickmusic.com. *http://www.warwickmusic.com.*

Wehr's Music House. http://www.wehrs-music-house.com.

Wessmans Musikförlag. Box 4, SE-624 21 Slite, Sweden. + 46 (0)498-22 61 32. order@wessmans.com. *https://www.wessmans.com.*

Western International Music, Inc. 3707 65th Avenue, Greeley, CO 80634-9626 U.S.A. (970) 330-6901. wimbo@wiminc.com. *http://www.wiminc.com.*

Wolfgang G. Haas – Musikverlag Köln E.K.. Rheinbergstr. 92, 51143 Köln, Germany. +49 (0) 22 03 / 98 883-0. *http://www.haas-koeln.de.*

About the Author

Dr. Patrick Lawrence is Professor of Trombone, Euphonium and Tuba at the University of Wisconsin-Stevens Point. He completed the Doctor of Musical Arts degree from Arizona State University where his dissertation Solo Literature for Trombone and Organ, an annotated bibliography, was recognized as an important musical reference for trombonists and educators. Dr. Lawrence also holds a Master of Music Degree from the University of Arizona, and Bachelor degrees in Secondary Music Education and Performance from The University of Mary.

An active performer, he is the conductor of the Wausau Symphonic Band, and principal trombonist with the Central Wisconsin Symphony Orchestra. A strong advocate for collaboration with organists, he commissioned and premiered "Resolution for Trombone and Organ" in 2009 and performed at the American Guild of Organists-South West Convention. He served as 2nd trombonist with the Tucson Symphony Orchestra and has given recitals in the United States and Canada. As a sideman, Patrick has shared the stage with musical greats Yo-Yo Ma, Louis Bellson, The Temptations, Doc Severinsen, Wayne Newton, Jerry Lewis, Linda Ronstadt, the Don Rickles Orchestra, Buddy Morrow and the Tommy Dorsey Orchestra, and the Artie Shaw Big Band.

Dr. Lawrence was the 2013 recipient of the University of Wisconsin-Stevens Point excellence in teaching award. He is a passionate educator, working with elementary through college-age students. He taught middle school band and orchestra in Arizona where his student groups received superior and excellent ratings at local, state and national music festivals. Dr. Lawrence is also an instrument repair technician, and teaches classes in brass and woodwind repair at UWSP.

Dr. Lawrence has articles and music reviews published in the International Trombone Association Journal, the International Tuba and Euphonium Association Journal, and Wisconsin School Musician.

Acknowledgements

This book could not have been completed without the help of many people to whom I am grateful.

Many thanks to organist and dear friend Janet Tolman who spent countless hours collaborating with me on these works in my Arizona days. Janet is a gifted musician and our time together was the catalyst for my interest in this music.

Thanks to my Doctoral committee at Arizona State University where this project was my dissertation: Gail Eugene Wilson, Sam Pilafian, Richard Mook, and Robert Oldani. Many thanks to the University of Wisconsin-Stevens Point for granting me a sabbatical to further this research, including the addition of euphonium and tuba with organ to this collection.

Thanks to my former student Jared Dalgleish, who was an exceptional associate lecturer while I was away for the semester.

Thanks to my amazing UWSP Low Brass Studio members, past and present. I love working with all of you.

I'm forever indebted to my many wonderful teachers: Gail Eugene Wilson, Michael Becker, Tom Ervin, and Dennis Gowen, who've set a high benchmark I strive daily to attain in my own teaching.

Thank you to the numerous composers and publishing companies who provided reviewer's copies of music for this research.

Lastly, to Bruce and Marie Trump for their hours of work proofreading and formatting to make this publication possible, I am most appreciative.

Notes:

www.ingramcontent.com/pod-product-compliance
Lightning Source LLC
LaVergne TN
LVHW091214080426
835509LV00009B/984